ATHENA RISING
A Memoir

By Heather Bond

ISBN: 9798656975346

The author of this book does not dispense medical advice or proscribe the use of any technique as a form of treatment for physical or medical problems without the advice of a physician. The author does not assume any responsibilities for injures that may occur in pursuing certain exercises. Please consult a physician before engaging in any of the physical exercises.

Woodbridge Press

Toronto, Canada

ATHENA RISING
A Memoir

Acknowledgments

I want to thank two individuals who have been mentors to me. They helped me to refuel my flame, passion, and clarity as a peak performer. William Poett, and Dr. Laura Ciel, are the founders of nineQ Consulting and Education. (https://www.nineqco.com) William is the kick-ass mentor with the True North Compass I refer to in the epilogue. William and I share similar backgrounds in pushing our physical limits through our sports and professions. I knew I needed a mentor and wanted to train with him.

A year or so later Laura joined William in co-creating their current business, nineQ. Laura, as a powerful and professional female, added another dimension that I needed to help navigate and support me through the nightmares of my relationship and custody battle. Many thanks to you both for all you do to help others remember their inherent worth.

One must stay focused and look for the messengers that are being sent to them. Doors begin to open and certain people are placed in our lives to help us progress towards our goals.

I want to thank my dear friend, Dr. Ginger Swanson, who came unassumingly waltzing into my life holding two cute pink three-pound dumbbells to a training session with me.

She and I instantly connected and it turned out she was a writer. I informed her I had been struggling with writing my book. She recommended that I read Lisa Lenard-Cook's book, "*Find Your Story- Write Your Memoir*." I ordered it that day in both hard copy and audio, and listened to it religiously.

I found out Ginger also hosts various types of retreats (AsarumRetreats.com), some of which are writing. She happened to be hosting a three-day memoir retreat that weekend. I was up to my ears and in the midst of the custody battle. My brain was scattered and frazzled, but I knew this was an opportunity knocking at my door. I gathered all my legal pads I'd been writing my story on, yes, in long hand, loaded them into one of my bags I'd acquired in prison that contained all my journals, and I became a student of writing.

When the other writers saw my legal pads I got some giggles. The notes looked like a puzzle with scratched out writing, arrows pointing to different areas; it was a mess. I did, however, have every person on the edge of their seat while I read snippets of my story. I felt this was a good sign. Unfortunately I had no computer to help clean up this tangled mess.

Again, thanks goes out to Ginger for believing in me so much she gifted me one of her computers she had written her thesis on. This brought a serious element to my writing. She and I made an agreement that I would start writing every day, and I did. Thanks to my amazing new computer I started my manuscript from scratch and day after day, hour after hour I clicked at the keys until I put the last period at the end.

I also want to thank a select few. Without your editorial expertise, your valuable opinions, professional reading skills, and various other tasks; Lea, Kara, and Ann, I could not have done this without you. Thank you from the bottom of my heart.

P.S. On a fun note, my thanks also go out to a myriad of wine makers. Your unique variations were a shoulder to lean on through the hard times of piecing this story together.

Cheers!

Table of Contents

Preface

Just as a rock in a flowing river will never see the same water pass by again, time changes our perspectives and reality. Through the process of writing this story I felt blessed to have my personal journals of in–the-moment experiences and reflections, as well as my mom's.

As I wrote a handful of the traumatic or high-energy scenes I relived the moments. So much so th at a few times I had to stop in the middle of the writing because I started profusely sweating and my heart rate spiked; I did however get a few interesting looks from some fellow coffee drinkers in our little café.

I spent nine years trying to force the process of writing this book. As I sat meditating on the rock after the October 11, 2017, court hearing and experienced the profound act of forgiveness wash over me I became a clear and open channel to the magnificent journey of writing this story. Although much of the writing was painful and haunting to relive I enjoyed every part of bringing it to life.

Athena Rising, a Memoir – Heather Bond

Part One
The Indian Promise

Athena Rising, a Memoir – Heather Bond

Chapter 1
The Calling

A ship in a harbor is safe, but that is not what ships are built for.

John Augustus Shedd

I smell my own fear as sweat drips down my back and adrenaline surges in my body.

My mom's transient glance pierces my soul.

My heart rate shifts into high gear in anticipation of conflict.

Desperation is painted on my mom's face as she leans into me and says, "Heather, if these men try to rape us we are going to run as fast as we can, they'll have to shoot us in our backs."

These words that softly slipped from her mouth will be etched in my mind forever and in that very moment sent chills that echoed deep into my being.

Ah, India. To my mom it had such an exotic allure. I on the other hand, well, Nepal called my name. It's a mountaineering mecca, home to the highest mountains in the world and the amazing Sherpa people. That was much more my speed and definitely on my bucket list.

For years I heard my mom talk about how exciting it would be to immerse herself in the culture and people of India. She wanted to walk through the colorful bazaars and bathe herself in the smells of the spice markets and experience all the humanity of mother India. This was her dream.

Around October of 2007, a trying time in my life, my mom came home from her morning walk and told me that Mrs. P and her daughter, Michele, were going on a tour through India. I've known Mrs. P since I was 9 years old; she's one of my mom's closest friends. She and Michele had traveled together many times. But this felt different. India was my mom's dream trip.

My philosophy is and always has been, "If they can do it, so can I." I remember the first time somebody called me a "Total type A personality;" I laughed and thought to myself *what the heck does that mean?*

I held an honorary position as a type1 Hotshot on a fire crew; rappelling out of helicopters and hiking into remote areas to face the fury of the firestorms. This helped earn me an esteemed position as a Los Angeles City Fire Fighter; they're the cream of the crop in the municipal fire department world.

For over a decade I pushed my physical boundaries adventure racing around the globe. The races lasted seven to twelve days. Twenty-four hours a day I pushed my mental limits to breaking points while racing on mountain bikes, kayaking, jungle trekking, glacier crossings, mountaineering, to name a few, all the while navigating a three hundred to four hundred mile course.

I had my fun go as a Hollywood stunt woman; performing high falls off two story buildings, getting shot with fake bullets in fight scenes that usually wound up with me being thrown through a window. Apparently this is what classified me as being a type A. I thought that was called a go-getter.

But given my physical and emotional state at that time, a trip to India would be quite an undertaking. It captivated me, however, because I was desperately looking for something I felt I had lost.

I remember the way my mom's energy shifted as she told me about Mrs. P's plans to go to India. I knew how badly she wished we were going. "Mom this could be us!" I told her. "There's never going to be the right time or enough money, and if you truly want to go I'll plan us the adventure of a lifetime." It brings tears to my eyes to remember that conversation.

My mom and I are so close that her body language tells it all. When I mentioned the India trip that day she didn't retreat from me; I knew she was serious about it. To my shock, she agreed to speak to my dad about going.

For my mom to consider a trip of this magnitude without my dad was unprecedented. After 41 years of marriage, they had only been apart for a week and a half in the 1960s. This was a big deal.

Athena Rising, a Memoir – Heather Bond

Chapter 2
Pseudo Backpacker

*Only by going alone in silence, without baggage, can
you truly get into the heart of the wilderness. All other
travel is mere dust hotels and baggage and chatter.*

John Muir

"Oh my gosh!" I shrilled through the phone. The lines around
my eyes became deep crevasses as my smile stretched across my
face. Excitement filled my body as my mom said, "Well, Dad said
yes!" I was beside myself.

I felt we were going to embark on the most magnificent mother
and daughter journey.

It turns out, my mom didn't actually have a face-to-face
conversation with my dad about us traveling to India. Nope, after
she agreed to speak to him, she wrote him a letter. Who does that?
I realized this is why she wanted to do errands with me at an odd
hour, so my dad would find the letter and have time to read and
digest the proposal.

Athena Rising, a Memoir – Heather Bond

There are not many things that excite me as much as adventuring to remote regions of the world. Like a child awaiting Santa's arrival, I get giddy when planning the logistics. From 1993-2003 my racing had me globetrotting to various countries. Fortunately, sponsors had supported my crazy lifestyle and my passion.

Planning foreign travel requires some homework. Do you sign up with a guided tour group and stay in some high-end hotels? Or do you go on a shoestring budget and tackle the country on your terms? We decided on an option somewhere between those two. I viewed myself as a guide and started planning a pseudo backpacker style trip.

I figured we wanted adventure. We wanted to immerse ourselves in the culture and the people, so we should be on trains, buses, rickshaws and tuk-tuks, and accommodations should be midrange hotels.

For the next five months I studied the history of the British Raj era and all the many cultures of India. I mapped out the regions of interest, picture after picture, and like a puzzle I pieced together the dream trip. I wanted to keep us off the tourist route as much as possible while still being able to experience some of the not-to-miss wonders such as the Taj Mahal. I looked into various options on multi-day camel safaris into the Thar Desert, as well as National Geographic-style jeep tiger tracking.

I took pride in the magnificent itinerary that began to emerge. A pocket-sized notebook stored all the moving pieces of our adventure. There were our bus and train departures and arriving times, as well as the routes we'd follow. I didn't want to leave much to chance.

During trip planning, I grew more and more excited about using "the arm." I had designed the piece of equipment to allow hands-free photography or video. "The arm's" functionality exceeded that of the now-ubiquitous selfie-stick, which didn't exist when planning my trip in 2007. It anchored from my backpack and extended over my shoulder and about two feet. I was able to swivel the cameras so I could capture video or pictures in either direction. I couldn't wait to walk through the bazaars capturing my mom's reactions.

As ingenious as I had originally thought the gadget was, there was no way we could have used " the arm" in a country teeming with millions of people. It hung on the side of my backpack, and now it's a fixture in my yard that always brings a great laugh.

Chapter 3
Nothing Is As It Seems

*It's not what happens to you, but how you react to it
that matters.*

Epictetus

Since this trip was going to require us to wear heavy backpacks, I suggested to my mom that we start a training regimen. My mom has always been in great shape and a fast walker. She and Mrs. P have walked for the past 38 years; however, they don't wear backpacks, which makes all the difference in the world.

On many of our training hikes, my mom and I would role-play, as though we were already traveling. We'd put ourselves into various situations and scenarios; some of them made us laugh and others made us ponder. I remember saying a few times, "Two American women arrested and put in prison for...? Could you imagine if we got put in prison in another country?" We'd look at each other and say, "Nope!" Then we'd pop into another scenario.

My mom and I were excited to embark on this mother and daughter adventure. However, my dad and my fiancé, Sean, voiced repeated concerns about the political climate. This put a bit of a damper on things at times, as did my overall strained relationship with Sean.

My mom and I have a gift of finding a silver lining in stressful situations. Leading up to our departure, my mom felt like she needed some cash for our arrival in India since she doesn't carry credit cards. So she went to one of our local dealers and got an impressive exchange rate on some Indian rupees. Later that afternoon when I stopped by to see her she was so excited.

"Heather I saved $89 on these rupees, come take a look." Her face was beaming with a huge smile. She pulled out an entire shoebox full of small denomination notes.

"Oh my gosh mom," I started laughing. "Where are you going to put all these bills?" I didn't want to discourage her enthusiasm. "I'm going to put the whole box in my blue polka dot pack." She said proudly. We laughed and laughed.

In our preparation, my mom and I went through every scenario we could think up.

We packed and repacked our backpacks several times. At one point I recall Sean saying to me in a rather annoyed voice, "You're not going to know until you get there. The books don't give you the full impact." Irritated, I responded, "Okay, well the book said..." I hoped those wouldn't be famous last words.

Through all my years of travels I've relied on the insight of the Lonely Planet guidebooks. For India, I noted a few warnings from Lonely Planet in my handy pocket guide. But I felt confident. I'd already journeyed through Africa, Australia, New Zealand, parts of Canada, Mexico and England, and all through the U.S. I'd done the research, and I was ready for India.

As our departure date neared, I started feeling more and more responsible for my mom's safety. I knew my dad was apprehensive about our trip and I wanted to reassure him everything would be okay, so one afternoon I stopped by their house to speak with him.

As I approached the door, I felt a powerful jolt of energy surge through me. The rush of energy was like nothing I had ever experienced. It seemed to have manifested in my gut, in my knowing, like a premonition this journey my mom and I were about to embark on was going to be far more of an undertaking than just a mother and daughter adventure.

I saw my dad working in one of his garden areas, and I told him I wanted to speak with him. After we'd walked for a bit, I turned to him with a full heart and said, "Don't worry, Pa, I'll bring Mom back safely, I promise."

I watched tears well up in my dad's eyes. The look of concern and reservation were so obvious. I felt tears flowing down my checks, and we embraced in a long wonderful hug.

Chapter 4
Expect The Unexpected

*The pessimist complains about the wind; the optimist
expects it to change; the realist adjusts the sails.*

William Arthur Ward

It was Saturday morning, March 22, 2008, and I saw that my
mom was calling. Excited and giddy, I answered the phone. She
asked a panicked question. I had her repeat it and told her to slow
down. "When do you think Sunday, March 23 at 12:10 a.m. is?"

I paused and slumped into the chair with a puzzled feeling.
Then, as if a fire alarm went off, I jumped out of my chair, panic
sweeping over me. "That's tonight!"

After five months of planning this trip, my mom luckily had
one of those dreams that wake you up in a sweat. Without it, we
would've missed our flight. The 12:10 a.m. departure had us
thinking we flew out on Sunday rather than Saturday.

We rushed about getting all our last-minute items together.
With no space left in my pack, I still managed to shove one last
item; an umbrella I thought might come in handy up in Darjeeling.

17

By 9 p.m. we'd arrived at LAX. Sean dropped us off in front of our departure terminal for Air China. He and I were to get married in six months and yet nothing was planned, and here I was taking off with my mom on a journey to India.

We said our goodbyes and my mom and I strolled off into the terminal. Once inside, I realized that instead of Air China we needed the China Air terminal. So we switched gears and power walked a few terminals away.

To our surprise, there was only one group in front of us. We checked in our baggage, went through security and had our boarding passes in hand. As we cleared security and headed towards our gate, a surge of energy rushed through my body just like the one I'd experienced before talking to my dad. I mentioned both of these power surges to my mom and we agreed that it must mean something, but what?

Our terminal gate was under construction and absolutely chaotic. Most of the seats were gone, and the few that remained were pushed against the other benches. This made for no walking space in between. People had to climb over the benches just to get around to the walkway.

My mom and I found a slice of wall to lean against with our carry on packs at our feet. Time ticked by, and I noticed I wasn't hearing the usual calling out over the intercom. "Mom, our connection in Taipei is just a little over two hours, and we are already an hour and 45 minutes behind schedule," I said with an anxious tone to my voice. The speakers weren't working. "Relax, Heather. One way or another it will all work out," my mom responded in a calming tone.

We had a long flight ahead of us. The first leg of our trip was 14 hours, the second seven and the time difference between LA and New Delhi is 12 plus hours. We hoped we'd have our wits about us when we arrived. My mom and I did laugh about our inability to understand what was happening because everyone at our gate was either Chinese or Indian, and speaking languages foreign to us.

Two hours behind schedule we started boarding the plane.

In our final approach into New Delhi, I experienced a first. The flight attendant walked down each aisle spraying disinfectant on people. However at the time I had no idea what the spray was. My mom and I threw our blankets over us. I later found out it was to kill any viruses we might be carrying.

I repeatedly returned to the notebook for the list of tasks we needed to get done once we arrived. I had everything in chronological order.

"Okay, Mom, first thing we need to do after getting our luggage is to find an Airtel to get our prepaid minutes on the phone. Second, we need to get a prepaid cab to take us to the New Delhi train station so we can purchase our tickets for our early-morning departure to Agra. After, we'll find our hotel."

The Hotel Vishal is located on the Main Bazaar Road, and we'll drop off our luggage. The last thing we need to do is to find a bank to exchange the shoebox full of rupees to larger notes." We chuckled as I said, "the shoe box." I was so proud of all the time I'd put into this little notebook.

I had written a few of the Lonely Planet warnings down in my trusty notebook. One of them was to note the number of your cab and give it to the airport police with your destination written on it. I thought this was a smart idea for women travelers; we didn't do that. Expect the unexpected.

Chapter 5
The Debacles

*If you don't like something, change it. If you can't
change it, change your attitude.*

Maya Angelou

Just like an episode of *The Amazing Race*, once the plane
landed, it was on. People pushed and shoved, smashing the
unspoken code of personal space. I quickly learned there's no
three-foot radius rule in India. As a matter of fact, for most of the
trip my mom was walking behind me rather than beside me.

Within the first 15 minutes or so I spotted a dilemma.

"Mom how could I have overlooked this? I must have been
thinking carry on, check in. What I should've been thinking was,
you have one back and so do I." Yet we ended up with four
backpacks and we needed the contents of each of them.

We giggled about my mom's little pack stuffed with the
shoebox of money. We felt we looked a bit suspicious but at that
point no one knew we had it.

21

Once we had our packs in place, at least for the time being, we were ready for task number one. We needed to find an Airtel stall where we'd get some additional minutes added to the cell phone our friends had lent us. They had just returned home from India. The phone was still active and had over 200 rupees on it. It should've been an easy task, but expect the unexpected.

Exhausted from our long trip, we still managed to wear smiles. We found the Airtel stall relatively fast but were met with attitude.

"So sorry," the young gal said in a thick Hindi accent, "you must pay extra start-up fee to activate."

We knew this wasn't true.

"Our friends we'd borrowed the phone from are Indian, and they'd just returned from a family emergency." I said as politely as possible.

The Airtel worker then turned her back on us. "Excuse me." I quickly said to her. "I have the paperwork to show the phone is active through the end of the month and still has money on it." She wouldn't budge. Had I known where we could find another Airtel I would've walked away.

Instead I kindly asked her, "How much?" She told me the price, and I agreed. I told the gal we'd like to put additional money on the phone for extra minutes, but this too became an issue.

After much back and forth negotiating we finally came to an agreement with the young gal. My mom decided to lighten her load of rupees in the shoebox and pay with her money.

What happened next was like a scene out of a comedy. My mom slowly unzipped her little light blue and white polka dot backpack and started fumbling with the lid to the shoebox. She didn't want to unzip the pack completely and expose an entire box filled with money. She awkwardly shoved her hand into the box and started pulling out random bills. The gal looked at my mom's handful of small denomination bills and, with her head bobbling side to side, said, "These bills are unacceptable."

Jet lag, it seemed, had interfered with my mom's typical surplus of patience. "What do you mean unacceptable?" she said through tightly pursed lips.

"Even beggars wouldn't take those low denomination bills anymore", the worker said. My mom, rather aggravated, reached her hand back into the box and pulled out a wad of bills. With every bill my mom held up, we got the head bobble, "No, no, no."

By then I'd become irritated. I grabbed my mom's pack and unzipped it fully, totally the wrong move. All the money started falling out. I quickly shoved the bills back into the box and zipped it up. We were drawing attention from others around us, we must have looked a bit suspicious, and I have to say, I was feeling suspicious.

I remember thinking to myself I just want to get us out of here.

With a slight bit of attitude, I reached into my wallet for the solution. I handed my debit card to the young lady, who looked down at it, then looked back at me and, almost in slow motion, tilted her head to one side then the other side.

"Sorry we don't take credit cards, cash only." She pointed to the money exchange window. Thank goodness, I thought. We shuffled over, and I asked the man behind the window to exchange just enough to take care of the phone. I handed him my card, and he replied, "Cash only."

What a debacle this had become, and we had just landed. Luckily, I had brought some American cash with me just in case. This was one of those cases. With our phone freshly filled with minutes, an hour of our time gone and our blood pressure slightly elevated, we were ready for task number two, find the pre-paid taxi stand.

By this time we were hitting the 20-plus hour mark of sleeplessness. We needed to get our next three tasks done, then catch up on some shuteye. The good news was our hotel and train station in New Delhi were only a 15 to 20 minute drive from the airport. We needed to purchase our train tickets in advance for the morning.

We told the gentleman at the taxi stall that we needed to get to the New Delhi train station. Without a pause, he handed us a receipt and pointed us in the direction of the doors.

As my mom and I walked to the doorway, I said, "I wonder how the cab thing works?" I wanted to be prepared and know what I was looking for.

"I'm going to let you lead the way Heather," said my mom as she fell in behind me to maneuver through the doorway.

Less than 10 steps out the door, a man rushed over to us, stripped the receipt from my hand, grabbed one of my mom's packs and quickly said, "Come, come this way."

We faced quite a spectacle with all the grungy little taxicabs and their drivers hustling about. The thought of the Lonely Planet's warning to give your cab number to airport police crossed my mind. But by the time the warning came into focus, we'd been whisked to the vehicle.

I gulped down a deep breath of air as my bottom came to rest on the taxi seat before our driver zipped away from the airport. My mom and I were sitting tightly together in the back of a cute but dingy looking little VW van. It was so tiny my big backpack alone took up almost the entire back seat. We managed to get out a few chuckles about the Airtel debacle before our white-knuckle welcome to the Indian road system. I'm not quite sure if the word "system" should be associated with the traffic and roads in that country.

It was more like Mr. Toad's wild ride at Disneyland. With sweat dripping from our foreheads and our clothes clinging tightly to our skin, we careened around the seat while our driver sped from one lane to the next. I've always been one for fast cars, and I've had motorcycles for the better part of my life, but this didn't feel safe.

My poor mom received the brunt of my nervousness as I squeezed her leg and hollered "Holy cow!" Nothing could have been more appropriate. I looked at my mom, giggled and said, "Do you get it? Holy cow." We both laughed softly.

I started noticing that the cabbies took their driving very seriously. I use the term poll positioning to describe when the drivers rally to take the lead in the front lanes. These guys were masters.

At the first major intersection we came to, I was pretty sure I saw two lanes marked on the pavement, but there must have been at least five makeshift lanes forming, and not all cars either. There were bikes, rickshaws, tuk-tuks, motorcycles and scooters, which usually had a man driving while a woman sat sideways holding her baby. There were even cows. When the light turned green and we jerked into motion, everyone poll positioned for a spot in one of the two lanes. It was absolute madness.

Our senses were assaulted from every direction, and fatigue added to the intensity. The noise pierced through to our eardrums; the horns constantly blasted, never stopping. The heat and humidity grabbed our lungs as the sweat poured from us. I felt like an amphibian.

As if we had been thrown into a loud rock tumbler, our driver came to a halt on the side of the road. Is something wrong? He hopped out of the vehicle, opened up the back and said to us, "I can go no further." As he unloaded our packs on the side of the road, I asked him, "Is this the train station?" "No." he said in a very short tone. He told us he could drive no farther into this particular area and tried to reassure us it would be no trouble getting there.

Confused, I looked around and saw other vehicles in the direction he pointed. He seemed rushed. I didn't have my bearings or my wits about me, so I asked him again to point in the direction we needed. Before I could understand what he was saying, he drove away. There we stood. Like lost, tired puppies in the middle of chaos. I tried to snap out of my funk, but I felt sick to my stomach. My mom's poor little feet were swollen from all the traveling, and I felt horrible about the backpack situation. I put my larger one on my back and the smaller one on my front side. The larger backpack my mom was using had wheels, so my mom put her little pack filled with all the rupees on her back and attempted to drag the other behind her.

With no sidewalks in sight and only half-paved and rubble-filled roads, my mom's pack presented a challenge. It kept twisting from side to side, making the wheels almost useless. She more or less dragged the pack down the road as we headed towards the biggest tangled web of humanity I had ever laid my eyes on.

In the midst of dodging rickshaws and avoiding cow poop, I tried to keep my eyes on my mom behind me. It would have been easy to lose sight of her in this turmoil, even with her red hair. Finally I got my first glimpse of the train station. Unfortunately, it was on the other side of the road. I took a deep breath and assessed the situation. We faced what appeared to be some sort of intersection, but I didn't see any stoplights or crosswalks. Huge numbers of people, animals and vehicles whizzed by relentlessly.

We must have stood there gawking for a solid 10 minutes. Eventually, I noticed an equally mobbed little side road, with a small sign that said Main Bazaar Road. Hmm, I thought. This sounds awfully familiar. I whipped out my little pocket notebook and there I saw in my own writing "Main Bazaar Road," the street name for our first hotel. The thought of navigating that crush of people made my head hurt. I closed my book and didn't say anything to my mom.

More determined than ever to cross the madness to the train station, I carefully studied the lanes and began to notice raised cement areas people could jump onto to keep from getting taken out by a vehicle. I counted eight lanes of traffic; four that went in one direction and were split with lanes going in the opposite direction. We needed to be extra cautious because the cars moved in the opposite direction from the U.S.

When I saw a slight break in the first section, I abruptly grabbed my mom's arm and pulled. "Quick, mom, let's go!" When we bolted out into the hectic road, my mom's pack twisted and fell over. I scooped it up and hopped onto the cement pad just in time.

I felt extremely emotional and so responsible for my mom's safety, in that moment, I wanted nothing more than to pick her up. My words for my dad flooded over me in the middle of that madness, "Don't worry, Pa, I'll bring Mom back safely." Then I saw another break, and we dodged people and cows until finally we stood smack dab in front of the gates to the New Delhi train station.

We paused to regain our composure and what little wits we had left at that point. I pulled out my notebook for the directions to the International Tourist Bureau. I had put a star by the Lonely Planet warning, "Do not let anybody tell you that the office is closed or has moved due to any reason, religious or not." The directions seemed straightforward. We were to look for a big sign on the first floor with the name on it.

Tour guides and beggars barraged us inside the massive complex. I finally got a glimpse of a sign in the distance with an arrow pointing through a gateway. "I believe this is the way," I said to my mom with relief.

Just as we were about to push the gate open, a young pleasant-looking guy politely asked us what were looking for. "The Tourist Bureau", I told him.

"Oh, so sorry, they are closed at the moment. We are celebrating a religious ceremony. But I assure you I most definitely can take you to where they are sold."

He was smooth, attractive and convincing. My mom and I, due to our delirium, did a double take. He was probably only 17 years old and just as polite as can be. Of course, we were apprehensive about it, but our fatigued brains failed us.

He told us he would get us a cab and safely transport us there. I had reached the point of exhaustion where my eyes took a long time to reopen after blinking. Just as they reopened, the young man waved us into a cab. He told the driver to only charge us a small portion of the usual cost, and away we went.

After a few hair-raising spins and sharp turns, we arrived in a small back alley. The driver slammed on the brakes in front of a tiny little building. On the door were words like travel, adventure and international, but I was pretty sure this wasn't the International Tourist Bureau.

Chapter 6
Three Cups Of Chai

First time you share a cup of chai you are a stranger.
The second cup you are an honored guest. The third time
you share a cup of chai you are family.

Various Cultures

By this time my mom and I felt like the main characters in a movie. We were about to meet a supporting character in our film.

There we stood in the doorway of a tiny office building filled with cubicles. We must've looked so pathetic and lost as we navigated the maze of cubicles, schlepping our packs behind us. But we were still alive, and we still had our passports and money, a whole shoebox of money in fact. The cubicles were so tiny, we had a hard time fitting our packs into the one we'd been directed to, but we shoved and maneuvered them and finally collapsed into the chairs.

"Hello, my name is Shafi. Shafi Shalla. Would you like some chai?" a young man from behind the desk said in a musically accented English tone. We accepted.

29

"You most certainly can call me Al." Shafi told us that most of his friends and family call him Al.

"Why Al?" I asked.

"Because many believe I resemble Al Pacino." His sincerity and the comical pose he struck put a smile on our faces and put me at ease. He extended his arm across the desk to shake our hands and asked both of our names. He had a kind welcoming smile and beautiful almond-shaped eyes to match. He wore a light colored long sleeved shirt with a button front and collar. Despite everything, I felt safe for the moment.

Smoothly he started into the conversation. "What are we trying to accomplish?" I sat there a bit dumbfounded until my neurons fired and I responded, "Ah, well, we are trying to purchase our tickets for an early morning train departure to Agra."

He acknowledged me with a simple, "Okay." I looked at my mom thinking, great, done deal, until he said, "What do we have planned for the rest of our trip?"

This time instead of me pulling out my notebook, I pulled out my folder with all our reservations in it. I handed it over to him and started explaining all the different modes of transportation I had planned on using.

As I explained, he sifted through the pages, saying things like, "Nope, no good," "Nope, bad idea," "No, not safe," "No, malaria area, I wouldn't recommend." In a few moments, he'd butchered five months of my research.

I wasn't mad or angry, but my ego was bruised. Shafi then pulled out a notebook filled with many thank you letters from satisfied customers stating what a wonderful experience he had created for them. The thought crossed my mind they could've been fake. I wanted to believe him.

30

He proudly showed us many pictures of all his wonderful custom trips. It really wouldn't be safe for us to take all these different modes of public transportation, he said, and we would have a much more enjoyable and memorable trip if we hired a car and driver.

I looked at my mom after Shafi suggested the car and driver. Her posture changed, but not in a positive way. In my research, I had looked into the option of hiring a car and driver but figured the best way for us to immerse ourselves in the culture was by way of public transport. But after our brief experience with our packs from the airport to the train station, the thought of an air-conditioned car with a private driver enticed me. I felt a mix of curiosity and tension from my mom.

"How much will this cost?" I asked. Of course it wasn't going to be that easy.

At this point another young man scurried into the cubicle and said, "More chai?" It was quite tasty, so we nodded our heads with a thank you. I could see it was going into the next phase as Shafi pulled out more three ring binders.

"You see here we have many options," he said, pointing from one page to the next. "We offer mid-range, luxury, budget, all to be guaranteed safe and not in bad mosquito area."

I wanted to burst out laughing. There sat my mom and I, barely able to keep our eyes open while a smooth-talking Al Pacino look-alike Indian tore our itinerary to pieces as he tried talking us into hiring a car and driver. At one point I actually looked around for the possibility of a film crew shooting the scene.

I'd planned for us to travel through Rajasthan for two weeks and to visit five different places. As I filled in Shafi on the towns where we'd planned on staying and the number of days in each, he once again responded in his very smooth manner, "No, no, no, you need not spend any more days than necessary in these places. So, I think it's best to visit a few more towns."

I sensed honesty in his voice, but my ego shouted, "Hey, Heather, you just spent countless hours and days piecing this trip together. Are you going to let this smooth-talking salesman change all that?"

My conscience and ego wrestled each other. I had already blown my first two Lonely Planet warnings, and there we were sitting in some back alley office with a seemingly nice man butchering our itinerary. As insane as it all seemed, I felt I was being guided by blind faith.

Shafi offered us more chai. After his first sip, he pulled his calculator onto the desk. We had both explained our sides. There were certain things that my mom and I weren't willing to negotiate. We definitely wanted to keep our jeep tiger safari in the Ranthambore National Park along with the camel safari and the elephant ride into the Amber Palace, and, of course, the jewel of India, the Taj Mahal.

Shafi's brain started churning out hotels that fell into our budget, his fingers punching the calculator buttons. Numbers got written, scratched out, recalculated and other figures added. He flipped that paper around so much we started to get dizzy.

The numbers looked high, really high, and the calculating continued until finally he circled a number and turned the paper to us. He had written it in rupees, and by the time the word "convert" came out of our mouths, he'd spun the paper around, tapped the calculator and came up with the total in U.S. dollars. He circled the number and spun the paper back to us.

There was silence from my mom. We looked at each other. I knew what her eyes said, and it was, "Let's stick to our original plan." My heart dropped. I knew this wouldn't put us in the poor house, but I also knew it wasn't what we had planned. I kept looking at our darn backpacks, and wishing that we didn't have the two smaller packs. I was having a very hard time visualizing my mom and me pushing, pulling and squeezing our way onto the packed public buses and trains.

Somehow my mom and I arrived at a mutual decision to put our faith in what Shafi was selling. Once the price was negotiated, Shafi leaned closer to us from behind his desk, looked us squarely in the eye, broadened his smile and said, "I give you my best driver." He had so many great lines.

What does that mean, his best driver? I guess we'd find out sooner or later. I was hoping he'd speak a bit of English since we'd be spending the next two weeks with him. But before we could meet our driver, we had to settle up on the money.

There we were, day one, and so much had happened already. But just when we thought it couldn't get crazier, it did.

My mom figured she'd use her shoebox rupees to pay for her portion of the new costs, but before we pulled out the box full of money we thought it best to tell them the story. When it was time to unveil the box, we all started laughing. Shafi laughed even harder when he saw how small the denominations were. He agreed that the beggars wouldn't take it. We all laughed some more.

Then came the enormous and quite humorous task of counting all the money, which became a two-person operation. Shafi loudly called out a name, and the fellow who had served us chai earlier appeared. The man's eyes widened when he saw all the rupees. By the time the sorting began, we were all laughing. The bills were inspected one by one.

Shafi started a pile for each denomination, and another pile for unacceptable bills. No one in India, we learned, would accept a bill that had been written on or partially ripped.

As we watched the "no good" pile grow, Shafi exclaimed, "This bill is counterfeit!"

"Counterfeit?" my mom shrieked. How on earth had we gotten counterfeit money? That pile started getting bigger too. Had I been not so fatigued I believe I would have been a bit more concerned but I didn't have enough reserved energy to really give a hoot.

We planned to exchange the bad bills at a bank. Shafi suggested hiding the other counterfeit bills deep in our luggage until we got back to the states and could return them to the moneychanger my mom had used.

It had taken over a better part of an hour to sift through and count all that money. In the end there were 32,000 usable rupees and over 40,000 non usable. We had negotiated for over four hours, consumed three cups of chai, seen numerous heads pop in and out of the cubicle laughing at us (or perhaps with us), and now it was time to meet the best driver.

We picked up our packs as the other employees gathered around us to say their goodbyes. I told them it was our honor to bring so much laughter to their office that day. Shafi swiftly reached to open the front door for us, and as we exited onto the street our eyes fell upon the cleanest imaginable brand new white car.

My mom and I smiled at each other and realized that perhaps the gods were on our side after all. From the front of the vehicle, a pleasant looking man appeared with a huge smile on his face and walked proudly toward us.

Shafi said, "I'd like you to meet my best driver, Kahn. This is the first tour for our brand new car. Blessings on a safe journey." My mom snapped a picture of Shafi and me before I hopped into the car. I will never forget our dear friend Shafi (aka Al).

Chapter 7
The Best Driver

Journal entry: "We were so tired from the flight and everything, but the sheer chaos of it all kept us awake. I just watched and stared out the window. It never ended."

My mom and I were absolutely physically and emotionally exhausted. I could think of nothing better than to close my eyes and fall asleep. I was also thinking the hotel we'd originally planned to stay in was just a few blocks away, but Shafi had recommended we get out of Delhi altogether and head straight to Agra, which is where the Taj Mahal is.

Unfortunately that meant another four hours on the road. Given all that had just transpired, I wasn't feeling comfortable enough to fall asleep. Everything we had planned had just gone out the window, so I started to surrender to what was happening and trust the journey.

The chaos and noise of the city faded into the distance as we headed out on an arid expanse of roadway. The sun was setting. The tall buildings fell away, and I started to feel at ease. I engaged our driver in conversation with some light questions.

We started with our names. His name was Kahn. He had been a driver for 10 years or so. We could tell he was very proud of his position; it was an honor for him. His English was broken but far better than our Hindi, and we found ourselves laughing together already.

He was small in stature, which didn't seem uncommon in this area. We had noticed many Indians have very beautiful almond-shaped eyes. Kahn's were the same, and kind like Shafi's.

The endless pulse of people stretched as far as the eyes could see. The sky was a sort of pinkish brown color, and people bustled on the roadsides for mile after mile. It was very surreal feeling. I remember everything seemed to slow down, and I was able to focus on the smaller things happening all around. A smoky smell permeated the air. I realized that the smoke columns I had seen earlier from the airplane were generated by tiny piles of trash burning all along the sides of the road. The darker it got outside, the more alive the roadsides became.

I drifted in and out. I was fighting a losing battle.

It was close to 10:40 p.m. when we arrived at our first night's accommodations. Kahn quickly and quietly announced our arrival. Packs in hand, we slouched towards the front door only to have a young boy rush over and swipe my hand from the door handle so he could open it for us and then stick out his hand for a tip. This began the unrelenting tipping requests that followed us throughout our journey.

By then we hadn't slept for over 30 hours. All I had been thinking about was laying my head on my pillow and falling fast asleep. But I'd reached the point of exhaustion where my brain wouldn't turn off even with the chance to sleep. Suddenly I had bionic hearing. Every creak in the floor, every sniffle and cough were amplified to feel like torture. We heard someone either gagging or vomiting, a plunger sucking open a clogged drain and a constant flow of footsteps right outside our door.

I said to my mom many times that night, "Are you still awake?"

As soon as I fell asleep, our morning alarm sounded. We'd clocked a whopping three hours of sleep. Welcome to India.

Chapter 8
The Indian Promise

Journal entry:
Raja, the king of India,
thank you for that gift.

Rise and shine felt much more like stumbling out of bed after an entire night of drinking and not knowing where I was. Kahn was quite punctual: 8 a.m sharp just as he'd told us he'd be. It was our first full day in India and we were going to tour its grand jewel, the Taj Mahal.

I had read it was a self-guided tour, and we were to purchase our tickets at the front gate. Like a professional race car driver, Kahn zipped around the streets of Agra. He abruptly pulled to the side of a busy little street, and a youngish looking man hopped into the front seat. He and Kahn shook hands, then the man turned towards us and in a fantastic smooth Indian accent said, "Hello, my name is Akosh. I will be your guide for the Taj Mahal."

I thought, Oh so this is the way they're going to get more money from us. How could I tell them we hadn't paid for a guide without sounding rude?

"How much do you charge? I asked. Kahn smiled at me and said, "Nothing, you just pay him tip."

My mom and I exchanged a "sounds like a deal" look.

"Are we good?" Akosh asked with a big bright smile. We nodded our heads in approval and off we went. Within a few quick turns on the cobblestone roads, the car came to another halt. This time Kahn had all three of us get out of the car in the middle of a very busy street, leaving all our belongings behind except our travel satchels.

"Come, come this way," Akosh said as he darted across the road in front of numerous vehicles.

I closed the door quickly and scrambled across the road with my mom. As we crossed, I watched a man we had met just last night drive away with our luggage. I was trusting Shafi's Indian promise for a safe journey, and I prayed in a few hours we'd be reunited with his best driver and our luggage.

Leaving my worries behind, I looked around and felt as if we'd been spit out of a portal and back in time. We were being led on a journey through the Taj Gang, a labyrinth of tiny cobblestone streets where cows roamed freely and children played in dirty water. Akosh painted us a picture of the history of the area as he wound us through the streets.

His family had lived in the area for generations, and he informed us the neighborhood had been built in the 1600s for the families of all the thousands of laborers that helped build the Taj Mahal.

We felt like the luckiest tourists in all of India. I remember thinking; I bet not many people get to experience this. About 10 minutes or so into our walk a sign reading The Shanty Lodge caught my eye. Why did that ring a bell? I pulled out my notebook, and sure enough, this had been the hotel I'd originally booked for us to stay in Agra. Akosh turned into the hotel and led us up three flights of stairs to a rooftop restaurant for a cup of chai.

The view was absolutely stunning. Smack dab in front of us towered the Taj Mahal, and for the next 40 minutes we got to learn more about both our guide and the magnificent history of the jewel of India.

In Hindi, Akosh means sky. He was educated and a great storyteller, well versed in the history. He was most articulate and spoke very good English, and like the two other characters in our zany movie, he too was a nice looking fellow. I captured his wonderful story on video.

Soon we were winding around a few more streets until we stood in front of the gates of the jewel. With a quick nod of his head and a gesture towards a ticket window, Akosh said, " I will meet you at exit gate in two hours."

And just like that he was gone. A feeling of abandonment crept over me briefly, and I thought to myself, you'd better be here buddy. Then I dismissed the thought and in we went.

It's truly a masterpiece. I felt quite small in this magnificent structure that took 20,000 workers 22 years to complete. As we walked the grounds, my eyes kept focusing on the angle of the Taj Mahal. It seemed to lean slightly to one side. I figured my three hours of sleep influenced my perception, but to this day when I look at the pictures I still see a slight lean. What I later found out is that the four minarets surrounding the mausoleum are indeed inclined outward so if they were to topple in an earthquake they'd fall in the gardens.

As we headed back to see if we still had a car, its driver and our luggage, we noticed a couple of men working in the gardens, with a beautiful oxen pulling a till. We thought this would make a wonderful scrapbook picture, so I had my mom turn towards me with them in the background.

After I snapped a few pictures, one of the men gestured to us to come closer. He indicated that the oxen was gentle and mom was more than welcome to stand beside the creature to get a better shot, so she did. After we thanked him, he put out his hand for a tip. We played dumb and thanked him three more times while leaning forward in a bow. We turned and walked away. I couldn't help but roll my eyes.

The moment of truth was upon us as we exited the grand estate. A familiar face appeared out of the crowd with a big smile. Akosh. He led us along a parkway lined with children begging and running beside us. I shot video as we strolled. We noticed the area had a multitude of handicapped people lying on the cement begging, a heartbreaking sight. I felt like I was in a separate glass bubble as we strolled along. I couldn't identify with it, but my heart hurt to witness it.

I asked Akosh's views on this almost harassing tipping expectation for tourists. I wondered how local working people felt about it and how they handle it. He kindly told us there are far too many tip-requesters. If they can walk and talk, Akosh said that he ignores them, but if they're physically handicapped he sometimes gives them money. It put me a bit at ease hearing him share this but it still didn't erase my irritation. The daily requests became a lesson in patience.

We had a long journey ahead of us. We were about to embark on a fast-paced two weeks. We were there to immerse ourselves in the culture and people of Rajasthan, which is located in the northwest region of India and much of it expands into the great Thar Desert. In our third week we were to head northeast into the mountains and the hill town of Darjeeling. There was plenty of time for reflection as Kahn drove us from one bustling place to another.

It took us over eight hours to drive to the location of our National Geographic-style jeep tiger safari. I made great use of my camera and video. But too late was the thought to utilize "The arm." It quite possibly could have worked in this situation. Our guide had well over 20 years of experience and an uncanny resemblance to Mark Burnett, the T.V mogul who made reality television mainstream with shows like Survivor. I had a connection with Mark through my adventure racing days.

I had reserved a private jeep as a belated birthday present to my mom. The other option had been a vehicle called a canter, which holds around 20 people. Our jeep held six including the driver and our guide.

The reserve was adventurous, like something out of "Indiana Jones and the Temple of Doom." Big beautiful Banyan trees towered over our heads, full of feisty and mischievous Langur monkeys. The 10th century Ranthambore fort shrouded the entire hilltop in the center of the park, the home of the royal Bengal tiger.

I felt like a cameraman for a nature documentary as I rode shotgun in our open jeep. I positioned the cameras while our skilled driver navigated the dusty and bumpy dirt tracks. There was no guarantee that we would glimpse a tiger in the massive reserve, but within moments we started seeing many other amazing animals.

Indian crocodiles sunbathed on riverbank rocks, and we watched one silently slip into the water. A large deer species called a Sambar was quite abundant in this area and the top choice on the tiger menu.

As we sat still listening to the cries of the wild peacocks and other birds, a call came over the guide's radio. He sounded the alarm to the driver and told us to buckle up and hang on. I braced the roll bar as our driver accelerated. He still managed to smoothly negotiate the terrain. I looked into the back seat to see my mom's hair flying in the wind and a smile stretching ear to ear.

For the better part of 10 minutes, we remained in hot pursuit. Of what exactly I wasn't quite sure but I guessed there had been a tiger spotting. We only hoped that we would make it in time. The guide signaled the driver, and we slowed down. Another signal, this time a clenched fist, and we came to a halt.

Intensity was written all over our guide's face. He was focused. I watched him watching and appreciated his alert awareness. It reminded me of when I was with my Hot Shot crew and I would guid the pilots in for an aerial fire attack to hit the target and avoid my crew. It took a lot of concentration.

After a few intense moments of silence, he said, "Look over there, under tree. It's a mom and her two cubs."

Yes! He found us the jackpot. "I found her, I found her!" I exclaimed in a giddy voice. Helping my mom spot her wasn't easy. She and her cubs blended into nature like a beautiful painting.

By then, we weren't alone. Other vehicles had joined in on the celebration, and we were treated to a grand finale. A large male tiger appeared, approaching us for a closer look. He stepped powerfully onto the road behind us with a confident swagger. He was massive.

He continued towards the canter parked behind us. The people in the vehicle looked nervous, and I couldn't blame them. Some of the passengers quietly shuffled in their seats, as if to get out of the tiger's jumping range. But his blood-pumping cameo was brief, and he then disappeared up the embankment through the high grass.

As we drove out the other side of the reserve reflecting on the beautiful creatures, we noticed a few tiny villages with families working. We felt a sense of happiness and peace from them. And like any great movie, we drove off the reserve into the sunset, the skies filled with magical colors and our hearts filled with gratitude.

Athena Rising, a Memoir – Heather Bond

Chapter 9
Evil Monkey Temple

*Journal entry: I was right. I knew this place was going to
be a bit spooky just by reading what Lonely Planet said
about it. But I've never felt such a gnarly dark energy in
my life. It gives me the creeps just thinking about it. I'll
never forget that man's face.*

We were feeling very comfortable with our arrangement with
Kahn. He always made us feel safe, and his humor entertained us.
As we drove into some of the small villages my mom and I
enjoyed watching Kahn and the other drivers hop out of their
vehicles in the middle of chaotic traffic jams. They'd often gather
in small groups, light up their clove cigarettes and chatter like old
friends.

Sometimes this could go on for thirty minutes. I wondered if
Kahn knew any of them. The moment the gridlock started moving
the drivers would jump into their vehicles and compete for the best
poll position.

Kahn soon came to call us Sister and Aunty, which suited us
well. We felt very fortunate to have him giving us the scoop on

what we might encounter. On the outskirts of Jaipur I told Kahn that my mom and I wanted to go to a monkey temple called the Galta Gorge. The Lonely Planet guide gave a warning to single female travelers visiting the area, especially in the evening, which I took heed of.

As Kahn pulled into the deserted makeshift parking lot for the temple, he seemed a bit unsettled. The 500-year-old temple was located deep in a mountain gorge. The sacred water tanks were set within the mountain and occupied by troops of monkeys. It sounded most intriguing.

Kahn informed us once we entered the gates we'd be approached by a person holding a red string, and they'd want to tie it around our wrists. The person would then want to lead us to an altar for a ceremony with incense, oils and more.

"No need to give any money," Kahn said sternly. He seemed concerned. Even though it was still light, the sun had set behind the mountain. I asked Kahn if he'd feel better coming in with us. He told us he wasn't allowed in the temple as a Muslim. This didn't sit well with my mom and me.

As my mom and I stood inside the eerily beautiful temple courtyard I felt very uneasy. We assessed the surrounding area, noticing monkeys perched all over the grounds. The temple was painted a burnt yellow color and was covered in intricate stonework.

We saw no other tourists, just a couple of people who appeared to be locals. I spotted a man dressed in robes peering down on us from a small lattice window and told my mom to slowly look around to see what I was talking about. Before she had a chance, the man was standing in front of us.

A soft creepy voice said, "Welcome." He then gestured for us to put a red string around our wrists. I didn't want to insult him, but something didn't feel right. He tied on the string then gestured for us to follow him through the courtyard. He then led us up a few stairs into a smaller courtyard. A number of unsettling images popped in and out of my head as we followed him.

Before we knew it we were standing inside a shrine area. The man proceeded to light incense and then anoint our hands and feet with oils. He then dipped his finger into a small glass jar and painted a red dot between our eyes.

He started chanting as he picked up an offering tray and rather abruptly shoved it at us. At that point, I heard Kahn's voice echo inside my head, "No need to give money, no need." Despite this, I reluctantly reached into my wallet, pulled out a few smaller bills and placed them on the tray.

The man looked at the money and back at us with an insulted expression. He told us in a rather suspicious tone that the money he receives goes towards the upkeep of the building and grounds. I told him we had no more money to offer and thanked him and stood up to explore the rest of the grounds.

We silently wandered around taking pictures. My eyes kept returning to the deep gorge where the sacred tanks were located. There was something enticing me to hike back towards them, so we headed in that direction.

The temple had an abandoned feeling. It sprawled out over a wide area, and the tanks were positioned at the farthest point from the main entrance.

The temple and surrounding area swarmed with monkeys. Dusk had set in as we walked up a few steps to another level. The monkeys started getting more aggressive, howling as we walked through. These weren't the cute little monkeys of storybooks.
These animals had long sharp teeth that can do great harm.

Athena Rising, a Memoir – Heather Bond

I told my mom to get closer to me as we proceeded, but loud monkey calls from further up the gorge stopped me in my tracks. I stood very still as I heard more monkeys getting closer. A cold energy crept over my body, and I felt the monkeys around us grow more assertive.

I started shooing them away, but it didn't faze them. I didn't want to agitate them more, so I started saying loudly, "No, go away. Stop!"

When that effort failed, I grabbed my mom's hand and said, "We need to get out of here. Something doesn't feel right." It was as if a voice was telling me, "You've seen the beauty and felt the energy, now you must leave!" We didn't sprint, but we did get out of there quickly.

With my mom's arm clutched in my hand, I headed straight back for the car. Kahn was sitting inside. We hopped into the vehicle post haste. Kahn had a concerned look on his face when he saw us jump in and close the doors abruptly.

"Sister, aunty are you okay?" He was turned in his seat with his eyes looking directly at us and not through the mirror like usual. "We are fine Kahn, we just got a bit spooked." My mom's words quivered slightly as she responded. Shaking off that dark feeling took a while. I don't use the word evil lightly, but that's my best description for the energy I felt. My mom and I reflected on the warning Kahn had given us prior to entering the grounds, and we understood why he seemed so uneasy.

Chapter 10
Colors In The Desert

*Journal entry: The constant begging is getting to me.
It's absolutely ridiculous. I want to feel bad for some
people and I do but then I get really pissed off.*

*I don't want anyone to do anything nice for me
because they ask for a tip.*

*Hold a door, expect a tip, hand me a paper towel
expect a tip. Good frickin' grief, I can't stand it.
Everywhere you turn. Tip, tip, tip!*

Rajasthan is a very colorful place, and the region is famous for its colorful saris. I wanted to give my mom a beautiful sari for another belated birthday present, so we headed to the pink city of Jaipur.

Jaipur is Rajasthan's biggest and most modern city, and its nickname (The Pink City) comes from its many pink-washed buildings. Often on our long drives we were entertained by visuals of village life. A few times we got to see amazing camel trains being led through the dry arid lands of the desert region. A couple of them had fuzzy newborn camels walking beside their mothers, a magical moment to witness.

At one point in our journey, my eyes fell on a beautiful and angelic sight. Standing inside an open door was a beautiful Rajasthany girl. She was dressed from head to toe in white. She arched her back and neck as she brushed out her long ebony hair, looking like an angel standing among the sea of dirt and crushed and cindered souls. Her eyes seemed soft and not yet jaded by her environment. Our eyes locked for a moment, and then she was gone. Her image has stayed etched in my mind.

Our long drives allowed for a lot of reflecting. In one of my journal passages I wrote that in three days we logged over 18 hours on the road. The drives gave me both a sense of freedom and sadness. I felt as though my soul was awakening from a long slumber given all that had transpired during the last two and a half years with the Fire Department, but my heart felt trapped in a red flag relationship with Sean. I was to marry him soon, so why wasn't I spending this time of reflection feeling joyful and excited?

The pink city of Jaipur is a bustling fast-paced place to visit, and it's where the magnificent red sandstone and marble Amber Palace is located. The palace was built in 1592. Many tourists come to not only admire its beauty, but to have the experience of riding up the hillside cobblestone road on the back of a massive elephant. We too wanted to enter the grand palace in style like the Maharajas of its early days.

As usual Kahn gave us the dos and don'ts and what we might encounter on our daily excursion. We got quite a kick out of listening to Kahn's warnings. They were always spot-on, plus we always seemed to get a few unexpected experiences. As Kahn was driving us towards the Amber Palace, he pulled off to the side of the road quite suddenly and said, "Roll up window!"

I looked through the front windshield and saw a massive wall of sand and debris barreling towards us. It had to be at least a mile in length and over 100 feet tall. It was as if our car sat inside a giant sand blaster. It shook and rumbled around. The sand hit the sides so hard it sounded as if it were scraping the paint off the new vehicle.

My curious side wanted to feel the force of the wind hit my body, but my smarter side kicked in when I saw huge pieces of debris flying through the air. Then, as quickly as it hit us, it was gone.

Kahn exited the vehicle to check for any damage. Thankfully we were good to go.

We weren't the only ones wanting to experience the elephant ride up into the palace that day. It was as though every country in the world was represented in the line.

After being assigned our elephant and handler my mom and I sat high above the ground on the back of a big beautiful 40-year-old female named Lechme, who was gorgeously painted and adorned with jewels.

As the massive creature slowly swayed and swished from side to side, we imagined what it must have been like in the early 1600s. We often had to remind ourselves that these palaces weren't props, and we weren't at Disneyland. Many lives had been lived and much blood shed in these regions. It was spectacular.

As the elephants assembled in an open courtyard to allow their passengers to exit onto a high platform, we noticed bananas being given to the elephants and thought it would be fun to feed the elephant. My mom was the first to get off of Lechme, and I followed from the opposite side.

I turned to the man to thank him, and he demanded, "Seventy rupee." I reached into my wallet, took out 70 rupee and handed it to him. Then an irritated voice to my right drew my attention. There seemed to be a disagreement going on between a tourist and a handler.

"Seventy rupee!" our handler repeated. I turned back towards him and informed him that I had just given him the money. He shook his head at me and muttered, "No, no, no," while looking at my mom with his hand out.

I told him firmly that we had already paid a good amount of money for the ride, and though we were okay giving him the first 70 rupee, we had no more to give him.

He wouldn't budge.

The voices to our right started getting louder and more heated. The female tourist spoke harshly to her husband, sounding very embarrassed at the situation. I then noticed the handler used an elephant to block the pathway with its trunk so that the people couldn't walk away.

At first we chuckled at this scenario; it was quite a comical sight. Sadly these people were getting harassed like my mom and I were, only their situation had reached a whole different level. We heard the wife say loudly to her husband, "For God's sake, just give him the money."

In his thick English accent, the man responded by saying he had already given the handler too much money and it was the principle of the matter.

I looked back at our handler and said to him again, "We have no more money for you!" He nodded his head in defeat, and we walked away. We weren't the victors either though; we never got to feed the 70-rupee banana to the elephant.

The pink city had a lot to offer as far as more modern conveniences, but it was loud and never seemed to sleep. Even when we were tucked in our hotel room at night, the noises permeated the walls.

Kahn seemed quite happy to be here. His village was on the outskirts of the city, so I'm sure he felt very at home. He knew of some wonderful places for us to eat. It took my mom and me quite some time to figure out the portion sizes of the meals. We had several hilarious mealtimes, including one at a spectacular rooftop restaurant of one of our hotels.

On one particular evening the sun was setting and the air was warm. We were both very hungry from our long day but still amateurs at ordering food. After a young boy took our order, he said, "Will anyone else be joining you?"

"No, no it's just my daughter and me," My mom said pleasantly. He looked at us with a puzzled expression, bobbled his head and responded, "Okay, no worries."

After a short wait, the young waiter reappeared with another boy and started lining up a multitude of dishes we'd ordered. We laughed out loud, the boys joined in the laughter. There sat eight decent-sized dishes, enough for a family of at least six. We then understood his earlier question.

One afternoon, Kahn took us to a textile shop to have our saris or shalwar kameezes made. We had really been looking forward to this experience. As we entered the shop, all eyes turned towards us. The male workers bustled over. "How can we help you?" At least four of them stood around us.

We let them know our shopping intentions, which gained more smiles from them. "Yes, hi. My mom and I are here to have an outfit made." The hot weather and the cluttered shop made me feel claustrophobic.

"Yes, yes come this way. We have most excellent quality fabric." This gentleman became my helper. Every wall around us had floor-to-ceiling shelves with bolts of every type of fabric. It was quite dizzying. Then it began. I had imagined an elegant experience; instead, it was a battle of the bolts.

One of the men started the show by pulling down the first bolt of material for our approval. We shook our heads kindly with a pleasant, "No, thank you." Then the next one leapt off the shelf and appeared in front of us. "No, thank you. Perhaps I can just look around a bit," I said as softly as possible.

Then bolts came flying out from different directions, pattern after pattern flung through the air, piled into heaps on the floor and draped over the chairs. The smile drained from my face. I felt like saying, "Leave me the f#@k alone." But of course I didn't.

I continued to stroll and tried to stay focused on the mission. My mom was having the same experience in another part of the shop. After quite some time in the store, my mom and I decided to sit down and take a break. Sweat dripped down our foreheads, and I felt a bit nauseated. We sipped on the chai we'd been served and then got back to business.

Over an hour later, my mom spotted a beautiful material. It was a rich regal purple with gold trim, absolutely stunning. I decided I would get the same fabric and pattern but in a beautiful royal blue color.

Then it came time for the body measurements. My mom's were taken very efficiently, but mine were not easy.

The salesman had the measuring tape turning and twisting in many different directions. He didn't seem sure of himself. At one point he even had another fellow come over to help. I felt like an animal in a zoo as all the workers gawked at the spectacle. They grabbed my arm muscles and looked at me smiling as if they had never seen such a muscular female tourist before. With the measurements finally written down, we paid half amount and would pay the remainder upon delivery. I informed the merchant that we'd be leaving the next morning at nine. He assured me they'd have them both done by that evening.

Throughout our travels, we never really settled into our hotels. We were always heading off to the next town, village and adventure along our journey. The relentless days of excessive horn honking, exhaust and the intensity of the pleading and scheming on the streets had begun to take a toll on us. At home, we live on five quiet mountainous acres, so India's crowds and constant activity put us on sensory overload.

That evening after the textile shop we were busy organizing our packs for our morning departure when the phone in the room rang. It was the man at the front desk.

He told us someone was here to see us. My mom and I ran down the two flights of stairs to find a young man holding two parcels. He handed them over as he informed us they were our outfits and he'd like for us to try them on. We were so excited.

Once we got to our room I put the pants on first and, bingo, they fit. My mom put her top on first, and, wow, it was beautiful. I tried to pull on my top, but my arms and head wouldn't fit. My mom suggested we turn the shirt inside out, where we discovered what seemed to be ample material for the seam to be let out. We ran back down to the lobby and I explained the situation as best I could to the fellow waiting.

He gave a few head bobbles and said, "Ok, I'll be back." Although it was already nearly 9 p.m. we knew there was no alternative other than to wait up. I laid in bed reading. My mom had already fallen asleep, when the front desk alerted me the fellow had returned with the garment. I quietly and excitedly ran downstairs.

The same young, tired-looking boy handed me a parcel and told me to try it on. I grabbed the package and ran back up the two flights of stairs. "Oh no!" I softly said under my breath. It still didn't fit. This time I got it around my head and part way to my shoulders, but it went no further.

Due to my moaning and groaning my mom was now awake and again told me to turn it inside out to see if there was any hope of enlarging it. Chances were slim; there wasn't much material left to work with.

I ran down the stairs where the young man stood waiting. I told him I was sorry, but it still didn't fit. His shoulders sank, but then he raised them and said, "No worries. I have for you by morning." I felt bad though it was no fault of my own. I was reminded of how concerned I was by the trouble they were having while measuring me earlier that day.

I informed the boy that we were leaving at 9 a.m., and he assured me he'd have it ready in time.

The morning came quickly, and the car was loaded as Kahn waited patiently for us. Just past the nine o'clock hour, the young man rushed into the lobby and handed me the parcel. I ran up the two flights of stairs, tore off my shirt and a smile of relief crossed my face. No room to spare but wearable. I thanked and paid him the balance. My mom and I hopped into the car, laughing as we headed off to our next adventure.

The golden city of Jaisalmer was to be our most westerly destination. Located in the heart of the great Thar Desert near the Pakistan border, Jaisalmer is home to the desert gypsies. At the center of this golden colored town, perched high on a sandstone hill stands the thousand-year-old Jaisalmer fort and its labyrinth of tiny cobblestone roads that housed people, shops and food establishments. It was spectacular.

There were various times through our adventures with Kahn that we got a taste of the discrimination between different religions, sects and the caste system. The hotel Shafi arranged in Jaisalmer wouldn't allow Kahn to stay in the servants or driver's quarters. This upset my mom and me to the point that we asked to leave. Kahn insisted it was okay and that he'd find himself another place, but he ended up sleeping in the car.

We saw Kahn as an extended family member. We relied on his keen knowledge and his enthusiastic personality. We were always inviting him to come along on our excursions, but that must have been taboo. So we enjoyed the long drives with him and sharing our experiences of the day. He always patiently awaited our arrival at the car. Most times when my mom and I got back to the car, Kahn would be buffing it, keeping it spotless. He was so proud.

In planning our journey to India, I had sought out a camel safari. Lonely Planet suggested avoiding the popular safari and recommended looking into an excursion another 80 miles into the Thar Desert that was far less tainted by the tourist scene. They painted a cleaner more serene sounding experience than the mainstream safari, where we'd be surrounded by mobs of people and a sea of plastic water bottles on the sand of the desert. Thanks to Lonely Planet, we chose wisely.

The drive out to the tiny village of Khuri was long and desolate. It was the great Thar Desert. In the distance, rain clouds appeared to be forming and moving in. This made us chuckle. We knew we'd be heading out overnight on the camels and thought what are the chances of it raining on us? We'd been praying for rain throughout the sweltering heat for days now, and it looked as though our prayers might be answered.

The desert has an amazing capacity to play tricks on your senses. Barren land seemed to stretch out for miles and miles around us, but after a quick left turn that seemed to lead to nowhere, my eyes fell upon tiny brown dwellings. Kahn pulled up and said, "Ok, we're here."

The village contained about 20 or so dwellings. It was very clean, unlike any of the places we'd visited up to this point. We noticed a handful of other tourists wandering about, six to be exact. Kahn walked us into a beautiful horseshoe shaped courtyard. It reminded me of a miniature western town.

We got checked in and pulled out our gear for a night under the stars. We were thrilled to find out that my mom and I were being led on a private camel safari with two guides. My guide's name was Mahesha, and the camels belonged to his family.

My mom's guide did not speak English and we didn't learn his name. He was the mystery man in the beautiful marigold color turban. Kahn made sure my mom felt safe and secure as she mounted her camel. I watched him give her a few pointers on camel etiquette. Before long we were on our camels, waving goodbye to Kahn and being led deeper into the desert by two men we had never met.

It's amazing how high up I felt on the back of my camel. They are called the ship of the desert for good reason. I'd never been around camels, and they're definitely strange creatures. Mine seemed to be in heat. She made a deep gurgling noise that was rather gross. I believe it was trying to attract a mate as it flapped its tail up and down.

Our guides walked methodically in front, leading the camels, and for the next couple of hours we strolled through villages and over dunes. The camels were loaded with our little overnight packs and all the provisions for our safari. Not far into the walk, the guides started collecting little pieces of firewood. We crested a final dune where the camels came to a halt and the guides set up our camp.

Surrounded by sand dunes, my mom and I ventured up to a high point to catch the sunset. I felt so lucky to be standing there on that dune with my best friend. Our camp consisted of two cots for my mom and me to sleep on. We hadn't paid for the Hilton, so we didn't expect anything more.

As we sat on our cots admiring the two men working in tandem to prepare a delicious hand cooked meal we felt safe. They sat on the hot desert sand as Mahesha cooked the meal and my mom's guide kept the fire burning perfectly with a constant stream of wood. The small sparks of the fire danced into the night sky.

Before dinner was served they made us two wonderful cups of chai .We chuckled when we noticed one of the small espresso looking cups had a broken handle. Then we noticed the men were drinking out of giant leaves they had picked and folded into a cup shape.

The camels lay grassing upon dried leaves on the desert floor creating a safety buffer for our camp. With our tummies full and satisfied, we welcomed the silence of the desert. The only sounds were the crackling of the fire and an occasional gurgle from the camels.

The desert night sky was magnificent with no lights around us to distract the stars. Our guides cleaned up the camp and settled down on the desert floor, tucking in with their camels. My mom and I had pulled our cots together, and we laid there staring up at the sky and reflecting on our journey. We were grateful for all the amazing adventures but also weary of all the other madness that had come along with it. We looked forward to a more peaceful time in Darjeeling.

I awoke suddenly to the pitter-patter of raindrops and moved my head under the blankets. Soon I felt one of the men drape a tarp over my mom and me. It was still quite dark out. My mom and I starting softly giggling like two little girls at a slumber party.

There were still a few more hours before daylight. The raindrops got bigger and louder as they landed on the blue tarp covering us. We were grateful for this covering, but eventually a leak formed right between us. Our giggles got a bit louder. We didn't want the guides to hear us so we tried to ignore the leak. There was no way we were going back to sleep.

We were soaking wet by the time we got back to the village where Kahn eagerly awaited us. We had huge smiles on our faces, as did the other tourists who had just finished their overnights. We all sat together in a simple and clean space and shared a meal and our stories of our rainy camel adventures.

Our journey had involved many different species of animals, from tigers to elephants, to monkeys, camels and rats. The rats weren't as exotic, but they were a sight to behold.

The Karni Mata Temple, better known to my mom and me as the rat temple, was home to 25,000 black rats. These holy rats are called kabbas, and many people travel great distances to pay their respects. Out of the many thousands of rats, there are a few white rats that are considered especially holy. They are believed to be the manifestation of Karni Mata, a female Hindu warrior sage.

The first thing that caught my eye at the temple was the pile of shoes outside the entrance. I don't mind mice, but I've never been a fan of rats. The only rat I ever like was Templeton from the classic children's book "Charlotte's Web." Just the thought of walking barefoot among the rats made me squeamish. Everyone has weak spots, and rats are one of mine.

But off went my sandals and in we went. The temple was very beautiful, with marble carvings adorning the walls and pillars. It had a big courtyard with many different smaller shrine rooms dedicated to various prayers and pilgrims. The courtyard was filled with locals bringing offerings of Prasad (gifts) to the rats.

People lounged on the floors, allowing the rats to run over them and sharing their food with the rodents. Rats lurked everywhere, many of them pushing and shoving and climbing on each other to get a good position at the milk bowls.

My mom and I heard some chanting coming from a small shrine so we poked our heads in for a peek. The people appeared to be in a trance as sweat beaded from their foreheads, and the chanting got faster and louder. I didn't understand how or why all these people could be praying to these creatures and feeding them their precious food. Then I realized, like many things in life, it's just the way it is.

Chapter 11
One Life - Many Chapters

*All that is gold does not glitter, not all those who wander
are lost; the old that is strong does not wither, deep roots
are not reached by the frost.*

J.R.R Tolken

One of the most profound attributes of the human being is that we are all perfectly unique. After exploring the Karni Mata temple it was hard for my mom and me to understand what faith drives individuals to pray to rats and share their food with them while so many fellow humans in this world starve, but like I said, this is what makes us all unique.

In a world teeming with difference I thought about my own personal belief systems and how my upbringing and geographic living locations have had influence on a variety of decisions I had made thus far in my life. But I also recognized as an individual unique from any other human I was born with my own dreams and desires, some from a young age that morphed as I fed them.

Athena Rising, a Memoir – Heather Bond

I was the curious and mischievous little sister. With skinned up knees and snot dripping down my dirty face, I had one doll named Sally. I wasn't much for dolls. I think I carried Sally around only so I could use her as a scapegoat and blame everything on her. I can still hear my mom frustratingly say, "Heather, did you get into my perfume?" Heck, it was never me it was Sally.

Shortly after my brother started first grade, (he's almost two years older than I am,) one morning before he was heading off to school he specifically told me not to go up into his tree fort because he hadn't finished securing the floor. It was built in one of our apricot trees. It was as if what he told me enticed and provoked me more. After he left I quickly scurried up the tree like a happy little squirrel stashing his jackpot of found goodies.

Agile but lacking the smarts I stepped off the high branch onto the flooring. With less time than it took me to climb up and a quick flip of the wood, I fell with a thunderous thump to the earth below and a clean snap to my collarbone. This was the beginning of pushing my limits but also learning that safety is first and foremost, especially if you want to live to see another day.

I came into this world with curiosity of body and mind. To experience the capacity at which the human body can physically be pushed and how we can control our mind and thoughts.

I believe this was innate within me from the beginning. I was fascinated and inspired by individuals who had mastered particular physical feats and challenged their limits, like Nadia Comaneci, the first Olympic gymnast to receive a perfect score of ten in the 1976 Montreal games. Gymnastics became my first competitive sport.

Bruce Lee was another person I fashioned my training skills around. Pound for pound powerful, agile and yet graceful, he is one of the greatest martial arts icons.

Then of course there was Mr. Jack LaLanne. I loved watching his shows in the 1970's. He was the Godfather of modern fitness. Seeing him perform his impressive almost humanly impossible physical feats was thrilling to me; such as the time at age 60 he swam for the second time from Alcatraz to Fisherman's Wharf. This time he not only wore handcuffs but he also towed a 1,000-pound boat. I am proud that my parents were in alignment with his nutritional philosophies. They definitely were ahead of the times.

My family spent a lot of time in nature either camping or out on the high seas with my diver and fisherman father. I was taught how to survive off the land if something were ever to go wrong. I knew from a young age how to handle weapons and became skilled and accurate with a bow and arrow, guns and knives. I was taught how to make weapons such as spears and traps to snare animals to eat.

My dad also had my brother and me learning new skills and I became proficient with machinery and woodworking. I could even tie a bowline knot with my feet. He would tell me to be like a sponge and absorb all I could.

I was exposed to many different types of animals from a young age. In the late sixties and early seventies my dad worked with the Santa Barbara Zoo. Not too many kids grow up with capybaras and tree kangaroos as backyard pets. Capybaras are the world's largest rodent; they look like a giant Mr. Potato head with four legs. One of my fondest memories was my brother and I sitting in the back bed of my dad's old light blue pick-up truck while transporting the Santa Barbara zoo's first gibbon. It was special. My brother and I were the two little kids behind the scenes and cages at the zoo. That sure wouldn't happen now days.

I didn't grow up vegetarian but we didn't consume a whole lot of meat, and what we did was mainly raised by us. This meant I had to learn how to slaughter or quickly kill the animals. My dad was very serious about the process. He didn't want to have the animals needlessly suffer. Looking back I am grateful for the experience and knowledge but as a young girl this was the last thing I wanted to do.

It started at the age of six. The smell of iron in the blood still haunts me to this day. My first job was plucking the feathers off the limp lifeless bodies of the chickens. My brother and I were in the 4H Club and we also raised hundreds of rabbits. I will never forget when I had to kill my first rabbit: I was about ten. I initially failed and not only got all scratched up by the rabbit but got a yelling at from my dad because I hadn't followed proper procedure.

Like I said, this wasn't fun, it was supper. Dinner of that nature was always hard for me to palate, and definitely not for the faint of heart.

By fourth grade I had become a dual sport competitive athlete. Gymnastics and track and field were my chosen sports. Much of my time revolved around these. At 13 years old I started weight lifting. I was fascinated by how powerful my body was and how the muscles developed through my discipline. My bedroom walls were adorned with posters of Bruce Lee, Arnold Schwarzenegger, Carl Lewis and other amazing athletes. I started earning my collection of various medals, ribbons and awards.

We all have a duality to our personalities. Mine was like, Mrs. Cleaver and still is, meets the extreme athlete. I made my first full turkey dinner with all the fixings for my family at the age of 13. It was delicious and I learned to ride a motorcycle right alongside that turkey dinner. My parents fertilized my childhood with many fond memories.

Once high school started I became more focused on track and field and I let my love for gymnastics become a fond memory for the time being. The summer before my sophomore year of high school I started dating Blue, my then friend of three years. He was rough around the edges and handsome as all get out. This was the beginning of the first fall and rise of teenage Heather.

I started hanging around a different crowd, fun yet a little more wild, actually, much more wild. I refer to this as the summer of '86. My sports started to take a back seat for the first time in my life. Talk about growing pains. Within a nine-month period I found myself suspended multiple times from school, arrested for being a minor in possession of alcohol, dabbling in drugs, and fired from a job-until finally I got kicked out of my high school.

I can remember so clearly my mom sitting in the schools dean's office telling the dean, Mrs. Maxwell, that as far as she was concerned I should just drop out of school and start working full time. Mrs. Maxwell leaned towards both of us and said, "Mrs. Bond I don't think that's a good idea." I am grateful to this day for her saying that.

That night at home got ugly. I had taken a toll on my parents and they had lost a lot of respect for me because of my poor choices. My dad verbally lashed out at me with a few truth bombs. I was so pissed off at him for saying what he did. I stormed away not noticing my mom in the beanbag chair and under my breath I made a derogatory remark to my dad.

Before I knew it my mom spun around, stood up, and pushed me into a wall, where I accidentally knocked down one of her favorite ornamental plates breaking it. When I hit the wall I reacted and shoved her back with a lot of force. And in that moment I lost respect for myself.

I did what I needed to do to get myself back on track, no pun intended. I worked my tail off at a continuation school until I made up enough credits to resume my education at my regular high school. I graduated with my class, no small feat at that time in my life. I also broke a school record as a discus thrower and continued thriving through college where I not only won a Western States Conference in discus, I earned a degree in exercise physiology and nutrition.

Athena Rising, a Memoir – Heather Bond

At twenty-two I had been waiting tables at a restaurant for seven years and then started coaching gymnastics with my former coach. I had finished my first round of college and I was looking to become a personal trainer.

One evening my mom and I were flipping through the T.V. channels at our house and stumbled upon a show called The American Gladiators. It was an athletic competition that vied the muscular athletic Gladiators that sported their famous red, white and blue spandex uniforms against the more common athletes from varied backgrounds.

As I watched with butterflies in my stomach, adrenalin surged through my body. I said to my mom, "Gosh, I would pay to do something like that!"

The universe responded to my request when at the end of the show the commentator said, "If you feel you have what it takes to compete against the Gladiators write to this address below to get a application." My mom had jumped up off the floor and grabbed a pencil and paper before my gaping jaw could close.

I grappled, ran, bled and fought my way to become one of 16 men and women out of 6,500 across the United States to earn a position to be pummeled by the Gladiators on television. I had two shows air in the fifth season in 1993. But instead of me paying for the experience, I got paid. It was my gateway to a decade long adventure that took me all over the world.

At the age of 22 it made me one of the youngest competitors. I instantly befriended the oldest female competitor, Cathy, on the show. She was a two time Olympic kayaker and fire fighter. Our relationship flourished and continued after the shows were completed for the season.

One day I received a call from her. She was super excited and started telling me how someone had recommended her to meet up with a U.S. team captain for an adventure racing competition. She proceeded to tell me the races could be anywhere from seven to twelve days long, 350 to 400 miles, in countries around the world and that various disciplines were involved such as mountain biking, mountaineering, kayaking and more. I was on the edge of my seat with excitement as she was explaining and felt a bit green with jealously.

Cathy proceeded to tell me how they wanted her to try out for the position of the lone female. She started laughing to me as she recalled the conversation with them, "Why would I want to do something that sounds so grueling? But I have the perfect gal for you,- her name is Heather Bond."

The country was Borneo, the third largest island in the world. The race was The Raid Gauloises. I was 23 years old and the lone female on a five-man team. We should have been called "Team Fun Gets It Done", but instead we were called Team South Bay.

We were comprised of a veteran racer, a New Zealander, former rugby player who happened to be a former teammate of Mark Burnett future Godfather of reality television. We had a former Navy Seal, and the rest of us had varied backgrounds.

Reebok became our main sponsor. Our team worked seamlessly together. We spent thousands of hours training and racing in smaller races. One of my teammates happened to be the president of the speleology club in San Diego, California and caving or spelunking happened to be one of the disciplines for Borneo.

I feel extremely fortunate that I was taught and became proficient in surveying cave systems. This gave us access to many caves throughout California and the Mexican border.

I had the honor of becoming the first female to navigate the entire system of one particular water cave. It was amazing. We spent countless hours exploring the subterranean world. I used to visualize myself like a snake.

Slithering on my belly through the narrow almost rib crushing crawl spaces. It was both physically and mentally strenuous. We schlepped ropes, climbing harnesses and hardware along with a lot of other necessary gear, food and water.

With only headlamps lighting our way, safety was always at the forefront. Some caves we'd rappel multiple times down or side climb between two walls not knowing if there was a bottom floor. Nothing was rushed. I got to witness the magnificent life that thrives in these environments. I had never seen creatures without eyes before.

A few times I was in charge of the anchor string. This was our lifeline to the world above. Eighteen hours was the longest I was down at any given time. I remember as we resurfaced my equilibrium was a bit off but I also felt alive.

When you are a part of a team you're only as strong as your weakest link. Being the youngest and only female on various teams I never felt like the weakest link. We all had our strengths and weaknesses.

As I became more experienced my confidence grew. By running in orienteering races I became efficient at navigating with a map and compass in the wilderness. I became a skilled rock climber, mountaineer, kayaker and mountain biker. I thrived in these elements.

In 1995 Mark Burnett launched the very first Eco-Challenge race in Utah. The same year the twelve top teams from that race came together in the Eco for the first X-Games. Again I was the lone female on a Marine Corp team.

Shortly after I was recommended to the race director of the Four Winds expedition length adventure race to help them with race logistics and run in a time trial of the course.

The race started in Durango, Colorado and ended in Taos, New Mexico. The course was close to 400 miles. I selected a good friend and my closest race partner, John, as a team member and logistics partner. I've known John since I was 15 years. When I was 24 he and I started doing crazy races and adventures together. He's now been inducted in the ultra running and cycling world hall of fame or something crazy cool like that.

One of my fondest memories on that time trial race was a particular morning when we hadn't slept in two days. The purposed course they gave us for the mountain bike section turned out to be a long slog of carrying our bikes on our backs on top of our packs up countless hills throughout the 50 plus mile section. The night prior the temperatures had dropped so significantly our water in our hydration packs froze.

When the sun rose that morning I felt a renewal of energy and I pedaled off ahead of my teammates. As the wind swept through my dusty braid in my hair I spotted a quick movement out of my left periphery. I was on a downhill run moving quickly. I glanced over to see what it was and to my shock I was looking into the ice blue eyes of a wolf. Up to that point in my life I had always thought wolves were kind of evil.

He steadily loped alongside me, not threatening. It was magical feeling. I couldn't believe what was happening. I remembered I had a disposable camera hanging from my pack strap and thought I better snap a picture of this once in a life time moment. As I reached across for the camera my bike started to wobble so I quickly grabbed back on to the handle bar. I remember thinking what would happen to me if I fell off my bike?

I glanced sideways towards this majestic looking creature and as we locked eyes for a brief moment, it was as if time warped. As the hill started to soften the wolf bounded behind me off the trail. I got to the bottom and stopped abruptly and saw nothing. Within a few seconds my teammates arrived and John said, "Oh my gosh Heather, you just missed a wolf on the side of the trail."

As I drifted in and out while being driven by Kahn across the long barren expanses of India I couldn't help but think of all the various people that became a part of my journey, some for a brief moment that quickly fluttered away while others left a lasting imprint.

My racing community was as such. It often felt like a family reunion at the next big race, meeting up in special places around the world such as Africa, New Zealand and British Columbia. It was always a guaranteed adventure. Back then there was no social media such as Facebook or Instagram, so there was always much catching up to do.

In 1996 Mark Burnett launched the third Eco-Challenge in British Columbia, Canada. It was set to be an epic course. My racing partner, John, and I had compiled a very skilled team of athletes for this race. One of the members had come in second place in the first Eco-Challenge in Utah. The others were equally, if not more, qualified.

Unfortunately after months and hundreds of hours of training together I got word our team sponsorship pulled out supposedly due to Discovery Channel taking over the sponsorship of the entire event.

I was so flustered. I couldn't imagine investing all the time and money not to race. So, I put my name on a list at the Eco-Challenge to see if there were any teams looking for a last minute addition.

I initially received a few calls from out of state teams plus a Spanish team, but they didn't seem like good options. I wanted to at least meet the team prior. Not more than two weeks before the race I received a call from a team that lost a member due to an injury. They were from Los Angeles, just a two-hour drive from me.

The team met up prior to the race but I only recall going out on one training hike with them; it was painfully slow. I wondered if joining their team would be a good idea. Part of me thought I could become a motivating force to help them get to the finish line.

Once we arrived in British Columbia it was apparent to me that the race organizers had possibly bitten off more then they could chew by allowing 80 teams to sign up. That was absolutely unheard of, perhaps 50 but not 80. I watched teams just slide through the proficiency tests. Not what you want when people's lives are on the line. I, too, was beginning to feel I had bitten off more than I could chew by hooking up with the wrong group of people for a race of this magnitude.

I remember Mark approached me and asked how I ended up with this team. I chuckled and let him know. I also let him know I wasn't overly confident with their ability and asked him if by chance my team members dropped out of the race would there be a possibility I could hook up with another team. He responded with a yes.

Within the first day it was evident this wasn't going to work out between this team and me. Since I was the last minute walk on team member they already had their appointed navigator, who in my book didn't know the first thing on navigation, it was so frustrating.

British Columbia is big grizzly bear territory and I didn't want to be scampering around needlessly in circles through the bear thickets. Unfortunately this is exactly what happened the first night. I was absolutely certain we needed to be crossing the river at a particular area but the team was afraid and untrusting.

They couldn't grasp the notion that this particular high log crossing the river was our only option, but it was. Day light ticked away as they squabbled. Their team captain blurted out, "We'll sleep here for the night." Irritated I said, "We aren't on a camping trip. This is a race with time cut offs." They wouldn't budge. I lay awake most of the night thinking about grizzlies.

The next morning one of the race helicopters landed and informed the team their only option to get across the river was indeed the log. I was so pissed off. We wasted nine precious hours. Once all members got to the other side of the river I took off solo. I had to get away from them. I was looking for the next checkpoint before we headed onto the Pemberton Glacier. I ended up reaching the checkpoint almost one hour before them.

Once they arrived, each one of them seemed to have a different issue or pain. I ended up taking a lot of their gear and carried it myself in the hopes they could keep up. That didn't happen. One by one they slowly fell apart. One broke an ankle, and another started getting sick and vomiting. It was over as soon as it began.

Out of nowhere a massive storm hit the high snowcapped mountains. Teams were being rescued and the race became a logistical nightmare. With many teams injured or pulled from the course the transition areas were packed full of racers. I was looking to jump on with another team to continue racing.

Talk about jumping out of the frying pan and into the fire. That's exactly what I did.

When the weather calmed down on the mountain and race officials got things more under control they allowed broken teams to hook up with one another for the canoeing section. I hopped in with two guys and another gal. She and I became canoe partners. It wasn't until after we launched the vessel into the water that I asked her experience. I'll just say it wasn't encouraging.

Canoes aren't as stable as kayaks when it comes to rapids even if they're only class 2. It doesn't take much to tip them over, and even an experienced kayaker can find herself floating down a river with out her paddle.

It was unseasonably warm for this time of year and the snowmelt was running into the river rapidly, increasing the volume of water. I had to get more assertive as I negotiated the rapids. Unfortunately my paddling partner was struggling with my basic verbal commands.

The river was plagued with branches and logs. These are called strainers and are known to kill paddlers who get caught under the branches in the water and drown.

The rapids started increasing. I looked down the river and noticed an obstacle sticking out of the water. I blurted out, "Back paddle left, back paddle left." She floundered in her actions. I back paddled as hard as I could, narrowly escaping a collision.

After we dodged that obstacle I saw a massive tree stretched across the water. The water swiftly churned and our canoe headed in line with the center of the tree. I yelled, "right paddle, right paddle."

But we didn't have the necessary horsepower to avoid this dam-like structure so we violently slammed against it.

The canoe started filling with water rapidly and began to get sucked under the tree. We only had seconds to get ourselves out of the canoe and on top of the tree. I steadied the canoe as much as I could to get her out first, then with a struggle I pulled my body onto this behemoth mass.

I watched as the canoe got sucked under.

How quickly things can turn. We could have easily gone down with the boat. I was grateful we came out unscathed. After I shook off the dopamine rush, I thought, well, now what?

Lesson number one, never race with a team you never trained with and never hop in a canoe with a complete stranger.

We were smack dab in the middle of the wilderness in Canada, a very remote region. This massive river we were stranded on didn't exactly have an abundance of access. My thoughts quickly shifted to how the hell are we going to get out of this mess?

I felt perhaps there would be another team paddling down to help us. Within 45 minutes we spotted a canoe up river. They looked so small out there in the distance. As they neared we started frantically yelling for help. But the scale of the river was massive and the water deafening.

They were now entering the unfriendly gauntlet section. "Help!" I screamed out, to no avail. I noticed the team struggle through the rapids as we did and with one quick flip the canoe capsized sending the two paddlers down the river alongside their canoe.

I wanted to help but there was nothing I could do for them. At least they had their canoe and were heading in the correct direction.

Down in the canyon the river wasn't as warm as it had been back in the transition area. Two hours had passed and we hadn't seen any signs of more teams coming. We sat hunkered down on the tree as the sun set behind the mountains.

The water constantly splashed on us from the rapids. Hunger kicked in. As I opened my pack to grab some jerky I realized I was carrying the emergency race team radio. I don't know how I could have forgotten it was in my pack.

Every team in the race is assigned one radio. It's not to be used unless it's an extreme emergency. I figured this definitely classified as one. I took it out of the waterproof case and followed the proper procedures to transmit an SOS. Once you engage the transmission a satellite zeros in on your co-ordinates and you get patched through to a dispatcher to inform them of the situation.

I was relieved to hear the dispatcher's voice. However I was a bit disheartened when I was told all the emergency crews were still extracting teams off the mountain due to the storm and wouldn't be able to get to us for at least a couple of hours.

With our body fat being as low as it was and the fact that we were sitting in wet gear our bodies began to shiver uncontrollably. Had we not been stranded on this precarious tree we would have done some physical movements to keep warm, but this wasn't the proper platform.

To keep my mind distracted I held onto the fact they'd be sending a rescue helicopter when available. This sounded exciting to me. I had grand expectations of seeing the helicopter flying down the valley of the river with a long rope attached. I visualized it coming to a hover above us while we each jumped onto the rope and clung on for dear life as it soared away. I thought that would be pretty cool and a great rescue story.

For the next two and a half hours my core temperature continued to plummet. It was now dusk and my grand rescue visions had taken a back seat to my constant shivering.

The gal and I, (I believe her name was Katherine,) huddled together the best we could. She had taken down the top portion of her wet suit to try and warm up a bit.

There was no sight of a helicopter anywhere. As our thoughts began to waver towards a more negative side I thought I heard the sound of rotor blades cutting through the air. We both looked towards the sound. Sure enough we saw the colored lights of the helicopter as it came into focus. I jumped up onto my feet quickly. I can remember how much colder I got once she and I unfolded our bodies from one another. But I knew I'd be warming up soon enough.

I strained to look for a dangling rope hanging from the helicopter or even a rescue basket, but I saw nothing. I couldn't figure out how they were going to extract us from this tree in the middle of the river.

The helicopter flew overhead. A rescuer acknowledged that he had spotted us as our arms waved towards the sky. Then the pilot did a quick bank to the right and it disappeared out of sight. I could still hear the rotors spinning for some time and then silence.

Within minutes we heard voices calling out to us from the distance. As we glanced towards the right side of the riverbank we noticed three figures standing along the edge. Needless to say it was very hard to understand what was being said over the thunderous sound of the water.

Fortunately there was just enough daylight left for a quick rescue, but how? One of the individuals stepped forward. He was holding what looked like a small chair cushion attached to something.

It didn't convince me this was a good strategic plan. Loudly the voice called out, "We're going to try to throw this life-line to you. Once you grab hold of it you're going to need to get into the water one at a time. Hang on as tight as you can while we try to pull you across the river like a pendulum. Then we'll get the next person."

We had been stuck on that tree for almost six hours. We had become hypothermic and certainly weren't thinking clearly. The last thing I could've imagined having to do was get back into the glacier fed river. Night was upon us.

Katherine and I decided that she would go first so I could help her on my end. I have to admit only three years prior I had started the process of getting over a water phobia and it started to rear its ugly head. I needed to focus on Katherine.

Her one-piece wet suit top was still dangling around her waist. I told her she'd better pull it up. Not just for the fact these waters were icy cold but it was dangerous and it could get snagged on something. She refused and snuggly tied the arms around her waist like a jacket. I couldn't convince her otherwise.

The waters were rated as class two rapids around this section, definitely not calm. It took four throws to get the rescue line to us. As Katherine prepared to enter the water I looked her in the eyes as she shook uncontrollably and told her to hang on with every ounce of strength she had left.

It was a daunting feeling. I helped lower her into the water while the swift current pulled at her legs. Her body took the final plunge and the water snatched her out of my grip sending her briskly down the river.

I quickly looked across at the three figures and watched as they struggled to reel her in. My breathing started feeling labored as I watched her head bobbing up and down under the water like a bobbin.

I frantically started yelling, "Hold on Katherine, hold on!" I saw her giving up. Then as if in slow motion, the river took her away.

I watched helplessly as she got sucked into the branches that were hanging in the water down river. Then the rescue team ran out of my sight.

It seemed like an eternity before the rescuers reappeared but it had actually only been 30 minutes or so. There was no sign of Katherine.

The men repositioned themselves further up river this time. I was struggling to keep myself together. My body was almost convulsing it was shaking so badly. I kept telling myself, "Focus Heather, just focus."

What little light there had been was less. My mind raced from one bad scenario to another. So much for the Hollywood stunt rescue I had envisioned.

Two throws and I had the rope in my clutches. The thing was, no one was there to help me into the dark waters. I was scared. I couldn't shake the feeling that I might die but there was no alternative. The only alternative I had was to convince myself if anyone could do this, it was I. I remember telling myself there was no other option but to hang on until I felt a rescuer grab me.

With my gear on my back and the pouch of the rescue rope welded to my hands I jumped in a layout position, feet down river landing on my backside. Upon impact the river swiftly whipped me down stream until I felt the slack get taut on the rope. The power of water wielded a force so strong I felt as if I was being ripped in two pieces.

I knew these three guys had to be struggling but I couldn't see them. All I could do was have faith in them as they pulled the rope in with me on it, and the faith in myself that I could hang on for as long as it took.

I glanced towards the dim lit shoreline and realized I was nowhere close. I saw a blur of the guys struggling to reposition. The rapids where taking a toll on me. I was getting mouthfuls of water by the second and started to panic. I had to do something. I felt helpless. Intuitively I thought if I'm going to have any chance of making it out of this alive I needed to flip over face down into the water.

As crazy as that sounded I wrestled with the water to turn over. Once I was on my stomach I somehow created an air pocket with my arms and rounded my spine towards the heavens. I clung to that rope with all my might. I felt my nails penetrating into my flesh as I gripped.

Within a few minutes of assuming this position I felt a hard object hit me in my head and heard a voice call out, "Grab onto the pole, grab on!" But I couldn't. I was stuck in a rapid about five feet off shore. Then I felt the staff hit my ribs, "Grab on, grab on!" the muffled sounding voice said. But I couldn't.

Then as if God's hand swooped down from the sky I was plucked out of the water.

As I drifted in and out of consciousness, I vaguely remember being loaded into the helicopter. The hypothermic conditions had not only taken a toll on my physical body but also my mind. I saw a fuzzy silhouette of a small framed body slumped inside the helicopter with their backside facing me. In my present state I assumed it was Katherine. No words were exchanged.

I woke up in the middle of the early morning hours in the hypothermic tent, thunder and lightening sounding all around me.

I caught a glimpse of Katherine as she slept in the cot next to me. She was a bit cut up, but we were alive. I never saw her again. I remember thinking it sure wasn't the rescue I had envisioned but it was going to make a pretty good story anyhow!

I am honored and humbled to say I've trained and raced with some of the most elite special force teams on the planet. Back in the early and mid nineties the Adventure Racing scene in the United States was sparse.

Being a female who raced in these types of events made me marketable and I was recommended to a Navy Seal Team, Seal Team One, out of Coronado, California to train with them for a race in South Africa. I was 26 years old and had various races under my belt. I was serious about my training and confident in my skills. I certainly never felt like the weak link on this team.

These team members had very different mentalities than any of my previous teammates. We were comprised of four Navy Seals, and the captain of our team happened to be their commanding officer. I get having a CO for military missions but I never thought it was a good idea in the racing arena. I often times watched him pull rank on the others, which produced a flawed team in the end. I actually had a hard time with him as a person. He arrogantly competed against his own team. This made for no real cohesion, and it turned out to the weak link.

As badass and intimidating as Seals are there never was a fun factor to our training. I deeply missed this aspect. Although we set out to perform a mission and accomplished it, I ended up admiring and feeling jealous of the French teams in Africa, who were laughing, eating baguettes and having a good time, while kicking butt. I don't recall having any fond memories with my team.

I do however have a treasured memory from an experience while staging in a transition area somewhere in the middle of the South African wilds. There was a village not too far away from our race camp. I had been noticing a native teenage boy walking about our camp with a beautiful staff. It had beautiful beadwork adorning the wood at the bulbous shaped top end. I had brought items from the U.S. like t-shirts to trade for just such an occasion.

I approached the boy who must have been around 17 years of age and gestured to him that I really liked his staff. He spoke no English but I made an effort to communicate through gestures, until he understood that I wanted to do a trade.

I had him follow me back to our team area where I took out a pile of t-shirts that had various logos such as Nike written on them. He stared but wasn't impressed. The negotiations commenced. I picked up three brand new different styled shirts and he swung his head side-to-side and responded, "No."

He continued to poke around. I picked up two more and said in an excited tone, "I'll give you all five of these for your staff." He looked at me and smiled, "No".

I continued to speak in English to him. I asked if any particular ones caught his eye. He walked a couple feet to the side and pointed to one of my personal race jackets. It was cool. It had all my official patches on the sleeves and backside.

He smiled as he looked at both the jacket and me.

The teams had just raced out of the Drakensberg mountain range where the elevation was over 11,000 ft. The weather had been cold, wet and miserable and he wanted the only thick jacket I had with me.

As he and I stood there in the midst of our negotiation I had beads of sweat profusely dripping from every pore on my body. It was Africa hot. The last thing I could imagine at that moment was wearing my jacket anytime soon. I also knew we weren't heading back into the mountains. I picked up my jacket and winced. I was letting him know I wasn't sure. I swayed my body back and forth in a contemplative stance. He stood smiling with a big bright white smile.

I relaxed my shoulders and bobbed my head front to back with a smile on my face saying, "Okay, let's do it."

He handed the staff over to me with a bit of reservation as I placed the jacket in his other hand. I put my hand out to gesture I wanted to shake on it and he obliged.

He had a grin from ear to ear as he stood in front of me putting on my race jacket. I gave him two thumbs up. We said thank you at least three more times before he walked away.

Throughout the entire afternoon I watched him proudly strut around in the triple digit heat wearing the jacket. I found out that the staffs are what the boys receive when they are initiated into manhood and the staff is then used for a prod for their livestock. I proudly display it on a wall. It was a win-win.

During the remaining hours we had left driving to our next adventure with Kahn, I stared out the window upon the vast expanse of Rajasthan and felt giddy. What a privilege it was to explore so many lands and cultures. To me it's a priceless education.

I started thinking about how incredibly blessed I had been to have a powerful body capable of pushing beyond limits which secured incredible sponsors that gave me the freedom to race all over the globe for a decade.

I had sponsors which included Compaq Computer, Nike, Teva, Oakley, Reebok, Camelback and others. I never had to buy my own socks. Heck, I even had a Brazilian millionaire foot my bill to New Zealand for the Southern Traverse race.

Now there was a fun team.

I befriended a racer name Joseph in the British Columbia race. He and I hit it off from the beginning and our friendship has never looked back.

He advised a Brazilian team, Team Senti Si Funds, that it would be a strategic idea to invite me to New Zealand to be their assistant crew person and use my expertise throughout the race. They were a lively team of seven Brazilians.

Talk about the complete opposites of the Navy Seals. The race was held on the South Island. We used the upbeat adventure gateway hamlet of Queenstown as our base camp. The race started in a remote region called Wanaka, home to high mountain views and a beautiful lake.

Besides my friend, Joseph, who was a smooth talker with a raspy voice, sexy really, and spoke Portuguese, only two of the others spoke English conversationally. On the flight over Joseph had prepped me for translations of everyday phrases. Such as, good morning, how are you etc. I still have four pages of a notebook I filled. I understood enough from the others to make it an incredibly memorable experience, and I picked up a little Portuguese along the way.

I was 27 years old and the world was my oyster. I have so many fond memories with this group. They were passionate individuals who knew how to have fun and live big and bold.

The highlight of this adventure for me was the day I bungee jumped from the second highest bungee in the world, Pipeline, with a few of my crazy Brazilian friends. Pipeline is nestled high in the glorious mountains outside of Queenstown.

Unfortunately some of us celebrated "Kiwi style" two nights prior at the after race party. Meaning we partook in a few too many libations.

The after party is always a highlight in itself. I don't remember much about that night of fun. However I do have fun pictures and recall the hilarious effort of Joseph trying to give me a piggyback ride back to our condo in the wee hours of the morning.

Because of our shenanigans, Joseph and I weren't healthy enough to race down the river in the speedboat the following morning. However we managed to recover enough to hop into a 4WD jeep for a hair raising 45 minute drive up the mountain to get to Pipeline.

Kiwis, as the locals are called, have a great sense of adventure, which I appreciate. However, the twisting and turning from the backseats of the vehicle were a bit hard to handle after a mild case of alcohol poisoning. The back tires seemed to edge off the sides of the mountain and gave me a nauseated feeling as I looked straight down into the abyss. Needless to say we were relieved no one vomited.

There it was, the bridge, spanning the gorge of the Shotover River 342 feet above. I was in awe. Interestingly in the past I had said the only way I would bungee jump was if I went to New Zealand and there I was.

I spotted a speedboat below me. From the bridge it looked like a bitty dot. I soon found out that that little itty-bitty dot would be picking me up at the bottom of the bungee and whisking me away to the other side of the river for a hike back.

There was fun, lively music playing at the launching station. The bungee riggers were having a blast and I was right there with them. I remember checking out every piece of hardware they used to make sure we were good to go.

New Zealand is very well known for bungee jumping, however when you're ready to swan dive off a bridge that is equivalent to a 34-story building you want to know that you are going to live to see another adventure.

With my feet shackled together with the bungee cord I shimmied out onto the one and a half foot wide wooden plank. The mountains that dwarfed me were covered with magnificent green trees. I could see the white churning water below. It took my breath away.

The fellow that was closest to me said in his cool New Zealand accent, "Alright Heether are you ready?" With a smile on my face I gave my most convincing response, "Yes I am." He told me to look out into the distance and give a big wave for the video camera.

"Four, three, two, one, go Heether," The guy belted out.

I took a deep breath and dove off the plank into a beautiful swam dive free falling through the air until the bungee slack caught up. "Wooohooo!" I laughed out at the top of my lungs. Pure adrenaline shot through my body. I wanted to go right back up and jump off that plank in a different style. Instead I got lowered down head first into the speedboat waiting below and in cool New Zealand style, swept away across the river to be let out the other side.

I appreciated my time with this fun new family. It made me realize that just because we come from different countries or speak a different language it does not mean we don't desire some of the same experiences nor does it mean we can't break the language barrier by holding joy and laughter in our hearts.

I met another special person in British Columbia that year of 96. His name was Marcus. He towered over me at about six foot three inches tall. He and I hit it off on a very different level. At this time in my life I had been in an eleven-year relationship with my high school sweetheart, Blue, when Marcus came racing into the picture. However things on the home front had been rocky for some time due to poor life decisions. As hard as it was, it was time to recreate.

Marcus was an absolute 180• from Blue. Even though Marcus and I had tons of fun at the after race party with our teams in BC, he was a straight-laced academic, physics and mathematics major, an officer in the Marine Corps and pilot. I was intrigued.

Marcus and I ended up having a relationship for about seven years but more than that he became a mentor for the continuation of my academic and fire careers.

Our relationship became more philosophical. I do have to say we did become quite the power couple. Between him being both a helicopter and fixed wing pilot and me breaking into the Hollywood stunt scene, it always got a conversation going.

I found myself making frequent long drives for auditions. A few months had passed in Marcus's and my long distance relationship and I knew it was time for me to start a new venture in life. I soon left my hometown of Santa Barbara.

In between auditions and races I was waiting tables at a wonderful family owned restaurant in Studio City called The Good Neighbor, a must stop place if you're in the area.

I was recommended by a customer in the film industry to check out a particular stunt performer workshop that was operated by a

90

veteran stuntman and coordinator, Johnny Miller, of Johnny Miller Stunt Productions. I signed on the dotted line. Soon I learned the ins and outs and the dos and don'ts of the stunt world.

The workshop was a four-month program. I absolutely loved spending extra time there. You could always find me either practicing two story high falls or learning the proper skills for camera angles for fight scenes.

After I graduated and had earned my SAG card, the Screen Actors Guild, I started helping other students that came to the school.

One day we had AMC, the American Movie Classic channel come in for a day shoot to capture some scenes of us performing various stunts. They captured all the preparation that goes into the behind the scenes. The show aired on AMC about the history of stunt people. I was stoked they captured me being thrown through a glass window in a simulated fight scene.

Unfortunately Johnny had warned me about what can happen behind the scenes of auditions and the industry. He let me know that it's not always how well you can perform the stunts but, sadly, how well you perform elsewhere. I definitely got my dose of it. It was extremely disheartening. I remember many times being asked to go to "lunch" with a stunt coordinator and "No" not being the acceptable answer. I wouldn't get the part.

One morning in 1998, I received a call from my agency, Bobby Ball. They were excited to tell me about a show CBS was going to pilot. It was to be a spin off of the American Gladiators. They were going to be holding auditions and tryouts for individuals that would be portraying the character parts like the gladiators. It was to be called Ultra Sport.

I was ecstatic. In their description they explained how the show wanted more natural looking athletes. Ones that didn't resemble body builders, such as many of the Gladiators did. I thought this was going to be my break.

I had already been training hard. I had a big 100-mile ultra race coming up in Colorado called The Hard Rock 100. But I went into beast mode to ensure I would be unstoppable.

At the tryouts I smashed it out of the ballpark. I was the only female that could do 20 one-arm pull-ups and flew through the rest of the events. I felt I was a shoe in. I sat on tenterhooks for two weeks waiting for a call back.

The call came early one morning. "Good morning", this very exuberant voice belted out into the phone. "I am calling from CBS studio and because you did so amazing in our tryouts we'd love for you to compete against the Warriors!"

My heart skipped a beat. My body tensed. I was hoping that my intuition was not correct about who I thought these "Warriors" were.

"Oh wow, who are the Warriors?" I asked in a watered down excited tone. "They are the people that will be like the Gladiators." the man continued to say in a jubilant tone.

You've got to be fricken kidding me, I silently screeched out to the universe. That was supposed to be my roll. That's what I tried out for. But as pleasantly as I could muster I said, "That sounds awesome, thank you for this opportunity." I hung up the phone in absolute disappointment. Then a master plan came into focus.

I spent the next month and a half upping my training regime. My mission and mentality was, if I can't be one of the Warriors, no one will defeat me. I'd beat them in their own game.

When I arrived at the Sony studios for the first day of practice and training I understood why I wasn't selected as one of the

Warriors. It was apparent that I didn't have big enough fake boobs. Everyone was checking everyone else out. This was another aspect to the industry that really got to me. There was a lot of testosterone exuding out of everyone competing. But I had my plan; I was focused, with or without big boobs I was ready.

I was pleasantly pleased and excited to meet our trainer for the show, Billy Blanks. Billy is the Godfather and creator of Tae Bo and a former champion martial artist. I felt most fortunate to have him there.

Once the scrimmages got under way the energy in the studio was off the charts.

First we were shown the particular events and then we'd get time to train. After the first hour or so I think these gals knew I was all business. I remember walking into the locker room that afternoon and one of the Warrior gals says to me, "Who are you?"

Like a comedian I blurted out, "The name's Bond, Heather Bond."

This gal looked at me and smiled as she said. "You did an amazing job out there today." She was the only one that didn't seem to have an attitude with me.

The day of the first taping was exciting. It brought me back to Gladiator arena. People in the audience were waving flags and cheering. At this point in the game I felt like a Navy Seal on my mission; ready to annihilate my opponents.

One by one I crushed them.

I was matched up on this one particular event with a gal who had given me a lot of stink eye throughout training. She wasn't much bigger than I but pound for pound she was no match for me.

Athena Rising, a Memoir – Heather Bond

In this particular event the contestant, me, was placed at a starting point approximately 15 yards out from the Warrior. She was perched on top of a two feet high platform made out of squishy mat. She guarded a 10-pound medicine ball that was on top of a high pillar. My objective was to somehow get around her in a breakthrough move and conquer the event by safely bringing the ball back to my starting position.

Billy was the referee. In his soft yet powerful voice he called out, "Competitor ready".

I stared that Warrior straight in the eye and never lost contact. I gave a nod. My teeth clenched down on my mouthpiece with force. I was pumping myself up by silently saying over and over, "You're going down," poor unsuspecting victim.

The whistle sounded. I sprinted head on towards her like a locomotive and when my arms could reach her body I swooped her into a fire mans carry on top of my shoulder and slammed her on her back to the ground with extreme force.

I could tell I knocked the wind out of her. She slowly got up. As soon as she did she pointed at me while looking at Billy and in a wincing voice blurts out, "she can't do that! She can't do that to me." I looked at Billy and said, "I didn't hear otherwise in the rules." She hobbled off and a bigger gal took her spot.

Now I had a bigger Warrior standing before me trying to intimidate me. I wasn't impressed. Just like the first one I stared her dead in the eye. I could tell she was getting ready for me to try to inflict the same punishment I had on the first Warrior. But she was wrong.

I could've easily lifted her. But I needed to be more strategic. "Warrior ready", Billy sounds out. She nods.

"Contestant ready" I thought oh yeah I'm ready. The whistle blew and like a racehorse I advanced head on just like I had done the last one. Her feet begin to shuffle and her body swayed back and forth. Just as I was at arms reach I extended my arms like I was, going in for the swoop and boom, I juke to my right and she tumbled off the mat to the ground. I quickly leaped onto the mat and grabbed the ball. She got disqualified for leaving her station.

This continued one event after another. I was unstoppable and felt a bit cocky.

Then the unexpected happened. During an event reset I was approached by one of the directors backstage. He began to tell me that they were going to set up some unplanned event and I was going to lose. I couldn't believe what I was hearing. As a matter of fact I questioned him a couple of times to make sure I heard him properly. That's precisely what he wanted me to do; fake a loss.

I approached Billy on the matter. Unfortunately this wasn't his call nor was it his show. I could tell he didn't approve of what they were asking me to do. But I kept my smile on my face and when it was time I jogged out into the arena.

I got the audience chanting my name. At one point Billy said to me, "do you hear them? That's all you." I really looked up to Billy and admired all he'd accomplished in his career and life.

Besides them having me fake that ridiculous loss, which by the way the audience saw right through and booed, I went totally undefeated. Mission accomplished. The crazy part to the story, is, I guess I must have ruined the whole pilot show for the female version. The men's show aired for I believe two seasons under the name Battle Dome but the female version never did.

After almost five years in the industry I threw in the towel. I definitely had some exciting moments but when push came to shove it wasn't worth me feeling fake or selling my soul. So I switched gears.

In 1999 I enrolled back into college, this time to earn a new degree in fire chemistry and wild land fire technology. I also enrolled in specific medical classes to earn my EMT license, Emergency Medical Technician. In one of my fire classes we got a visit from two U.S Forest Service fire fighters, who were Smoke Jumpers.

No sooner had they started into their talk then I thought, boy oh boy, how awesome would that be to become a smoke jumper. I'd get to jump out of planes into fire-ravaged areas and get paid for it. This type of lifestyle definitely got me excited, and my heart pumping.

Shortly after the visit by the smoke jumpers we got another visit from the Forest Service. This time they were offering five positions to become fully-trained full-time fire fighters while continuing to earn our degree. I felt a tug in my heart. This was always my indicator to go for something. If I could secure one of those coveted spots it would be my shoe in, and it was.

After much testing and many interviews I was selected for one of the five positions. I immediately got hired with the U.S. Forest Service on the ANF, Angeles National Forest, in Los Angeles. My new adventure started on an engine crew. I quickly learned the ropes.

Actually it took time to feel fully confident in this unpredictable world of fire. But just like in any of my sports I started collecting awards and certifications, only this time it was academic. I even made the honor role.

During the off season I enjoyed donning my dress uniform with my badge and name plate to help educate the inner city youths on the hazards of fire. I became ranger Heather and my crew wouldn't be complete without my dear friend, Smokey Bear.

"Hi boys and girls, my name is ranger Heather. Can anyone raise their hand and tell me the name of my big brown fury friend?" The kids would get so excited. I really enjoyed the fire prevention side.

After the second season I was selected to become a member of a prestigious type 1 Hot Shot crew called Bear Divide. We were an elite team of fire fighters. Being on a type 1 crew meant I was gone for weeks at a time on fires all over the country. Many times we'd be the first in on an initial attack fire and make magic happen.

We were a specialty crew, which meant we had the authority to carry various types of explosives, which were always in demand.

On one particular fire in Washington State, near the border of Canada, we had been spiked out on the fire for about ten days. Spiked out means you have no access to the outside world like toilets, showers, good food, you get the idea.

On one particular day I was asked by one of my captains to transport some gel explosives to another part of my crew who had split off on another section of the fire. I remember as I walked down the dozer cut fire line with walls of flames on each side, I thought boy I feel pretty vulnerable walking with explosives in my pockets.

Later that night the fire jumped the line. The sound of a full-blown crown fire is deafening. It's hard to put into words the energy that resides within those swirling flames. It's actually mesmerizing to watch. Not so much when you're getting cut off from your escape routes and safety zones.

I had studied many reasons why a fire fighter can lose their life and it can happen in seconds. No one can out run a fire when it's charging. My crew that night did a hasty RTO, (reverse the order) and got the hell out of Dodge. Those were intense times.

It sounds cool and it definitely was for the first couple of years. When we'd roll into towns, people treated us like heroes. They'd be holding up and waving signs they made saying things like, "hot shots rock" or "thank you, we love you." Sometimes if we'd go into a bar or store people wanted to buy us a drink.

But at 29, 30, 31 and 32 years of age it wasn't glamorous. It was some of the hardest manual labor work I'd ever done in my life and the pay sucked. Since the day I had been hired with the Forest Service I heard many of my fellow crewmembers calling the municipal fire fighters, "pavement princesses".

When I asked what they meant they responded by saying, "Look at them down there sitting in their engines." I said, "Isn't that structure protection?" One of them responded, "They rarely even pick up a tool. You'll never see them out doing what we do." I thought, isn't that the point? We're wild land and they're structure? The job descriptions are different. I was starting to like the sound of getting a hotel to sleep in at night while continuing to be paid.

Instead, I was stuck out sleeping on a rock while trying to keep warm near a small burning part of the fire. What was degrading was the fact that when our crew came off the fire line and possibly had to sit in fire camp, we wouldn't be getting paid. I thought more and more about becoming a member of the pavement princess clan.

I had an epiphany on one particular fire in Arizona. It was around the San Francisco Peak, which is Arizona's tallest mountain. Most of my crew was sick. Now this wasn't your typical sickness. This is what they called "the crud." I compared it to having bronchitis all the time and continually hacking and spitting up phlegm. We never got a break from sucking smoke into our lungs.

When municipal fire fighters go into structures or vehicle fires they wear breathers and masks. Not us. I wasn't as sickly sounding as some of my crew but it was enough for me to realize that being a wild land fire fighter definitely went against my healthy living philosophy.

Later on that fire I barely managed to escape the wrath of a massive burning log rolling through the night down the hillside. Had there not been a rock outcropping five feet away three of my crewmates and I would've been obliterated. This was the moment I decided to start the testing process with L.A. City Fire Department, AKA, "The Pavement Princesses."

My reverie was broken by Kahn's announcement that we would be arriving at our next destination. I wondered what adventures lay ahead.

Athena Rising, a Memoir – Heather Bond

.

Chapter 12
The Holy City

Journal entry: Poor mama, she's got a bad case of Delhi belly. The crazy thing is that we split and shared our meal. Usually she's the one with the ironclad stomach.

She took three anti-diarrhea tablets and went to sleep in the back of the car. I feel so bad for her. We had a long six-hour drive today. It wasn't pretty for her. Kahn kept the AC on the whole time to keep her cool

Fate or a higher power must have wanted my mom and me to end up in the holy city of Pushkar.

It is a pilgrimage site for Hindus and Sikhs with many temples and ghats. The town is located on the shores of Pushkar Lake and is surrounded by 52 ghats where people bathe in the holy waters.

When I planned our trip, I saw photos of the town and thought it would be fascinating to go to the ghats but opted against it because we wouldn't be there during the famous camel festival. Shafi had put it back into our itinerary during the negotiations.

We arrived in Pushkar mid-morning and settled into our room. Since this wasn't in our original itinerary, I had nothing planned, but we were very curious about the ghats.

We loaded up a few provisions and told Kahn we'd be heading out to explore. In great Kahn fashion he told us that at the ghats someone would try to give us a rose. "Do not take it." he said with a mild headshake. "Another person will want to bless your rose before you put it in the water," he continued. Then he gave us that look that only he could give. "Do not take rose unless you pay tip."

Our hotel was in a quiet area just outside the hustle and bustle of the tiny narrow street town. With no map or directions we set out on foot, following my intuition that we'd find the lake and ghats towards the center of town.

Shortly into our walk our hotel road merged into the main town and I decided to stay on it hoping we'd see signs to follow to the lake. I noticed that a man seemed to be following us on the opposite side of the road, but initially I didn't say anything to my mom to save her from unnecessary worry.

Finally I felt she must know. "Mom, stop," I said to her with concern in my voice. "Don't look until I stop talking to you. I've been watching a man follow us." I described where he was. He had also stopped.

We continued along and I told my mom to look over in his direction as we kept walking. I've always taken pride in being highly aware of my surroundings. As a firefighter and an adventure racer, it was my job and responsibility to know all the dangers and hazards around myself, and my team members. It felt like such a cliché thing to say, "Look, but not now."

Throughout this journey and all of my other travels I am respectful of the dress etiquette for the regions I'm visiting. My mom and I wore long sleeved Indian tops, long pants and scarves at times so we were confused as to why this man was trailing us.

At this point I was quite positive we were being followed, but why? It definitely felt creepy. The quiet road started getting louder and louder. People were hustling around as if an event were about to take place.

Both sides of the narrow street were lined with tiny stalls. I told my mom to stop at the next stall and look at the wares. The man stopped as well and pretended to be engaged as my mom looked at the goods. I deliberately made eye contact with him to inform him that I knew he was following us, but I still couldn't understand what he was doing.

We continued to walk through the maze and mob of people congregating on the road. We found out that a holy day parade was getting underway.

I started getting a bit more bold and animated with the man. I directed my camera towards him and took pictures, but this didn't seem to shake his nerves one bit. He kept with us. I pointed my index and middle fingers towards my eyes and then directing them towards him. "I see you watching me, buddy," my gesture said. I did this multiple times while shrugging my shoulders and mouthing, "What? What is it you want?"

Music started sounding through the streets, and he disappeared into the ocean of people. Just as I was about to take a deep sigh of relief, a little beggar boy walked up to us. "Food, please."

His big brown eyes stared up at me. I had quite a few things to offer him, but he refused.

"Food, I'm hungry." He started tugging on my arm. I put a bar in front of him again and he still refused. "Chapatti, I want chapatti."

103

At that point I got a bit short with him. I told him if he were truly hungry, he would take what we were offering him. "No, no chapatti." I pulled my arm away from him as he tugged and pulled on my shirtsleeve. He ran away.

My mom and I crossed to the opposite side of the road and tried to rationalize what just transpired. Then I saw the same boy talking to the man who had been following us.

My mom and I stopped to watch a transaction between the two of them. Then they parted ways and disappeared into the crowd.

I finally saw a small sign on the road that said ghats with an arrow pointing down a back street. We turned off the hectic road and found ourselves on an almost too quiet back street. I found it perplexing that a holy city known for its bathing ghats had such a private entrance to it. After what I had just experienced I was apprehensive.

The road we continued on had a slight uphill slope. We couldn't see the lake yet, but I saw the ghats in the distance, so we continued. As we crested the top of the road I noticed a group of men near the ghats. My pace slowed, and my hackles went up. I stepped in closer to link arms with my mom as we began descending toward the lake.

Suddenly a man stepped out of the group and started walking towards us yelling something. It was the man that had followed us through the streets. Rattled by this I stopped.

He moved towards us quicker and quicker yelling, "Evil woman! Evil woman!" As calmly as I possibly could, I told my mom to start walking backwards up the hill and not to turn around until we reached the top.

Other men in the group started advancing towards us. Our pace quickened. "Evil, evil woman, you don't belong here." His dagger eyes pierced into me. We got to the top and I said, "Turn!" Arm in arm, my mom and I started to run like the wind.

At this point it became a blur. For all I knew I could have been dragging my mom and wouldn't have noticed. We wound our way back into the chaos of the holy parade. The sound of drums were beating and beating. My heart was pounding just as fast. I could barely breathe as I dragged my mom through the sea of people, cows and madness. I felt like Cornel Wilde running from the natives in the film *"The Naked Prey."*

Not caring what people thought, I pushed and shoved my way through the crowd. In the distance I spotted an older white couple standing watching the parade. I ran up to them and put my arm around the older gentleman's arm.

With snot dripping down from my face I managed to slur the words, "I'm sorry! There are some men chasing us. Can we stand with you?" With the sweat dripping from me profusely I trembled as I looked around for any sign of the men. Nothing.

After I caught my breath and felt safe, I unclenched my hand from my mom's. All I wanted to do was leave that town. The two people that we'd latched onto were named Sarah and Jack. They were definitely good sports. Can you imagine what they must have thought when a frantic 37-year-old woman with slobber and spit flying from her mouth ran out of a crowd and latched onto Jack's arm in the middle of a holy parade in India. I didn't see him flinch. Perhaps I was too shaken to notice their response.

Jack told us that they were hiking to one of the sacred temples on the surrounding mountains and thought it would be a great way for us to shake off what just happened. Plus they said they'd enjoy our company. I thought this to be a far better option than running from a crazy man back to our hotel with our tails between our legs. I had never felt threatened like that in my life, and it wasn't the welcome we'd been looking for.

Athena Rising, a Memoir – Heather Bond

Jack and Sarah led us through the winding streets and out of the chaos. Once the noise gave way to more silence it allowed our conversations to flow. They were very curious as to what had just happened to us, and we told them. Sarah told us that they'd visited Pushkar five or six times and were quite surprised by our story. I let them know that we too were quite surprised but we didn't want it to stain our view of the town.

Jack pointed to the temple on the top of a volcano-shaped mountain that we were going to hike to. There were four similar temples surrounding the town and lake. He also however informed us that this was their first time hiking to this particular temple and they didn't have the exact directions. Jack assured us it shouldn't be difficult to find the trail.

Sarah, Jack, my mom and I enjoyed fantastic conversations. They were my kind of people. They'd tackled two items on my bucket list: the trek to Everest base camp and the Anapurna circuit. They lived in Canada. I believe Jack was originally from Australia and Sarah from England, and have lived very active lives.

We took a left turn onto a dirt road and kept heading towards the mountain. At one point it seemed like we were going through villagers' yards, so Jack asked a woman if this was the path and she gestured in the direction we were heading.

Low shrubs grew sparsely in and around the poorly maintained trail. The trail began to fade as we continued upward. We were all wearing sandals as we climbed the steep path full of thick shale and sharp outcroppings of rock. I was in the lead and I asked if everyone was still okay with the terrain. I am a professional hiker and recognized this wasn't a trail for the weak hearted. As a matter of fact I was beginning to realize that we weren't on a trail at all. I couldn't imagine others trekking up this.

Jack, I'd learned, was 70, and Sarah in her late 60s. Sure, they were tough as nails, but by then we were using our hands to climb.

I looked up and noticed that at the top there was a small rock ledge to climb over. I knew it would be a slippery scramble for me, so I hoped the others would be okay.

As I grabbed my last handhold before pulling myself to the top, I set my eyes on a pair of feet in sandals. With a quick heave-ho, I jerked myself up and there in front of me stood a monk. I turned to help the others over this crux, and as I did the monk said to me, "Why come such a hard way when there is an easy path made for you?" We looked to where he was pointing and saw a marked trail. I turned back to the monk and said, "Why, that would've been too easy."

So as in life, do you take the well-walked path of others or do you blaze your own trail and create your own amazing adventure? For a few hours of an adrenaline pumping day, Jack, Sarah, my mom and I created a joy-filled adventure.

As for those 52 sacred bathing ghats, we made it to them the next day. That time our walk did not include a man stalking us and calling us evil woman, and on that day we found the main entrance that was just as I had originally envisioned, teeming with life and humanity. The universe even threw in a few snake charmers and the chance to perform the sacred rose ceremony.

Chapter 13
Not Shangri-la

*Journal entry: Today when I performed my sacred ritual
I prayed to have a child. I know Sean doesn't want to
have a family, but somehow*

*I am going to have a child. I guess even if that means I
raise one myself, who knows. It was so cool how it
started raining on us right as I started this ritual. God
was telling me something.*

Around 1995 my mom came across a National Geographic special on the great railways of India. We must have watched that VHS tape a million times. There was a section on the Darjeeling Himalayan Railway, also known as the DHR or the Queen of the Hills.

Built in 1881, the DHR is the oldest running coal burning Narrow Gauge toy train in the world. Its 48-mile route climbs over 7,000 feet in elevation, ending in the hill town of Darjeeling, our next and final destination.

When planning the trip, I was so happy to see that the train was still running its route. I couldn't wait for my mom to experience this small-but-mighty train in all of its majesty.

It was a bittersweet goodbye to Rajasthan. We were excited and relieved to be heading up into the hills of Darjeeling and its surrounding environs, but we had reservations about leaving behind our dear friend Kahn.

We were from very different cultures and ways of living, yet that meant nothing because he was a kind-hearted, caring human and the best driver ever. For the past two weeks he had looked out for us and taken care of us, and we really enjoyed him as a person. He had nurtured my mom a couple of times when she wasn't feeling well, which was the case on the day we parted ways with Kahn.

My mom had been battling her second bout of food poison along our journey, and she wasn't in top form.

We wrote a letter addressed to both Shafi and Kahn to thank them for keeping their promise. I wanted Shafi to know that we agreed with him about Kahn 100 percent. As I wrote my portion of the letter I reflected on two weeks prior when my mom and I sat in Shafi's cubicle. I visualized him as he tore both my ego and our itinerary to shreds. Thank goodness. They were both godsends.

With my mom still feeling weak, we endured a full-day's journey of planes, rickshaws and a cab to reach our destination of Kersoung, where we would start our long journey up the mountain on the little toy train. I felt bad for my mom, especially since this was the journey that she'd be dreaming about for years. I also knew we were both tired and ready to go home. We had another seven days until our flight home, and we looked forward to a peaceful and spiritual experience in the mountains.

Kersoung was home to the highest railway station at 5,000 feet. The third leg of our journey to the station was a tiny cab. As we headed up the winding, narrow mountain road we watched the landscape change. We had left the barren brown desert of Rajasthan and started heading into a semi-tropical mountain region in West Bengal, northeast India. The mountainsides were covered in tea plantations and we could see ladies out cutting the tea leaves. I was grateful my mom didn't vomit as the mountain roads twisted and turned.

Our train was to leave the following day at 3 p.m. My mom and I decided to splurge and go with a first-class ticket. It cost us a whopping R's140, about $3.25 U.S. at the time. General seating would have cost 10 rupees, and we never discovered a difference between first class and general.

The engineer had that little train stacked with hot coals burning. The smoke billowed from the stack as we backed our way out of the station. Puff, puff went the thick black plumes into the air.

My mom had given me the window seat so I could take pictures and capture our journey on video just like we watched so many times on the National Geographic video. The brakes squealed and made loud shrill sounds as people continued to jump on.

The train never really picked up much speed. It seemed to take all her might just to keep a steady slow pace. As we made our way higher and higher into the mountains we got to witness the young school boys in their uniforms running alongside the train and hopping on just like our NG video.

The whistle sounded as we neared a hillside village. This gave warning to the shopkeepers through the narrow corridors. At times the track was so close to the shops and homes one could lean out the window and grab some supplies.

The little narrow gauge train was old and required numerous stops to cool down the breaks or for the mechanics to bang and clang around different nuts and bolts. Some of our stops were longer and allowed some of the young local girls to run out of their homes with cast iron buckets and a tool to collect hot burning coals from the train to use for both cooking and heating their homes.

Sadly the novelty of the little train started wearing off about 45 minutes into our three- hour journey. The higher we headed into the hills, the more we were assaulted by the sound of share jeeps (local tour drivers) honking their horns for no apparent reasons. We thought we'd left behind the loud chaos of Rajasthan and were heading towards tranquility.

My mom was slumped down tenderly in her seat. Her neck seemed strained as she twisted to catch the view of the landscape. My mind drifted in and out of various thoughts and reflections on my home and career life.

Though my window seat served its purpose, it had turned into more of a burden and something of a metaphor of my life. There was no glass protecting me from the elements. My bloodshot eyes burned from the smoke billowing in. Tears rolled down my cheeks, and little blisters formed on my skin from bits of coal burning through my shirt and sticking onto my skin.

Quite agitated, I realized that throughout this entire journey I had kept a play-by-play journal of the daily events, my thoughts and feelings, but I hadn't written anything about the man stalking us in Pushkar, and neither did my mom. This wasn't a little event. It had really struck fear in me, and why did I feel I should hide it?

What was it that allowed me to feel that this type of behavior was acceptable or okay and I should just brush it off like nothing?

112

The words I'd written in my journal that day read: Our ghat experience got interrupted that day.

These thoughts provoked deep painful feelings I had stored towards my task force commander and other high-ranking individuals at my last fire station and within the department. I had spent the last two and a half years fighting for my truth to be heard.

I struggled with self-doubt and rage, while seeking my higher self. I saw the parallel between these two scenarios.

My task force commander regularly assigned me to drill on a particular ladder that physically was hurting me, and I said nothing. Over and over I sucked it up and didn't speak my truth. I worked to make everything look good on the outside, but I struggled on the inside.

In my relationship with Sean, too, I was stifling my truth. I could see the lie that came from creating a Pollyanna front, hiding my real feelings in order to avoid being vulnerable.

At the beginning of my relationship with Sean I felt red flags at a gut level, but I was busy with my fire career. When I visited him back in my hometown we'd always have a fun motorcycle adventure. I also knew from the start that Sean had no desire to have children or a family, and I certainly wanted both. I started to see that I had placed myself in these situations because I wasn't listening to my inner voice.

My epiphany was this: because of all the loss I'd endured around my racing and fire careers, I had settled with my relationship. I was a broken woman accepting a broken relationship and searching for answers.

Profound thoughts flooded my mind. I flashed to an experience I'd had eight days earlier in a tiny back-alley silver shop in Jaipur. Standing in the back of a shop, I was watching my mom haggle with the clerk when a man walked out from behind a curtain. I remember feeling his energy directed towards me. He approached me, and we caught eyes. He said in a thick Indian accent, "You have great crown chakra."

Unsure I understood, I asked him to repeat himself. He did, adding that it was a very high compliment. I thanked him.

"You have great problems with your neck, low back and knee." He started gesturing to the left side of my body and this got my attention, especially after he accurately noted when the issues had started.

I had always thought it would be cool if a healer or medicine man appeared out of thin air to confront me with powerful truths, past, present and future. For 30 minutes, the man, Ajay, told me truths that no one knew or could have made up. He told me I was to conceive a child on April 17 and I would return to being "Heather." As it happened I gave birth to a baby girl on April twenty fifth the following year, but the due date was the 17th.

The man also informed me I should stay away from eggs. Two weeks prior to the India trip I'd had an overwhelming urge to stop eating eggs. So much so that I had mentioned it to both my mom and Sean. I never found out why. As an interesting side note the Avian Bird Flu became big news shortly thereafter.

Finally, the man told me that my fifth chakra was closed and that I needed to work on opening it. The fifth chakra is your throat chakra. I now know this had to do with me not speaking my inner truth.

By the time we finished, I felt emotionally drained. I'd cried and laughed, and I was now speechless. Ajay gave my mom and me two beautiful silver and garnet pendants to hang from our necklaces. They would protect us on our travels. Like many things in India they came with instructions. In two days I was to begin a cleansing process that would conclude with a ceremony 15 days later. I was not to touch the pendant until then. I thought it was fitting that we'd be high on the mountains just below the Himalayan range.

Along the train ride, my back and neck felt the toll the trip had taken on them. The sun was getting lower and it wouldn't be long before it went behind the mountains. The last 30 minutes or so were my favorite; all the loud noises subsided and I spotted a couple of magnificent monasteries and waterfalls on the hillsides.

When traveling, I try to arrive at my destination during daylight hours, particularly in unfamiliar places. It was just after 6 p.m. when we pulled into the Darjeeling train station. The sun had set and my mom and I were the last two people on the train. We grabbed our large mountaineering packs off the floor and hurled them onto our backs. The window at the station had already closed. No one was around to help with directions.

I pulled out my headlamp and we proceeded to the nearest road. We located our map of the area. Hunger had set in as I scanned the map. I noticed one main road and a labyrinth of smaller ones on the steep hillside town. I forgot I had marked a Thai eatery called The Park Restaurant back in the states.

We proceeded up the main road, and along the way, a few people assured us we were heading in the right direction. Within 20 minutes or so we found ourselves warm and toasty enjoying a well needed meal and having a conversation with an older English gentleman in The Park Restaurant.

Partway through our meal I mentioned to him we had just gotten off the train and I felt a bit disoriented and unsure of how to get to our lodging. We told him the name and he said he'd walked past it on his way to dinner and he would be glad to walk us there after our meal.

With no street signs or lamp posts we set out winding our way through the puzzle of narrow cobblestone streets. Higher and higher we climbed for over 30 minutes.

I felt like I was on a stair stepper at the gym. Then, at just over 8,000 feet elevation, our new friend stopped in front of a dwelling marked Andy's guesthouse. We'd made it.

With holes burnt in our clothes and sweat dripping from our foreheads, we walked inside but found no one at the front desk. I was exhausted and felt very annoyed at facing another hurdle. I looked around for a bell or something to sound, but we saw nothing. I remembered I had the phone number to the guesthouse, so I called. The phone just rang and rang. Deeper frustration crept in.

We finally found a buzzer and pushed the button. Within a few moments we heard a voice that sounded as though it came from outside. We walked out the front door and saw a woman on the third floor. She told us she'd be right down.

Within a few minutes Matilda appeared. She was expecting us and also happy to see us. Her voice, however, had that tone of slight irritation almost like the mother of a teenager who is late getting home. It was only 8:30 in the evening, but once the sun went down in these parts, so did the people.

Our first morning in Darjeeling was a bit strange. We had nothing scheduled, nothing really planned and no Kahn. We looked forward to a nice hot shower, but discovered that not only was there no hot water, the shower had no water at all. I realized this after I stripped down, hopped in and found tape across the

116

handle. Who needs a shower anyhow? Through Rajasthan we had gotten used to little water and daily electricity outages.

Matilda and her husband, Genesis, owned the guesthouse and occupied the third floor as their home. They informed us they had a deck on the roof with views of all of Darjeeling and Kangchenjunga, which, at 28,169 feet tall, it's the third highest peak in the world and highest in India. I was so excited to hear this I zipped up to the deck to take a look. Unfortunately the mountain was shrouded in clouds and we weren't able to see a thing.

Genesis gave us the history of his hometown. He told us that when he was a little boy Darjeeling was a Shangri-la, but the growth in tourism and population had taken a toll on the once pristine hillside town. He suggested that we hike and venture towards the north side where it was much more tranquil.

We quickly learned our way around the little town. It had a bustling center square called the Chow Rasta. This is where people congregated and socialized. The square was lined with little stalls selling food and other goods. The narrow streets above the Chow Rasta seemed to be off limits to bigger vehicles and were lined with fruit and vegetables stands.

The roads below were plagued with tourist-share jeeps and felt suffocating. The smell of exhaust and the continual honking of the horns assaulted our senses. We came across two places that became our go-to eateries. Glenary's was the first and it provided us with luxurious flaky croissants and lattes that put a smile on my face. The second was a place called the Ailement. It became our dinner and breakfast spot.

I really enjoyed our visit to the Himalayan Mountaineering Institute. It was dedicated to Sir Edmund Hillary and Tenzing Norgay, the first two men to summit Mount Everest. It gave a great perspective of how time changes things. I had witnessed my race gear change over the years, but it shocked me to see the difference between their gear and mine. This was Tenzing's hometown. He was a hero to many, and he was buried in a shrine on the institute grounds.

The day before I was to perform my sacred pendant ceremony, my mom and I came across an amazing climbing area dedicated to Tenzing. It was spectacular. The rocks were dramatic. We found a perfect spot for the ceremony. It was lush, surrounded by green foliage and a waterfall.

After exploring a bit more around that area, we headed off to find the Tibetan Refugee Center. It was a steep mountain road and we were heading a number of miles downhill. I kept an eye on my map to keep from missing the turn to the center.

Realizing that street signs were unlikely, we asked a few people along the way to make sure we were still on the right path. The locals all smiled, stretched out an arm and pointed a finger forward, as if to say, "Yes, my child, you're on the right path."

Along our hikes we had noticed a number of political-looking signs hanging from walls. They had an unsettling energy to them. Words such as Ghorkaland and Revolution were written on the signs. We didn't understand what they meant at the time, but we'd soon learn.

We enjoyed our visit to the Tibetan Refugee Center. We wandered around the different rooms and watched many of the older refugees working on looms, spinning wool and tapestries. I felt as though we had stepped back in time.

I got a kick out of one of the little old ladies who stopped her spinning and posed for a photo with her little apple face and no teeth.

There was a particular room dedicated to the massacres of the Tibetan people. It was heartbreaking to see the photos. Another room was dedicated to his Holiness the Dalai Lama. Viewing all the needless suffering made my mom and me feel even more grateful for our lives.

We felt fortunate and glad that we could help support the center by purchasing a few special handmade items. As I'm writing these words I am sitting on top of a beautiful hand woven wool blanket I bought from the ladies.

Perhaps my place in my own life's journey added to the impact India had on me. I had been to other impoverished countries before, but watching the local people in India struggle daily for their next meal, clean water and shelter was affecting me on a different level. I had never known the feeling of extreme hunger, nor had I ever struggled to find clean water. Never had I intentionally lived without electricity to run my refrigerator, and I most certainly had never experienced deep suffering.

I was starting to see how much people from the western world, including myself, put themselves through needless internal suffering brought on by our own egos. There are too many people who settle for "good enough is good enough." They never live their truth to reach their full potential.

By the time we'd hiked back up the steep mountain from the refugee center, we were hungry and ready for a good meal. We decided to head to The Park Restaurant where we ate the first night we got into town. As we neared the Chow Rasta Square we heard the sounds of chanting coming from the direction we were headed. People in the square were uneasy and moving quickly about. The doors of the little stalls and shops were shutting.

We asked a man what was happening and he abruptly said, "Ghorkaland strike!" Then he turned and quickly walked away.

The square and streets became hauntingly quiet. My mom and I weren't sure what to do as the loud sounds of the chanting got closer and closer. We found another man who informed us that the whole town and the surrounding areas were going on a political strike and all the businesses were closing down indefinitely. We tried not to panic as he too shuffled away through a tiny door.

We feared that we'd be stuck here and miss our flight back to New Delhi or worse. Then the thought of food and drinking water popped into my head. Without hesitation I turned to my mom and said, "Mom, quick, we need to find someone who will sell us food and water." With none of the businesses open we'd have no access to food or drinking water.

The marchers were now becoming visible as they pushed and shoved their way up the road. The hostile chants were so close to us my heart sped up as if I were fleeing from a battle. We had to find a shop that would sell us some provisions, so we quickly headed towards our guesthouse to avoid the mob coming towards us.

Louder and louder and closer and closer the mob came, while our feet moved quicker and quicker. As we rounded the bend in the road I noticed an older gentleman struggling to get all his produce put away. We rushed over to him.

With my hands in the prayer position I ask him if we could buy some supplies. He must have noticed the desperate look on our faces and hesitantly agreed. We grabbed cucumbers, water and crackers. We gave him money and said thank you without taking the change. Now that we had the food we felt a bit more at ease. If worst came to worst, we could ration this food for the next couple of days.

Our next concern was for our flight in a couple of days. We felt very uneasy about being foreigners who didn't speak the language and had now landed in the middle of political turmoil shutting us off from the rest of the world.

The next day we cautiously made our way to the climbing area and performed the sacred pendant ceremony. I was determined to complete it. There was a specific order and sequence I was to follow.

Three times I cleansed my pendant with milk and three times with water. As I cleansed, I chanted the words Om Shanti Deva Nama over and over. The Gods added their blessings by opening up the heavens with rain. After hiking many miles down to the sacred area we cut our visit short because the rains were getting heavier and heavier.

Soaked to the bone, we started our ascent up the long steep hill. Water soon began to flow deeper and deeper on the road we were traveling. There weren't any sidewalks to take refuge on from the small river that was forming. Soon debris started floating by us as the waters were nearly knee high.

We finally saw a tiny overhang stretching out over a decrepit looking platform that was connected to a few dwellings, so we hopped up and hunkered down. The rains kept coming and coming. Soon the thunder and lightning started up a show. It looked like we'd be there for quite some time, so we took out the little food we had packed.

Standing under the eve I noticed a youngish looking guy pop his head out a door. He gestured to us to come in out of the rain. Feeling a bit uncomfortable, my mom and I walked into what turned out to be his grandmother's house. There we stood soaking wet and apologizing for dripping water all over their floor. They made us a nice hot cup of tea, and we felt welcome. The rains let up about 40 minutes into our visit, and we knew we'd make it back safely.

We thanked them for their generous hospitality. Actually, given the fact that the fellow was close to passing out from being intoxicated by alcohol, we were grateful for the rains softening. By the time we got back to our guesthouse it was dark and Matilda had been concerned. It had taken us five hours to return, but we were now safe and sound.

Even though my mom and I trusted that we would make it to the airport, it came down to the wire for us. The evening before our flight, the strike lifted. We were filled with relief and ready to go home.

Matilda knew a man who would take us to the airport at 7 a.m. We said our goodbyes to Matilda and Genesis and met our cab driver down the road.

As we drove away from the Rasta, I turned back to say a final goodbye and was struck by the most magnificent sight. The peak of Kangchenjunga stared right at me, bidding us farewell. Away we drove.

Part Two
A Twist of Fate

Athena Rising, a Memoir – Heather Bond

Chapter 1
The Pickle

Your pain is the breaking of the shell that encloses your understanding

Khalil Gibran.

It had been a long winding two-hour cab ride down the mountain to the airport. We were so excited to be flying back to New Delhi, where we would spend the night before we flew back to the states the following day. Before visiting Darjeeling, we had left two of our packs in New Dehli at our hotel we'd be staying.

My mom and I were surprised that we didn't see a soul as we walked into the airport that morning. It was awhile before we even saw a worker. We asked if anyone was there to check us in. Apparently we were early, and we needed to wait.

We wandered around the upper floor to see if we could spot a place to grab a tea or something to snack on. All our snacks had run out, and we hadn't eaten since early the prior evening. We walked around but saw nothing. When we noticed a worker near the Deccan Air window, we walked over and checked in.

Athena Rising, a Memoir – Heather Bond

As we turned from the ticket window with our boarding passes in hand, the worker instructed us to put our packs through the x-ray machine. By then, there were a few other people shuffling around the lobby. We walked up to the x-ray machine and my mom plopped down her pack, then I set down mine. We walked to the other side of the scanner.

My mom grabbed her pack and flung it over her shoulder, but as I went to grab mine the man put out his hand and stopped me. We looked at each other. "Excuse me," he said to me sternly. "Excuse me, do you have an umbrella in your pack?"

I thought that seemed like a strange question. "Yes, I do have an umbrella," I replied as I reached into a small outer pocket. I grabbed my umbrella and went to hand it to him.

He brushed away my hand, reached into the same pocket and pulled out a gun cartridge loaded with bullets.

My jaw dropped as I look at him holding the bullets in his hand. I look at my mom, her eyes wide in disbelief. My first thought was holy shit! Then I looked at my watch and thought that if we missed our flight we'd be able to catch the later one. My second thought was oh shit!

The man started talking fast and loud in Hindi on his walkie-talkie. Before we know it people were coming out from behind doors and gathering around us. They seized our packs and start pushing and shoving us towards a door.

The room was tiny, like a small bedroom. White painted walls and not a single picture hung. There was a tiny desk that was backed up towards a window that had a view of the airstrip. People came in and out of the door. Every time a person entered, the door latch would fail to catch and the door would slowly creep open. My mom was closest to the door and repeatedly closed it.

At one point my mom counted 14 people stuffed in the minuscule room all speaking a different language than us at the top of their lungs.

I started feeling claustrophobic. At one point, my mom cracked the door ajar and held it with her foot just so we could get air. I felt that if I could just speak to the right person I'd get this whole situation under control. We watched the cartridge of bullets and our passports get passed around from one person to the next. Every time a new person got a hold of them they'd shake their heads and look at us in disbelief.

The door opened abruptly. In walked a broad-shouldered man with a very intense and serious look on his face. We found out he was the senior investigator. Later, my mom and I privately referred to him as S.I. Fat Boy. He wasn't actually what I consider obese, but he was much larger than most of the other men.

He was followed in by three of his cronies. Most of the other people left the room when S.I. Fat Boy entered. He was handed the cartridge, bullets and our passports.

I tried to explain to him that it was all just a big misunderstanding and I had permits in the states for these.

He didn't seem interested in what I had to say. He leaned into me with a piercing gaze and informed me that only military and terrorists carried such types of ammunitions, and in India it was a very serious offense. He also told us that he was capable of taking care of the situation.

My mom and I turned our attention towards getting a hold of Sean. We were trying to imagine how on earth the bullets could've made it out of LAX and then on through Taipei and New Delhi in the first place.

First I tried to call Sean. There was a 12-hour difference, and I hoped he'd answer the phone. It took a while to connect, and then the phone just rang and rang.

His voicemail was full, so I called again, still no answer. We really didn't want to call my dad and needlessly worry him. We thought if we could find Sean he could fax paperwork to the proper authorities, and the whole thing could be settled by proving he owned the nine- millimeter gun.

Fat Boy grew impatient after numerous unsuccessful attempts to get Sean on the phone. I told my mom to call my dad so he could find Sean.

My mom was nervous to call my dad, and with good reason. I couldn't imagine the thoughts that would churn in his head when news that his wife and daughter were being held by the police in India on a possible weapons charge. Or worse. These policemen were talking to us with the word "terrorists" being used in the conversation.

My mom got her nerve up enough to dial my dad's phone number. Within a few rings he answered. I was on the edge of my seat wondering how my mom would deliver the news to my poor dad. Then, without a stumble or hesitation my mom said, "Larry, we're in a bit of a pickle!"

My jaw dropped as I heard her words. A bit of a pickle I thought. More like a F-ing mess. My thoughts spun like a whirlwind in my head.

My dad wrote in his journal that day, on April 13, 2008, "The room was pitch dark, and as I jumped up, simultaneously groping for the light switch and the telephone, I got the most excruciating cramp I have ever experienced in my right calf muscle. This caused me to trip over a pile of pillows and clothes that were alongside the bed, and as I fell I pulled the light. I had been fumbling for everything around the light and it came crashing down on top of me.

As I was attempting to stand up, I heard Monica say in a plaintive voice, "Larry, are you there? I hope you're there. We're in a bit of a pickle."

My mom muttered softly to my dad; I could barely hear her speaking. She got off the phone and reported that he was going to drive up to my place where Sean should be and let him know what was happening. Sean relayed to me later that he was fast asleep when my dad arrived. My dad knocked on the door with so much force and concern that Sean thought a SWAT team was trying to break down the door.

After being loaded up in a small paddy wagon, I frantically began searching my notebook for an emergency phone number for the United States Embassy. This was the reason travelers are advised to write down these numbers. I had every other number, but not the embassy.

I remembered seeing it in my Lonely Planet, which thankfully was in my pack. By the time I pulled out the book we had arrived at the local police station.

We were escorted into a station that looked much more like a one bedroom house. The main room was nothing more than an open space. S.I. walked straight back to his desk and plopped down in his seat. The desk was surrounded by file cabinets and located towards the back of the office.

The office was painted in headache green, which made me feel quite nauseated. There was a picture of the Hindu god Ganesh hung from the wall with garlands of marigolds draped from the frame. An open back door revealed a vacant lot behind the station. The windows had a few bars across them and no glass.

We were told to sit in the chairs near the side of S.I.'s desk. He asked us for our flight papers and tickets. I was extremely reluctant about handing the items over. I didn't want to, but I did. He set them down within arms reach of me when he was done looking, and when I asked to get them back he said he needed to hold onto them.

I found the number for the U.S. Embassy located in Kolkata. We had very few minutes left on our cell phone and knew we needed to get help. I was quite nervous when I dialed the number to the embassy. What was I going to say? How would the embassy react?

The phone rang and rang before being transferred to a waiting line. I waited for a bit but it was burning our last precious minutes. Once those minutes were used we'd have no connection to the outside. It was our only lifeline. So I hung up.

My mind raced back to an event 20 years prior. I was racing with the Navy Seal team in South Africa and Lesotho. We were heading into an area that was under massive civil unrest in the Lesotho region. It was close to two o'clock in the morning and we were driving in our vehicle, slowly approaching a border stop. There were many armed men. I started feeling very uneasy about the whole situation and remembered how concerned my dad was before I left home.

The energy in our vehicle quickly shifted into high alert status when one of my Navy Seal teammates said to us, "Get your weapons ready." I thought holy crap I'm not sure if this is a good thing I'm with these guys or not.

We pulled up to the gate and at least four armed guards approached our vehicle. Adrenaline was pumping through my body. One man spoke up in very broken English and asked us why we were coming to this area.

We had special permits to enter this territory but I started to think it wouldn't really matter. The other men were peering into our vehicle and poking around at all our gear. They looked and me. It was intense. I had horrible visions of us being murdered right there in that spot and thought no one would even know what had happened to us.

Back in the police station in West Bengal there were journalists and photographers showing up on the front porch sneaking photos of us through the bars. They waited for any movement.

More of S.I.'s cronies showed up and leered at us like animals in a cage. Guns slung over their shoulders, they walked inches from us while talking to one another in Hindi and then looking at us and laughing. It took every ounce of my restraint to keep my mouth shut. I wanted to ask, "What's so funny, you piece of shit?"

It went from uncomfortable to distressing when S.I. leaned into us and said, "Tell me your thoughts and feelings on terrorism!" What was he talking about, "our thoughts about terrorism?"

What we didn't realize at the time is that we were sitting in a communist and terrorist region. Then I had flashes of the political strikes in Darjeeling.

"What do you know about Al Qaeda or Osama bin Laden?" My mom and I looked at each other in bewilderment. Then he brought up corruption in the U.S. He went into a long rant about how we Americans are so rich, and he was just a poor Indian. We didn't even know what words should exit from our mouths.

131

Creepy and overbearing, the man appeared to be in his late 40's and had very bad body odor. He seemed dishonest and kept questioning us harshly for some time. Thankfully it was interrupted by the sound of our phone ringing.

It was Sean. I hadn't been as pleased to hear his voice in a long time. He informed me that he was looking for the paperwork on his gun but was having challenges.

Back in the states it was close to midnight. I told him that I'd tried calling the embassy but couldn't stay on hold forever. I asked him to contact the Kolkata branch and let them know what had happened.

Sean mentioned that perhaps we could pay our way out of this. I told him that sounded like what S.I. was getting at when he was on his rant about us wealthy Americans. I felt that if I did offer him a bribe it would backfire on us, and then what? My gut told me not to do it, and I listened. Sean wasn't happy with my decision.

Hours went by and the harassment continued. Then, as if he knew we wouldn't offer money to get out of it, he stated that he would have to hand it over to a higher authority. Personally, I had never met a dirty Tijuana cop who asked Americans for bribes, but I knew people who had. It is possible S.I.'s crazy rant wasn't a roundabout way of asking us for money, but it felt like it was.

It had been around six hours since we'd been detained when two plain dressed men entered the station. They were handed our passports and flight itinerary along with the bullets and cartridge. One of the men escorted us into another small room, and the whole process of questioning continued. "Where did you get bullets?" the first man asked.

I was really pissed off by then. I had been asked that same question for six hours. With my jaw clenched I said, "Like I have been saying to all the others, they're my fiancé's." They looked at us suspiciously.

"How could bullets travel from U.S. without being detected?" he asked over and over. I shrugged my shoulders and responded, "That's a very good question." The looked at us like, Yeah, right.

I asked the two civilian looking cops for a fax number so that when Sean found the paperwork he could send it.

We were given one and learned the hard way that it wasn't a working number. We were taken back out to the two chairs in the main office and never saw those two men again. As we sat, we heard the phone ring and ring. No one in the station would answer.

We received a few calls on our cell from the embassy stating that they were having a hard time getting a hold of the police. I informed them that the police must have been playing a game because we were listening to the phone go unanswered.

Time ticked by. There were mosquitoes flying around us, and that really began to agitate me. My mom and I sat like stiff mannequins in the uncomfortable metal seats, my whole body tense. It was humid and sticky out, and we were hungry and thirsty. The guards continually lurked around us. We were emotionally exhausted.

About 12 hours into the ordeal, a female guard led us back into the smaller room and unfolded a makeshift cot. Thank goodness, we thought, we can actually lie down.

The woman gestured to the ground and plopped down on the cot. I wanted to grab her and throw her on the floor, but thought better of it. The ground was cement. In one section they'd thrown down some awful looking red astroturf. I wanted nothing to do with it, but there was nothing else in the room.

I perched my mom's pack in the corner and mine next to it. We had finally been given a small cup of water. Soon enough I regretted drinking it. I asked the guard if there was a toilet because I had to pee. She pointed to a door. As I walked in I was shocked to discover how foul it was. The American style toilet had no plumbing connected to it, and yet it had been stained with dry feces. I gagged so badly I threw up in my mouth and in my hand.

When I tried to wash my hands in the small dirty sink, no water came out. I looked underneath and there were no pipes hooked up there either. My eyes continued to tear from my gagging as I walked from the putrid room and explained the situation to my mom.

Our brains were exhausted and fading. "Mom you lie down in the corner, there's no way I'm going to fall asleep," I said in a very concerned voice.

She responded back in an equally concerned tone, "Heather, you really need to try to shut your eyes too, we both need to get some rest." I created something of a barrier to protect her. We leaned against our packs and fought to keep our eyes open. I told my mom to close her eyes and try to rest.

I felt so low. I watched my mom fade in and out, and I was wondering if she was angry with me. It felt like it was my fault. I started silently breaking down. Tears flowed from my cheeks as I sat on the filthy floor trying my hardest to keep it together. I needed to be strong to protect my mom. So I thought.

As I lay there staring at this beautiful amazing woman I thought how lucky am I to have such an awesome strong woman for a mom. What was it that made her so strong and resilient? She was never an athlete. She didn't strive to do crazy physical feats. Heaven forbid her ever thinking about doing a high-fall from a two-story building and yet she's got grit. She'd had plenty of crazy adventures on the high seas with my dad and let me not forget wrangling animals and building dreams.

My mom is the youngest of three kids. She grew up in the small town of Santa Barbara, California in the 1950's. This is where her mom, my grandmother landed after the depression to put herself through nursing school.

My grandmother was a tough old bird. When Pearl Harbor was bombed she wanted to help and be a part of it, so she tried to enlist in the Army but was told she was too skinny. She joined the Red Cross instead and off she went for a year to help the wounded soldiers. This is where she met my granddad.

It was a whirlwind war romance that produced three children. Unfortunately my grandfather, who came from a very wealthy Ohio farming family, was the black sheep of his family. He'd just as soon be riding the trains and playing poker at the hobo junctions. The liquor took precedence, which left my grandma a single mom of three.

But like I said she was tough and smart and climbed her way to becoming the head nurse of the Pulmonary Disease Unit at the Santa Barbara General Hospital. I always felt she lived vicariously through my adventures. I remember one time when I told her I got selected to train and race on the Navy Seal team in Africa she said, "Well for God's sake don't kill yourself"

Back on the cement floor I struggled to stay awake to protect my mom and myself. At times my eyelids got heavy, and I felt myself doze off. Then, without knowing how long it had been, I would wake suddenly as if I had fallen off a ledge or mountain. This had been the longest night in my life.

Throughout that night I heard the ringing of the phone, over and over. I knew that our family was doing all they could to get us help. Unfortunately we felt like pawns in a sick game. They told us if the proper paperwork could be produced, we'd be released, otherwise an arrest warrant would be issued.

It was April 15, 2008. We saw no one until one of the officers waltzed into the room around 10 that next morning and set down two official looking papers. My mom and I glanced down to read them. They were two arrest warrants, one for me and one for my mom. "I am not signing these papers!," I immediately told the man.

I couldn't understand how they could arrest my mom. As my rage grew, I started getting louder and bolder. "You can't make me sign these!" I looked at my mom like what the F-k is going on. At that point I needed to alert the embassy myself. I didn't care how many minutes we had left.

The man that brought us the paperwork left the room. Just as I got patched through to the embassy, S.I. burst into the room enraged. He pushed the paperwork towards me as he aggressively said, "You will sign these papers!"

I looked him in the eye and say, "No, I wont!" I was then having two conversations, one with the embassy and one with the police. I told the embassy that we needed help now. S.I. kept speaking loudly over my phone conversation. The embassy informed us that they'd contacted a local advocate and he should be arriving any moment. They also let us know that if my mom and I felt comfortable with him, it was our choice to retain him.

I got off the phone and told the police we wouldn't sign anything until the advocate showed up. My hope was that he spoke English.

Within minutes I watched through the barred window as a vehicle pulled into the lot in front of the station. A man quickly emerged and shuffled his way into the station. We must have looked a mess standing there.

"Hello, I'm Mr. Chatterjee," he said in a very thick accent. I couldn't understand his name, so I had him write it down. I told him there had to have been some mistake going on. He looked into my eyes and said nothing.

Eventually, he told us the paperwork was just a formality. Internally, I questioned his judgment but we signed the papers and were escorted to the back of a police car.

"Where are we going?" My voice was tired and nervous. "To face judge," a random police officer said to us in a harsh tone. I looked at my mom in absolute disbelief. Our passports, plane tickets and itinerary had been taken, and now they separated us from our backpacks.

Thankfully I still had my smaller satchel purse with our phone, my camera, journal and money. It lay across my chest. It's my old faithful travel companion. Mr. Chatterjee then told us that we were being taken to the court to face the judge about our crime.

My mom and I both sunk down in our seats close to each other. I drifted in and out as the car's motion lulled me to sleep. We were beyond exhausted and didn't know what lay ahead. After being on the road for around 30 minutes, we pulled into a chaotic parking lot adjacent to some buildings. We assumed it was the court.

The courtyard was mobbed with people. As our vehicle pulled into the parking lot, a crowd of spectators separated like the parting of waters. Two unknown female guards opened the vehicle doors and grabbed my mom's and my arms.

The mob of people closed in on us as the guards pulled us through the middle. Members of the crowd chanted our names. Photographers and journalists got in our faces taking pictures trying to ask us questions in both Hindi and English. It was absolute insanity. It was as if we were celebrities, but this was definitely not a red carpet event.

We were taken to an eight-foot-square holding cell. As the guard closed the bared door behind us, I started gagging. I have a sensitive gag reflex, and certain unpleasant smells can set it off.

The cell had old worn paint. It was a sad yellow color splattered with betel nut stain from people spitting on the floors and walls. The smell of old urine was so pungent I couldn't stop gagging. There was a squat toilet in the corner stained with dried feces on the sides. It was the foulest of the foul.

In a couple hours, two guards came with Mr. Chatterjee to escort us to what I can only describe as a circus. It was the courtroom, and it was bursting at the seams with people. We were shoved through the crowd toward a cage of male prisoners. I thought, Oh, hell no!

Thankfully someone decided it was too full even for Indian standards. It must have been the men's faces smashed up against the wire that was their gauge. So we were stuffed between two male guards like sardines. The judge had old looking ledgers stacked in piles on each side of him. People stood in the doorway and against the walls. They walked in and out of the door and spit their betel nut all over the hallway.

It was unbearably loud and hot in the room, and the smell of body odor filled the air. I thought, surely once the judge starts talking people will stop talking. That wasn't the case.

Mr. Chatterjee approached the front part of the room to address the judge, but then quickly turned away and motioned for the guards to bring us back to the cell.

Chapter 1 - The Pickle

Silence descended when the guards stuck us back in the cell. My mom and I looked at each other like, what the heck just happened? We thought maybe they were getting our stuff and planned to release us. My thoughts had me panicked.

Mr. Chatterjee came back a few minutes later and said, "This is a very serious offense. You're being arrested and charged under the Indian Arms Act." A shroud of darkness fell over me and I looked at my mom.

"What does that mean to us?" my mom questioned calmly.

"It is a charge that holds a sentence of three to seven years," Mr. Chatterjee said earnestly. "You wait here while I find out information."

I've had many crazy, thrill-seeking and heart-pumping experiences in my life, but in that moment, something snapped within me. I lost it. I didn't get angry, but I physically and emotionally lost it. I turned pale and started sweating profusely. My heart pounded as I struggled to breathe.

My mom went into action mode. She grabbed a hanky from her pocket and poured some water on it. I grew dizzy and my vision narrowed. We both worried I was having a heart attack. My mom made me sit down on the dirty floor as she placed the wet hanky on my forehead. She caressed my hair like only a mother can do. "Breathe, Heather, just breathe." She continued rubbing my head as she sat beside me.

My beautiful mom sat beside her daughter whom she feared was having a heart attack in the filthiest conditions she'd ever experienced on the floor of a cement jail cell in India after hearing she may be facing a prison sentence. I would do anything to protect my mom, but the tables had just turned and now she was protecting and nurturing me.

We later managed to sneak in a last call to our family. Sadly the news we gave them was grim. It was a description of the conditions of the cell, my ailing health and a mention of a three-to seven-year sentence.

We waited, our bodies stiff and sore from the last 40-plus hours. Around 8:30 p.m., Mr. Chatterjee somberly walked to the holding cell door with concern etched on his face.

He shook his head in a defeated manner and said, "Not good news. Not good news at all." I felt my heart clench again. I braced myself and clutched my mom. "So sorry. They are sending you to a prison. It's a correctional facility."

Tears flowed down my cheeks as I looked at my mom.

Chatterjee continued, "If you must go to prison, this is the one you want to be at." If our current conditions were any indication, prison would be no better. Now add prisoners.

Two guards came to collect us for transport. A thought popped into my head. "Can we at least grab something from our backpacks?" I asked in a rushed manner. The guards passed a few words in Hindi back and forth between each other and then abruptly turned us in a different direction. They unlocked a door to a storage room where our packs were being held. One of the guards told us to quickly grab whatever we were after. We grabbed our toiletry kits; conveniently my mom had a pair of pants rolled around hers. The guards ordered us to come, but my mom turned back once more and grabbed her deck of cards.

We were escorted outside and directed to climb into an old paddy wagon packed with male prisoners. One of the guards jumped in and closed a wire-windowed door that divided us from the male prisoners. My mom and I were sandwiched between four armed guards in the back section.

The windows had no glass and were covered with thick gauge steel. The vehicle looked like something out of World War II. I wrapped my arm around my mom's shoulder as we drove away.

The piles of burning trash on the sides of the road gave way to darkness. The full magnitude of the situation finally hit me. The truck moved erratically, the brakes suddenly slamming and lurching everyone forward. I looked deeply into my mom's eyes and told her I was sorry. I was fighting back my tears. I felt that any minute I would start breaking down again, so I looked for a distraction out the window.

Peering out through the bars, I felt the whole world shift into slow motion. I locked eyes with a man sitting near a burning pile and I sensed he felt my fear. He kept gazing deeply into my eyes, seeming to say, "Don't worry, God will take care of you." Then he was a distant blur.

After what felt like a few quick turns, we were backing up into a dark yard where armed guards waited. The door swung open and the guards motioned us out and escorted us to a lit room with the other prisoners. My mom and I sat on two chairs, and the male prisoners sat on the cement floor across from us. Every guard in the room was staring. It made me uncomfortable. No one spoke, which made it oddly quiet. I felt as though the men were undressing us with their eyes.

A guard came in, gathered the male prisoners and led them out a door. My mom and I softly spoke to each other. Instead of putting us more at ease, when the prisoners left it only intensified the tension. The senior officer demanded we turn over all our money, credit cards, wallets, cell phone and camera.

His attention then turned to our jewelry. One thing after another got stripped away. When my mom was told to take off her necklace, she refused. I looked at her like, what?

"It would be bad luck and it's against my religion!" she told him forcefully. She'd summoned the deepest, most demonic sounding voice I had ever heard from her.

He turned to me and noticed I was wearing an identical Celtic eternity pendant. I followed suit by saying, "Me too." My confidence, however, was a watered down version of my mom's. It was a minor victory. We were allowed to keep our necklaces.

The guard grew extremely agitated by our behavior. He grabbed our belongings and walked out the door. Four other guards entered the room, which made us squirm. These guards looked intense.

Adrenaline surged in my body, and my heart rate shifted into high gear in anticipation of conflict. That's when my mom leaned into me and said, "If these men try to rape us we're going to run as fast as we can. They'll have to shoot us in our backs."

I thought, Holy shit, did she just say that? My eyes frantically searched for options, and scenarios played out in my head. None of the apparent options had acceptable outcomes. A female guard stepped towards us and motioned for us to go through a door.

I felt dirty and violated. The dank smell permeating the air was almost unbearable. I tensed every frightened muscle and bit down on the fear that circulated throughout my being. My breathing was labored. I was having a hard time walking and clutched onto my mom's arm and as were led down a long dark corridor. The narrow beam from the guard's flashlight faded into the darkness, and the clanging of her keys turned our footsteps into what seemed like a methodical march into the unknown.

Chapter 1 - The Pickle

We hadn't slept in over forty hours and I thought perhaps this was actually a nightmare and surely I'd be waking up. We were stopped at a set of massive metal gates. The woman inserted a big medieval looking key. As she pushed the gates open with her body weight she directed us through, and the gates slammed behind us.

First we were led to a massive central courtyard with high walls on every side. The guards stopped us at two more double gates. The sound of an old fashioned bell rang twice. I heard locks open, and then the bells sounded again. More locks clicked into place. The gate in front of us opened, and two female guards gestured us through. We were now standing in between two locked doors. I thought, where on earth are we being taken?

Two more bells rang out, and the second gate opened.

As we walk through the darkness of the night towards a dim pool of light, I caught my first vision of all the female prisoners as they sat on the cement floor. Their eyes stared through the barred windows to get a first glimpse of my mom and me. As I watched, their intense, almond-shaped eyes came into focus.

A guard met us at the door of a cell holding one grey woolen blanket. We were ushered in.

Two of the prisoners directed us to a space in the corner of the cement cell. We unfolded the blanket and collapsed onto the floor. My body and brain swayed back and forth as I lay there. It felt as though I'd been on a boat for days. We were confused, uncertain, and I had nothing left in me. I remember thinking, there's no way we can stay here.

Chapter Two
Initiation

Journal entry: I can't imagine what it would be like to have to stay here. There's no way we can. It's fricken nasty and dirty. We don't belong in here. I hope someone gets here quick to bail us out.

April 16, 2008, I woke to the feeling of something scratching over my face. I quickly tried to brush it away while my swollen and puffy eyes slowly opened. As I focused, I saw two prisoners standing above us quickly rolling up this net substance. They shuffled away and one of them buried the object into a pile of their belongings.

I sat up on the itchy grey wool blanket, and tried to stretch the stiffness from my back and my shoulders. My face and eyes were gritty feeling. My mom and I observed the other women for a moment and noticed them forming into a single-file line in the center of the cell. Then they dropped down into a very submissive squat position. A few of the inmates motioned to us to fall into the end of the line and do the same.

My body felt as though I had been beat up. My spine hurt, and I was stiff. I was having a hard time getting my body into this position due to my bad knee and my spine injury sustained a couple years prior. One of the female prisoners who must have felt it was her duty started pushing down on my back. She pushed and pushed in an effort to make my body drop lower to the ground.

My knee buckled painfully, and I said to her sternly, "My body doesn't like that." She had no idea what I was saying and continued to shove me down. I looked at her resentfully, daggers coming from my eyes, spoke the universal language necessary for her to back off.

Twenty plus women huddled into little balls with their heads towards the ground so no eye contact would be made with the male guards in the room. I felt outrage, anger and humiliation for the prisoners who were treated as lesser beings.

I felt like standing up and shouting in their defense, but I played the submissive game. My knee throbbed with pain as the guards kept us in this tight huddled position for some time. When they walked away, the women slowly unfolded. I stood up and exhaled a big forceful snort that sounded like an agitated horse.

The two same prisoners that had shown us to our corner space the night before, gestured to us and said in a thick Indian accent, "Come, come." My mom and I joined them in their personal space on the floor. They were located directly across from us in the opposite corner of the cell. It seemed as though they may have been leaders of some sort.

They handed us two small teacups, two metal bowls and one metal plate to share.

The cell was a big open cement room 15 feet wide and 50 feet long. There was no glass on the barred windows. They were open to the elements and any creatures that could fly in and out.

Chapter Two - Initiation

The two girls walked us to the opposite end of the cell. Behind a door was a tiny space with two repulsive, keyhole-shaped squatting toilets.

Thankfully there was a partition of sorts between the two squat slabs. Unfortunately it was so low you could look right at your neighbor. There was no toilet paper or sink, just six rusty pots and containers filled with water. "Wash, wash," one of the inmates said while pretending to rub her hands as if she were washing them. It looked to me much more like a mosquito breeding habitat.

That was it. Our cellblock tour was complete. I was exhausted from the hell of the past couple days and wanted nothing more than to go back and lay down. But somehow I didn't think that was going to happen.

My mom and I decided to see what the other prisoners were doing outside. All eyes turned to us as we entered the courtyard. We didn't know how to react. I noticed a few steps attached to this little out-building, and we sat down on them. A cement structure at the top of the steps turned out to be the trash burning area.

Three of the inmates and one of the female guards came and sat down on the ground at the bottom of the steps. The guard we later came to know as Matajee had a newspaper bundled up with objects inside. My mom and I watched as she rolled out some good- sized green leaves, a few hard nut-like objects and a dirty little bottled filled with a white substance.

We watched as they grabbed one of the leaves and dabbed it with the white substance. They then placed the hard looking nut at the center of the leaf. We had no idea what they were doing. They watched to make sure not many people saw, then continued folding the leaf up into a tiny green package. We realized it was betel nut when one of them shoved the entire thing into her mouth. A smile warmed her face as she began the disgusting ritual of spitting the red-stained substance from her mouth.

147

They continued making the little green packages. At a certain point, one of the prisoners who had given us our bowls and tour handed us two of the little packages. "Take", she said as she gestured for us to put it in our mouths.

We later came to know this prisoner as Bobbi. I thought perhaps this was a trick or a trap. I certainly didn't want it, but I also didn't want to offend them so we accepted the little leaf packages.

I planned to chuck it later, but they insisted that we put it in our mouths. Given all the issues I had with my heart the day before, a stimulant was the last thing I wanted in my system. The packages included tobacco leaves, the white bicarbonate and the betel nut.

My mom and I looked at each other and counted, one, two, three go, and into our mouths went the betel nut. The three ladies laughed. I wasn't sure if that was a good sign or not, but I was pretty sure I'd watched them make all the bundles the same.

The betel nut really stimulates your salivary glands; my mouth filled with spit almost instantly. I felt a bit frozen in uncertainty. I didn't want to swallow this horribly bitter substance, nor did I want to start spitting on the ground.

The women continued to monitor our every move and gestured to us to start spitting. I look at my mom and nodded. I spit out what seemed like a half a cup of red brown muck and my mom followed suit. The women gave us that look like we'd just been successfully initiated into the prison system.

The small group wandered away, leaving my mom and me sitting alone. I wanted to get the stuff out of my mouth, so, I suggested my mom and I take our first solo walk around the prison courtyard. The eyes of the women followed our movements. I walked us behind the structure where we'd been sitting. We pulled the soggy little packages from our mouths and chucked them into the plants, chuckling softly. Here we were sucking on betel nut in an Indian prison.

Chapter 3
Bail Halona

Journal entry: When I woke up this morning I just laid there staring at mom. All of a sudden, like she's talking in her sleep, she says, "Are all the nuts still here?" Once she came around, I put my finger to my mouth in a shhh position. We giggled when I told her what she said. I think she meant the inmates.

Within a few days my mom and I began to understand the daily pulse of the prisoners and the tasks we needed to perform at various times. There were three submissive lineup counts a day. The first count was bright and early at 6 a.m. The second count came midday with a cell lockdown, and at 5:30 p.m. we had our last count and lockdown of the day.

For some prisoners the mornings were a race to get their illegal mosquito nets down and put away before the guards came. Somehow we were blessed with a mosquito net from one of the other prisoners. We always hoped not to oversleep and get busted with it.

The prison was located in a highly populated mosquito area, and unfortunately not all the prisoners had a net. Every evening at lockdown one of the inmates would be given the task of walking with a bowl burning with herbs. She'd walk up and down numerous times the length of the corridor. The thick grey smoke choked everything in sight including the women, but it did help keep the mosquitos briefly at bay. At night the cell would turn into a web of strings; nets hung like cocoons from one side of the cell to the other.

The morning hustle continued after count. It was always a mad dash to the courtyard to gain a poll position on one of the three water spigots. Our water came from metal pipes sticking out of the ground with small valves on the end to open and close them.

The water was on for only certain periods of time throughout the day, and most of the time only two lines had water. The number of prisoners fluctuated between 20 and 26 women, so when the cell gate opened the women pushed and shoved to get out. Water was a precious lifeline. We used it for washing dishes, filling plastic water bottles, cleaning our bodies and clothes for those who had extra. On a couple of days there was no water access at all.

In the early days I had only the clothes on my back. I had a dark pink tank top that I wore underneath my Indian styled shirt, my pants, two black sport socks and my underwear. I would watch the other women wash their colorful saris by scrubbing them on the sandstone and hanging them to dry in the courtyard. The colors were so vibrant and beautiful in contrast to our environment.

After we'd been in prison for a few days, representatives from the embassy in Kolkata arrived to speak to us. We were informed that we'd be meeting in the prison warden's office. We were thrilled. Great, we thought, they're here to pick us up.

The guards escorted us from the cell to the office. Mr. Chatterjee was among those waiting for us. The opportunity to see and speak to the embassy officials raised our spirits.

As the meeting commenced, the embassy reps did a lot more listening than speaking. We were given the opportunity to ask questions to both Mr. Chatterjee and the embassy.

"We need you to know that we feel the arresting officer deliberately didn't answer the phone calls that were coming through to their office on our behalf." I said this with much irritation in my voice.

"We understand your concerns at this time. However it's out of our authority," responded one of the embassy officials in a watered down tone. We learned the protocol for how the embassy operates in such a situation. We were informed that we'd be going in front of the judge the next day for bail, and the embassy would be there to support us.

That evening my mom and I felt great optimism. We gathered together our few belongings so they'd be ready after we made bail the next day. That evening sitting on the floor I got so excited about the possibility of going home,

"Oh gosh ma let's have a huge homecoming party." Smiles crossed our faces, "Let's," my mom said. We visualized all the different foods we'd have. We spoke about how wonderful it would be to take a long hot showers and how nice some shampoo and conditioner would feel in our hair. We spoke about lotion for our skin and the use of other daily items that we'd taken for granted. We couldn't wait to get back to our family.

The next day arrived and we said our goodbyes to a few of the gals before the guards came to load us into the paddy wagon and take us to the dingy little holding cell at the court. This time we were prepared with some old newspaper to sit on. We stuffed a few crackers that the embassy had brought us into our pockets for snacks.

Around 2:30 p.m. my mom and I were escorted into the chaos of the courtroom and squished between two guards. We saw the two embassy representatives sitting among the crowd as well as Mr.Chatterjee and another attorney from a different district. I then noticed the original arresting officer standing against the wall, looking heartless and suspicious.

The noise never subsided. It was the same chaos on repeat. People walking in and out spitting their betel nut juice on the wall in the hall. The fans on the ceiling turned loudly and rapidly, looking as though they might take flight any moment. The defense and the prosecution for our case finally approached the bench.

We saw Mr. Chatterjee open up the show but heard nothing. When he finished, the prosecution started, but again we heard nothing.

The judge never seemed to look up from his papers. He seemed uneasy. A few comments went back and forth between the groups, and then a strange silence fell over the room and I thought I heard the judge say, " Bail denied!" I must have heard it wrong.

"Bail denied?" I queried my mom. She hadn't heard what I'd heard. Perhaps I'd imagined it.

As the guards escorted us back to the holding cell, a journalist with a video camera approached us, "What are you going to do next if you make bail?" he stated as the light of the video blared in our faces. "We'll just have to wait and see what happens," I said with fading confidence.

I was grateful to my mom that she had thought to bring newspaper to sit on in this holding cell. We waited and waited hoping someone would come inform us it had all been a big

154

mistake and we were free to go. What reason could there be to deny our bail? I kept thinking, we're not terrorists; we're tourists.

Eventually Mr. Chatterjee showed up. With a somber look on his face, he said to us, "Well, it is not very good news. Your bail has been denied." "Denied!" I squealed out in horror. How in God's name can our bail have been denied? I thought to myself.

My mom's face saddened in disbelief. We were dumbstruck. In situations like this the body can go into shock. "I don't understand," I blurted out, questioning to my mom whether or not this was reality or if I was stuck in another dimension.

I could see on Mr. Chatterjee's face that he too was in disbelief and felt badly for us. "I will try to get more information and come back," he said in his soft kind voice.

As my mom wandered in dizzying little circles, I sat and sobbed. Now what? I thought. Perhaps they'd made a mistake. That's what I hoped. My thoughts drifted to the previous evening, our giddiness and excitement over going home. Hope faded away.

We sat somberly on the newspaper inside the holding cell. Thankfully my mom had snuck her playing cards in her pants, and for the next four hours we tried to keep our minds occupied by playing different games.

Mr. Chatterjee's friendly face appeared late in the evening, perking our spirits. Unfortunately he had no good news for us.

For the next 45 minutes Mr. Chatterjee sat outside our holding cell talking with us. It allowed us to get to know each other a bit better. As the conversation unfolded, we could tell his optimism was for our sake. He didn't want us to worry more than we already were.

"Please, please don't hesitate to ask me if you need anything." His words were comforting to us. He had spoken to both my dad and Sean, and he gave us both the impression that his conversation with Sean was a bit uncomfortable.

Mr. Chatterjee is a proud and professional individual. Through our time in India, we came to know him well. He and his wife had been practicing law for the past 15 years and had done a lot of work with the Mother Theresa Foundation. He was in his early 40s and a pleasant-looking fellow.

On every finger he wore a ring that represented a particular aspect in life. Each of his rings was adorned with a stone that had meaning. He had a big heart, and we felt we were in good hands with him. Despite the circumstances, he made us laugh by telling two stories in his thick Indian accent about two other foreign prisoners he'd helped.

As the guards came to take us back to the prison, Mr. Chatterjee said, "Tell the ladies in facility, bail halona." "What does this mean?" I asked, and he replied, "Bail denied."

Chapter 4
The Women Behind The Walls

She wanders silently, glides really, around the compound.
She's crazy they say; her husband beat her in the head.
She has a seven-year-old child but she herself is a child
in a woman's body.

Most of the time her face is expressionless, but
sometimes in the early morning hours when the others
are asleep she quietly sings to herself while she
gracefully dances, her hands twisting and turning to a
song she probably knew from childhood.

In the daylight she will sit alone to escape from the
yelling of the others: She pulls the paint off the wall near
her barred window- She wanders the courtyard quietly
trying to be invisible, and sometimes when the others
sing and clap she will dance.

A smile will cross her face and for the moment she is
happy. But even when she tires they prod her for more.
The smile is gone and she dances like a trained monkey
while they clap and cheer. Her name is Lela.

Written by Monica Bond in Prison

157

There were more than a few shocked faces when my mom and I trudged back into the prison cell that night.

Most of the women were sitting on the ground eating when we arrived. I didn't feel much like talking so I headed straight to our corner, unfolded and laid out the itchy wool blanket to rest on.

One of the prisoners spoke a bit of broken English. My mom told her what had happened, and she passed it on to the others. I didn't always trust her interpretations, but she was the closest thing we had to a translator at the time.

As the night drifted away, the words "bail halona" echoed inside my head. I'll never forget those words as long as I live.

Morning sunlight soon poured in through the barred windows. Nights and days were becoming hot and humid. The skin on my face was supple thanks to the humidity, but the lack of nutritious fruits and vegetables, and the lack of hygiene, had taken a toll on the rest of my body.

We settled into our daily lives and routines. Though the prison lacked amenities, its structure was aesthetically pleasing. It was originally built in 1962 to house Tibetan refugees. Now it was called a special correctional facility.

The grounds housed a medical facility that specialized in cataracts and a few other conditions. Prisoners with special medical challenges ended up there. We got the impression that prisoners felt fortunate to end up there, and they stayed on their best behavior to avoid getting sent back to other prisons.

A younger woman stayed briefly in our cell while receiving medical treatment, and was treated no differently by the guards or the other inmates.

Chapter 4 - The Women Behind The Walls

The building and walls of the facility were persimmon color. They were constructed out of something stucco-like. Lush vines and trees grew in the courtyard. Some of the walls had beautiful moss and flower-producing vines growing on them.

The walls surrounding the ward stood over 10 feet high. One large tree in the yard created a bit of shade and had a low stonewall around it, which made for a good place to sit. This is where our morning chai was served.

Our housing structure for the women's ward was two stories. At this point in time only the first floor was needed to house prisoners. There was an internal central walkway in front of both the cell dorms connecting the lower and upper floors.

On our ground level there was a small room that the guards occupied and slept in. During the day, the women were allowed to sew by hand in the room. A small narrow walkway surrounded the building and had a cement gutter that wrapped around its length. Many of the women used it as a place to urinate. They would walk out of the cell, squat and pee. I ended up calling it the urination station.

Just like in any community there was a pecking order. It's human nature to classify people based on their personalities and status. This was no different in the prison system. There were the women who were friendly, the wallflowers, and then the ones you wanted to stay clear of.

I felt like Diane Sawyer. I wanted to know who these women were. What were their stories? Before the woman who spoke broken English was released on bail I asked her a handful of questions about the other women.

Our days included interactions with key characters. Bobbi, was my age, 37. She looked Samoan to us, but came from a district up above Darjeeling. She was sturdy and just a little taller than I am, which was unusual. She had a keen way of observing others and not reacting in unnecessary dialog. But when she spoke it was powerful.

She appeared more modern than the others. She was one of the prisoners who knew how things were done and how to get them done; she'd already served five years of a life sentence for some kind of murder charge.

We really liked her, and at that point we didn't know other details. She was helpful, and I wanted her on my side.

Bobbi spent most of her time with her floor mate Hridicka, a 24-year-old who also wore western style clothing. She was a sweet natured girl and very attractive. Hridicka was smaller in stature with long slender hands and shiny black hair that nearly touched her rear end.

The old donated television that was perched near my mom's and my area would be blaring for about an hour and a half on Sunday evenings, of course on only one station, in Hindi.

My mom and I would watch Hridicka touch the screen anytime she saw a baby on it. This seemed to make her sad. I believe she had small brothers and sisters at home. She always gave her best effort to speak a few words in English to us. We learned that she'd been framed on a drug charge of some sort and was facing ten years and had already done three.

Good or bad there's always someone in a group that stands out from the others. In this instance, it was Yogamaya. She was cunning, calculating and intriguing to watch. She was a character. Hollywood's best writers couldn't have invented a crazier one if they tried. We came to call her "madam monkey" because she reminded us of the man we'd seen peering down on us at the evil monkey temple earlier in our trip.

Chapter 4 - The Women Behind The Walls

Yogamaya was the head prisoner of the women's ward. I guessed her to be in her mid-30s. She kept her cell space impeccable. We figured her family must have had some money, because she had stacks of beautiful saris. They were organized by color. She even had a few matching shoes.

She seemed to thrive by intimidating others with her sadistic behavior. The women feared her but didn't respect her. Her story was unclear but it had something to do with kidnapping. She had skinny, hairy legs and her belly popped out like a basketball. When she walked, she clasped her hands behind her back and swayed like a captain on a ship. She was the only prisoner with an indoor altar honoring the god Ganesh.

I developed a soft spot for two particular inmates. One was the youngest, the other the oldest. I knew the moment I first laid my eyes on Bimala that she was a good person. She had a strong physique and kept her grey hair pulled back in a tidy bun. She was a compassionate and wise medicine woman with still a bit of twinkle left in her eyes. Bimala was around 72 years old and sadly living out a life sentence in the prison. She had been locked up for two years. We found out she had been a nurse by profession. Her offense that landed her in prison was a tragedy.

Though Bimala spoke no English, we had conversations that I will treasure for the rest of my life. We shared the special bond of people who break the language barrier and manage to connect on a deep level. We laughed, we cried, we spoke and we listened and connected to each other's soul. Bimala had a playful sense of humor. I remember one day as I power walked around the cell for exercise, she flashed me her boobs as she bathed at the water spigot. She sure made me laugh and I often think about what became of her.

The other inmate that touched me deeply was Roksona, an 8-year-old girl from Bangladesh who had landed in prison with her family for illegally immigrating to India in search of a better life.

161

They had already been locked up for six months and were waiting to be deported.

Roksona was every bit a female version of Mowgli from the jungle book. She was a scrappy, intelligent child of the slums. Her eyes were a beautiful deep shiny brown, almost black. Her hair was cut short like a boy and her little ears were adorned with colorful stud earrings.

She had no formal education, yet she could read Bengali and was learning to write in both English and Bengali. When I think about it and as odd as it may sound to some, prison could have actually been a saving grace as she was getting an education she most likely otherwise would not have been given. She was a lovable and capable little girl.

When her mother allowed it, we spent a lot of time with her.
Sopia was Roksona's mom. She was physically strong and fierce looking. Her eyes were a beautiful but penetrating green. She spoke no English and was illiterate.

She was proud and protective of her daughter. I estimated Sopia to have been in her late 30s, and she was handsomely beautiful. She'd probably be a force to be reckoned with, but she knew her place in the system and it was at the bottom of the pecking order. I always felt she and I would have been good friends in another time.

One of the saddest cases was a gal they called Lela. She resided at the opposite end of the cell in the corner spot. Originally from Nepal, her tragic tale remained a bit unclear to me. We gleaned that she had mental issues caused by being beaten on her head severely by her husband.

You could see the scars on her temples. We heard she had a 7-year-old daughter, but she herself behaved like a child. She was graceful and tall. Most of the other inmates didn't treat her well. This prison was no place for her to be.

Every Monday and Wednesday the women's ward was visit by two representatives from a church organization. They would spend time in the early afternoon hours teaching the inmates sewing or reading.

We became close to Sister Elisha Gurung. She appeared to be in her mid-20s and had a welcoming warm smile. She spoke softly in broken English, but was confident. We began to utilize her as our interpreter to gather as much information as we could. She was a generous and giving human who volunteered with many organizations and we were grateful for her presence.

Strangely, out of the six guards who rotated shifts, we really only got to know one of them.

Matajee was the 57-year-old guard who rolled up the betel nut on our initiation day. She was a strong, capable woman who had worked in the prison for many years. She was proud that she was able to help financially support her family. She seemed to have befriended a few of the inmates and sympathized with their circumstances and yet had a zero tolerance for those inmates that treated others poorly. We were soon to find out she was also a good cook.

In addition to these main characters, there were the other women who we learned to stay away from during our time in prison. Four of them were in on murder charges, and we didn't want to provoke them.

Athena Rising, a Memoir – Heather Bond

Chapter 5
Pick Your Battles

Journal entry: This is so crazy. Sometimes mom and I look at each other and just start laughing almost out of insanity or disbelief.

We look around and say, "What the heck are we doing here?"

These women eat so much rice. I haven't been able to go to the bathroom in a few days. My stomach really hurts.

Murderers, kidnappers, drug smugglers and two Californians all rolled up in one 50- by 15-foot cement cell. Days started shedding away. On one day during midday lockdown I remember sitting on the floor writing in my journal. The cell was unusually quiet. I was in a philosophical mood and writing about my observations.

As I sat and watched how these cellmates of mine moved, spoke and interacted with others, a realization came over me. I thought to myself, I am no better than they are. What makes me think these ladies are any less than me? I am on my life's journey just as they are. I had begun to see that the geographic circumstances we're born into make our journeys incredibly different.

Day in and day out our mornings started off the same. By 5:45 all the mosquito nets had been pulled down and hidden. By 6:00 the male guards had sounded the bell to announce they were entering. The women scrambled to the submissive positions, and at times I noticed women scatter to grab a scarf or wrap to throw over their head and shoulders.

One day it was unbearably hot and I was in the yard working in only my tank top. When the bells rang out a fellow inmate of mine threw her shawl over my shoulders. Our shoulders were not allowed to be bare in front of the male guards.

Then came the humiliating and painful part to me, having to squat down like you're defecating to show your submission to them. I hated doing it. Emotionally it never got any easier for me, but physically it did. It started breaking down old scar tissue in my left knee from my last surgery, making it more flexible. Who would ever have thought?

After morning count was over it was the race to the water spigot.

At around 8 a.m. a guard brought in a tin of chai. It was lukewarm at best, but it was the highlight of my morning. I do embrace my English roots and love my tea. One tiny cup was allotted. There was no milk, but every few days I'd spot a gross looking little brown chunk of something being passed to certain prisoners. It looked as though someone had chewed it up, formed it into a small ball and spit it out. We later found it was raw sugar cane. I got to indulge a few times.

We received one main meal a day. It was usually brought in around 1 p.m. by two male guards who would bring two large dirty vats filled with the leftovers from the male prisoners and hand them over to one of the female guards and usually Yogamaya. It wasn't much, mostly rice and a watered down version of dhal. It was rarely warm, and never hot but this was our lunch and dinner.

The rice was nothing we were used to. It was the stickiest white rice I've ever tasted, like eating glue. It eventually started to wreak havoc on my intestines.

It was a free for all at mealtime. No one formed a line, and no one practiced patience when it came to food. All bets were off as elbows lashed into torsos and women scrambled to get something to eat.

I was reminded of the old saying, "One man's trash is another man's treasure." After our bail had been denied, the embassy brought my mom and me some approved provisions. We were grateful they supplied us with a towel, a couple of pairs of much needed underwear, a few bottles of water and some grapes and crackers.

The towel they supplied us with became a tool for many things over time. I slowly shredded it and repurposed it into various things, such as a liner for my underwear while I was on my period even though I was told I could obtain some prehistoric looking pads from the medical infirmary.

In the yard I had been watching the crows pecking at something gross and at times bloody looking. We learned that these obscure objects were the women's used sanitary pads that were discarded in a pile. It was rather disgusting, but reality. As the days slipped away and I continued to lose weight, I also used a strip of the towel to make a belt to keep my pants up. I still have this warn piece in my belongings.

When we were given items from the embassy the inmates would flock around us as we carried them back from the warden's office. Even though families of the prisoners were allowed to leave money for their loved ones to have certain supplies purchased, there were only a few inmates who had this luxury. We felt uncomfortable walking in with new items and felt obligated to share them with the others.

I noticed that Sopia and Bimala both had some of their personal belongings stuffed into dirty looking plastic bags. My mom and I thought it would be a kind gesture to give each of them one of our new plastic bags, which we no longer needed. Big smiles spread across their faces as we handed them each a bag, and we knew they were grateful.

Unfortunately Yogamaya put a damper on our cheerful moment. No sooner had my mom and I started walking back to our space, she started screeching at Sopia and Bimala, She then rushed across the cell and grabbed the bags out of their hands.

This pissed me off. I wanted nothing more than to rush up to her and grab them back. Still screeching in Hindi, Yogamaya briskly followed and confronted us in our corner. She continued speaking as if we understood what she was saying. She waved the bags in our faces and dropped them at our feet.

This got my blood pumping quicker. I looked at my mom and said, "Should I hit her?" My mom looked at me wide-eyed and held her hand in front of me. "I'm just kidding mom, I wouldn't hit her but I feel like it." I bent down and grabbed the bags.

Frustrated I sat down on our itchy wool blanket and my thoughts drifted back to a situation when I was around eleven years old. At the time I was neglecting to keep my room clean and my belongings were stacked up in piles.

My dad had given me many warnings but I was becoming a bit defiant. On one particular evening my dad came into check on my room status and noticed I hadn't tidied up. This didn't sit well with him.

He extended his arm and swiped all the items that were stacked on my dresser to the floor and said, "You don't realize how lucky you are. When I was growing up I owned two things, my bird egg and stamp collection and they both were stolen from me."

After the frustration with Yogamaya settled I started pondering just how lucky I was. My parents were happily married and always here for me. I couldn't rationalize how my dad's mum could have just up and left her four boys. I always said it was because she was gypsy but I don't believe that had anything to do with it.

I did however have the opportunity to meet her. The first time, I was seven years old when we visited our whole family in England, including my dad's father.

My grandma in England, as I called her, was a fascinating person. A Romany Gypsy by birth who spoke both the Yiddish and Cockney languages. Unfortunately we don't know much else about her non-papered family history but she sure left an impression. My dad's father was a workingman and his father a sheepherder.

It was the height of World War II in England. My dad was the second youngest of the four boys. Derry was the oldest, then Sam, my dad and Ken. They were evacuated from a small village called Tring. From that time on my dad, five years old at the time, and Ken, three, were taken to live in an orphanage.

I think of my dad's story much like the saga of Oliver Twist. My dad was not an orphan; he had parents who were still alive at the time. Unfortunately they were not able to raise the two youngest boys. My dad ran away many times from the orphanage to find his parents only to be brought back.

He learned to survive on the streets. I couldn't imagine being a five, six or even seven year old child trying to help take care of myself let alone my younger sibling. But that was their reality.

One of many heartfelt stories my dad has told me through the years was about the time he and his four-year-old brother Ken had run away again from the orphanage and were wanting to catch a ride on the bus to find their mum.

So my dad, then seven years old, devised a plan in his head without telling Ken. As the conductor of the famous double decker bus came around collecting the money or tickets, he stopped and asked my dad for the fare.

My dad quickly turned to his little brother and said, "Ken give the man the money." Ken pulled out all his dirty little pockets and started crying. "What did you do with the money?" my dad said in a frantic tone. Ken looked at my dad, tears flowing down my uncle Ken's cheeks and said, "I lost it." As people watched this sad episode unfold, a nice couple gave the conductor the money needed. My dad thanked them and grabbed Ken's hand and hopped on the bus just as he had planned.

Ten years my dad lived in that orphanage.

I tucked the plastic bags away for the evening and got ready for another long night.

The following day I stealthily delivered the bags to the ladies. I learned to pick my battles wisely.

Chapter 5 - Pick Your Battles

It was hard to get accurate readings on some of the personalities. I had to remind myself that I didn't know these women to begin with, and we were all living in a stressful environment. We also were in an impoverished country where the lack of daily resources could take a toll.

The weather was sweltering and getting hotter with each passing day. We were 20-plus women that slept on a cement floor, had no privacy from each other and were together 24 hours a day. It was hard enough for me to keep up with my own mood swings let alone the others.

On one terribly sultry day, my mom and I had finished some time in the yard and were excited about being given a chance to utilize a grimy little piece of soap to wash our faces.

We headed to the back water pipe for a quick wash and to fill our water bottles. Three others were using the spigot, so we stood and waited. One was our little friend Roksona, another was Bisanti, the woman who was there temporarily for a medical treatment, and one other woman. They allowed us to step in and share the spigot.

We offered Bisanti the soap, and as she took it she turned to little Roksona and said something to her. Roksona's eyes welled up with tears and her face expressed anger. She tried to communicate her feelings to my mom and me but grew frustrated at our lack of understanding.

After trying to communicate with us for some time, Roksona took off running back to the cell. My mom and I finished with the water and headed back in to check on her and try to understand what had happened. As soon as we entered the cell, Sopia started speaking aggressively to us.

She was intense, but we had no idea what she was saying. Sophia put her daughter behind her back, as if to protect her, which indicated to us that she didn't want us to interact with Roksona.

With frustration written on my face I turned to my mom and said, "I want to know what Bisanti told little Roksona to make her so upset with us. To help us solve the mystery,

I searched for Gauri, the woman who spoke broken English. When I told her what happened, instead of helping, she made matters worse. My mom, just as agitated as I, replied softly to me, "How do we even know when they're telling us the truth?"

Gauri approached Sopia and started yelling at her. I felt bad, but I also was getting really pissed off. All I wanted to know was what Bisanti had said to poor little Roksona. The other women started gathering around the feud, and the intensity kept building. All the women glared at my mom and me.

After Gauri finished her verbal bashing, she turned to us and simply said, "It's nothing." I called bullshit on her, and she responded once more, "It's nothing."

We decided to walk away. To this day we still don't know.

That evening I reflected on the day's event. It brought up other scenarios in my life that I had chosen to walk away from. I realized many times in my life I've tried not to create waves in order to keep the waters as calm as possible. I was beginning to recognize the fine line between maintaining calm and allowing others to mistreat you.

I started examining my personal life and my relationship with Sean. I missed him and looked forward to seeing him, but the warning signals sounded when I thought about our long-term future together. It concerned me. I knew I had let him verbally abuse me. I certainly didn't like it, so why did I allow it to continue?

These thoughts swirled around in my head, keeping sleep away for hours.

172

Chapter 6
Dress Up Doll

Journal entry: All I can do is shake my head and laugh. It's like a rollercoaster of emotions and energy in this place.

Up and down, around and around. As strange as today's event was it also made us laugh, entertained us and broke up the long day of usual boredom.

Some days weren't as intense and crazy as others but that could change in a blink of an eye. It was around 2 p.m. and we were all in the cell on afternoon lockdown. I heard Madam Monkey call out to me. As I turned to acknowledge her, she was intently telling Hridicka something and gesturing to me.

Hridicka glided to me across the cement and softly said, "Makeup." At first I assumed Yogamaya wanted to use the mascara I had in my toiletry bag and my first thought was, pink eye. Of course if she wanted to use it I would just let her have it.

I handed Hridicka the mascara and she waved her hand and said, "No." I pointed to the mascara then gestured towards Yogamaya as if to say, "Does she want my mascara?"

Hridicka started laughing. She grabbed onto my hand and pulled me up off the floor.

We walked over to Madam Monkey's space and handed her my mascara. With a few grunts and moans Madam insisted that I sit down. I looked over to my mom who looked puzzled. I shrugged my shoulders and gave her a look that clearly said, "What the heck is she going to do with me?"

My hair fell onto my sweaty skin as she took the bun down from on top of my head. Over and over she brushed my hair until she started to braid it. When the braid was complete, she turned me towards her and said something to Hridicka, who then pointed to the mascara in my grip and subtly said, "Makeup."

Through gestures, she communicated that Madam wanted to put my mascara on me. I felt uncomfortable and didn't know how to respond. I didn't want to offend her or start a riot, so I reluctantly agreed.

I could tell she felt empowered when I said yes. A hierarchy was being established. However, I didn't want her to feel threatened by me, nor did I want to seem subservient.

She proceeded to make me up with my mascara, her black charcoal eyeliner, lipstick and even a double bindi between my eyes. She worked on me with a strange, sinister smile on her face. Almost all the women in the cell watched us.

After Madam finished the makeup, she said something to Hridicka, who turned to me, and awkwardly said, "She says you are like doll." I smiled a fake smile.

Yogamaya stood up and gestured for me to get up. "Thank you," I said to her.

Thinking we were done, I looked for an escape route. "No, no, no," she blurted, grabbing my arm and spinning me around.

I wanted to keep it as light and positive as possible, so I kept playing along. She walked towards her stack of beautiful saris, then turned back towards me and scanned me from head to toe. She knelt down and pulled out a beautiful red sari, and with a quick gesture, she had Hridicka up to lend her a hand.

Yogamaya started the ritual of wrapping me up in the beautiful material while Hridicka held onto the other 15-plus feet of material. She wound and wound and wound me up before flipping the last bit over my shoulder.

Then she gestured for me to take off my shoes. She debated between two pairs, eventually bringing back the pair with a tiny heel. I slipped them on.

She marveled at her creation. Her hands clasped below her chin in delight. She looked towards her audience for approval. Quite a crowd had assembled, and most of them started clapping and chanting. I looked towards my mom and she was smiling. But I could see the underlying look from her. It wasn't the look of, oh look at how beautiful that crazy women just made my daughter. I figured since I was made up glamorously I might as well put on a show.

I strutted into the center of the cell and struck my first pose. Then I walked the catwalk in my beautiful red sari. I shook my hips and stepped in line, left foot in front of the right. I sunk my shoulders back and made a sassy face. I sang, "I'm too sexy for my sari, too sexy for my sari." I started laughing and laughing, and so did everyone else.

After several minutes of fun, I knew it was time to wrap things up. Unfortunately Madam Monkey hadn't had enough. She tried to get me to put on another sari, but I politely gestured and said, "No thank you." She wasn't taking this for an answer.

She started to unwrap the red sari from my body while her face took on the strange look she would wear when performing her sadistic acts. I was really feeling like her little doll. I kept being as pleasant as I possibly could.

The other women were still looking on, which meant I needed to get my point across without verbally disrespecting Madam. So I turned the tables on her by exaggeratedly thanking her. I patted her on the back as I walked back towards her space. I graciously smiled and bowed with my hands in the prayer position. "Aw, thank you. Thank you so much. That was fun." I think this confused her enough to back down.

I finished the disrobing process and returned all her items. Then I walked back to my mom rolling my eyes. As I sat down on the blanket, my mom turned to me and said, "You did good Heather."

"I'm definitely not her bitch," I responded. We chuckled.

Chapter 7
Life In The Yard

Journal entry: My brain woke up this morning at four with a terrible headache. My neck has really been bad. I managed to fall back to sleep until 5:15, shortly after the most nets came down.

I have to say last night was a challenging night for me. I had a horrible headache and I started crying. I really struggled to control my crying. My body doesn't feel well and I am so homesick.

I try so hard to block everyone back home out of my mind. It seems to make it easier for me. I can't even imagine what my bed back home feels like. I just need to stay strong.

If the pulse of the prison came from the inmates, the daily life in the yard was the heart. It was where we worked under the heat of the sun and where we sat to contemplate. On rare occasions I could slip around a corner of the cellblock for a moment of silence.

I spent a lot of time watching and observing my cellmates. Many times I felt like an animal locked in a cage.

177

Athena Rising, a Memoir – Heather Bond

I visualized myself like a lion, alert and on guard. I watched the way the other inmates went about their chores, and they reminded me of monkeys. They worked while squatting primitively. Some just sat and would stare dead-eyed into space and others busily swept the dirt with giant leaves.

Every now and then a woman who wasn't a prisoner showed up in the yard to perform the unpleasant task of cleaning the cement gutter around the perimeter of the cellblock. Its content was a stagnant sludge, a mixture of urine, small leaves, scraps of food and who knew what else.

The first time we came across her performing this duty, my initial thought was, thank goodness that isn't my job. She reached into the gutter with her bare hands and scooped out the foul mixture and slopped it on the walkway beside the gutter. We watched for sometime thinking she'd remove those malodorous little piles that were gathering, but she never did. We found it kind of humorous. She seemed familiar with many of the inmates and they with her.

She was definitely intrigued by my mom and me. One day she even brought us a couple of biscuit crackers. We never found out her story, but we believe she must have been a former inmate. She had a knife scar that stretched from her mouth to her ear.

The spigots in the yard were regularly in use as a laundry station. For me, laundry wasn't a big task because I only had a pair of pants, a tank top, two socks and a sheer Indian shirt. The first time I washed and dried my little pair of black socks, one went missing. We thought perhaps a big crow took it away. From that point on, I had only one sock. My mom, on the other hand, had two pairs of pants, and one of her favorite stories came from a day she decided to wash her black cotton sweats.

Sitting in the squat position, she got her pants wet at the main water spigot. She noticed Sopia, the fierce mother of Roksona, peeing in the gutter. After she finished, she made eye contact with my mom. As my mom tells it, "Then Sopia nodded at me. As she nodded she walked towards me and gave me the look of, I'm going to wash these for you." The look implied that my mom's easy life had never included labor like laundry.

The way my mom described it cracked me up. "Sopia grabbed the sweats out of my hands and threw them flat on the ground. She grabbed a rock in one hand and a tiny piece of soap in the other and started scrubbing on them with the rock. Then she picked them up and beat them on the ground over and over, almost like a baker working the bread dough. She twisted and smacked them abusing the heck out of them until they were spotless."

My mom later told me she was quite mesmerized by the whole experience and hoped there were fibers left in her pants after all that. She wrote in her journal, "Although the pants were spotless I wouldn't trust her with my cashmere sweater."

Growing up in a country like America made certain things we witnessed hard to understand. Sure, we were in a prison and certain behaviors are expected from inmates, but it was hard to watch the submission the women demonstrated towards the men, or even certain women towards other women.

One particular event that took place was very hard to watch.

Sopia had been struggling with the way certain inmates treated her and Roksona. One afternoon the warden visited the women's courtyard. After he finished his business, Sopia threw herself on the ground at his feet. She cried and begged him for something. He looked at us and tried to get her to stop. She repeatedly crawled back to his feet, pleading over and over.

I started tearing up at the horrible sight. I had such compassion for her. I wanted to pick her up and let her know it would all be okay. Of course, I couldn't. The warden turned around and left her crying on the grounds as he walked out the gates.

This type of behavior is unacceptable and left a bad taste in my mouth. Though not the same, it reminded me of the hurtful hazing that happens within the Fire Department and how I was abandoned when I got injured.

Sundays were different. After count, the sound of acoustic Indian music filled the air. We originally thought, what a treat, we get music. But it was extremely loud and after a while it grated on my senses. What seemed pleasant at first became a form of torture.

The music belted from a few large central speakers mounted high in a banyan tree, which created a dome-like effect that rained the music down on both the male and female inmates. The music didn't stop until evening lockdown and became our least favorite part of the day.

Sundays were visitation days for families to visit for 15 minutes. Inmates with visitors would be taken to the double gates of the women's ward where they spoke through a small-barred window in the gate. As far as I could tell, few inmates had visitors.

A Sunday luxury was the coconut oil ritual, partaken by a few of the prisoners. This was quite a sight. One person giving the treatment slathered oil onto another's hair starting the scrunching process. Once the hair was saturated, head massaging started producing a rhythmic drumming on the head; over and over they drummed. Once that was complete they switched. My mom and I experienced this firsthand. It was heavenly.

Heavenly wasn't a typical description for our daily life. It was quite the opposite. I remember the day the guards brought in at least seven or eight bags of uncooked rice.

The bags were about 70 pounds each. Our job was to sift through the rice and separate it from the chaff. We were given flat woven baskets as our tools.

The women sank into their famous squat position, and the rice was poured on top of the flat basket. With the basket in both hands, the inmates gently glided it forward through the air at about arm's length. Once their arms were fully extended they performed the rhythm section. The motion reminded me of a boat trying to crest a wave but falling back down. It was repeated over and over. These experts made it look easy. I was mesmerized watching the timeless and beautiful ritual.

My mom told me later that as she watched these women in their beautiful saris she felt as though she had been transported back in time.

My rice sifting skills, however, lacked their finesse. A couple of the ladies grew impatient with us, but we tried to learn the process. I knew that I wouldn't be perfecting it any time soon.

The women rotated the duty because baskets were limited. Each woman would spend around 40 minutes on the task. My respect for them deepened as we plugged away in the 100-degree heat.

We had no shade, and the dust from the rice stuck to our skin while sweat beaded from every pore in our bodies. I remember looking at all the bags that needed to be sifted and thought to myself, holy rice, we're going to be here all day, and we were.

One morning my mom and I were on our cellblock power walk, and as we rounded the corner to one of the side areas we came across Lela standing close to the wall and staring up. Lela is the gal who should have been getting help for her mental wellbeing. It wasn't unusual to find her staring off into space, but on that day she was gesturing at something.

We stopped and looked where she was pointing. We thought at first perhaps it was a bird or something that caught her attention, but we saw nothing. She moved her body as if she was trying to fly. My mom kindly said, "Bird?" guessing that a glimpse of one had triggered her strange behavior. Lela didn't answer, and after a while we started walking again.

We walked past Lela at least five more times that morning. She never changed locations, and she smiled each time we passed her. Later that afternoon we found out that she tried to sneak out of the prison yard by tucking behind sister Elisha. We had to chuckle a bit. Lela was taller than everyone, but she'd made her best attempt at escape.

Unfortunately for Lela, the guards caught her and gave her a bit of a talking to.

That evening my mom and I realized that when we'd seen Lela that morning she must have been trying to tell us she planned to break out of the prison over the wall. And there we thought she'd seen a bird.

In the 24 hours of the day we were allocated seven to eight hours in the courtyard and the rest in the cell on lockdown. Our yard time was spent doing our necessary duties and chores and the rest was spent mostly sitting and passing time.

It was taking an emotional and physical toll on me. Once our bail had been denied my mom and I knew that we needed to start engaging ourselves in an exercise and stretching regime. Squatting and sleeping on the cement floor day after day began aggravating my spine, my hips and knee horribly.

Four months prior to our departure to India I had finished an 18-month formal spinal rehabilitation journey.

I'd spent a few hours a day, four days a week working with a neurological and spine specialist to regain proper function on the left side of my body. In India, the intensity of my pain was starting to concern me. I realized I was the only person that could help myself.

My mom and I found a corner in the yard and claimed it as our gym. No frills, just dirt and a wall to lean on, but it did the job.

The first morning we engaged in our program we had no idea what it would become. We started off that morning with a power walk around the cellblock and yard. I remember many of the ladies watching. Around and around we went. It didn't take long to work up a sweat in this climate. We had no way to tell the time except by the sun, so we just did what felt right.

After our power walk we headed back to our corner. We engaged in exercises that opened up our joints to full range of motion and increased our flexibility. With my back facing the prison cell, my mom said with a big grin on her face, "Don't look now, but we have quite an audience."

I turned to begin another exercise and noticed many women standing across the yard with their eyes wide open watching us.

The next morning my mom and I noticed a few of the ladies out for a power stroll. This put huge smiles on our faces and filled my heart. Once my mom and I had started into our routines that morning, we noticed a few more women showing interest in what we were doing. When we left our makeshift gym area, two women shuffled over to us and started pointing at various spots on their body. They spoke no English, but universal sign language doesn't have borders.

One of the women pointed to her belly and giggled. Then the giggle subsided and turned into a more serious face. I put my hand to my mouth to let them know that it starts with food or nutrition, but then I realized that in the prison environment we didn't have options when it came to food. Instead, I turned our attention to strengthening our stomach. I found a place on the hard cement and demonstrated a few exercises that could help the woman strengthen her belly.

I firmly believed that all the white gluten rice they consumed had caused their distended stomachs, and I knew it wasn't good for their intestines. Without fruit or vegetables in our diet we were lacking the necessary minerals and nutrients for a healthy system so it seemed a moot point. Instead I focused on strengthening the body.

A few other women joined in on the conversation that day. One of them pointed at her arm, waving around the flab on the underside near her tricep muscle. I realized we are all the same. There are the women concerned about their health and appearance both in America and here in an Indian prison, and there are others that don't seem to care.

The exercise program became a morning ritual for many of us inmates. I became the cellblock trainer. Bobbi braided a jump rope out of a plastic material that inmates used to make handbags. Between little Roksona and Bobbi it got a lot of use.

My mom, Bobbi and I started walking and jogging the stairs to the second floor. This became our version of stadiums. Over time I started noticing that with all the attention I was putting on helping the other women the pain in my own body started diminishing.

My mom and I became a wonderful distraction for Roksona's loneliness of prison life, and the 8-year-old girl was a valuable distraction for us too. She was always a pleasure to be around, though some days my mom and I didn't feel much like interacting with anyone.

Roksona was a beautiful, smiling ball of energy. I cherished the times we got to share with her in the yard. She was a great listener and caught on quickly to everything she put her mind to.

In the early days we taught Roksona a fast form of patty-cake. We counted, one, two, three, four, while clapping hands, and as we repeated it our cadence and movements quickened until one of us messed up. This could go on for long periods of time.

She also enjoyed learning the hokey pokey. We would point to all her little body parts and sing the song over and over. I even went back into my old roots of coaching gymnastics with Roksona. I started teaching her cartwheels and handstands. In no time I watched her performing cartwheels in succession on her way to fetch something.

At one point we found out that Roksona's 9th birthday was approaching. In my satchel pocket I found a special silver eternity knot pendant I had bought in Darjeeling. When I presented it to her, her reaction was priceless. I doubt she'd ever been given a present in her life.

We had regular participants in our exercise program. Matajee, the prison guard, wanted a flatter, stronger stomach so she'd participate. Bimala, the oldest inmate, liked to do push-ups against the wall. A few times I watched her trying to instruct my mom on proper form.

This was an entertaining part of the day. Many of the inmates wanted nothing to do with this unusual activity, but it brought us closer to the ones who did. That was special to my mom and me.

Life in the yard was hard, it was hot, and it could be entertaining. Above all, it was what we made of it.

Chapter 8
Sixteen Hours Of Cement

Journal entry: The one wonderful thing mom and I got
this morning was the rain. We took that as a sign that
it's time to leave.

We got rain as we were leaving Rajasthan. We got rain
as we were leaving Darjeeling, and now it's time here.
We've got a full cellblock of inmates now, and tension is
definitely mounting.

My other side is starting to poke through.

The nervous system is fundamental to human life, and the 15-by 50-foot cement cell shared by the women represented this system. Our lives, our belongings, our anger, our resentment, our hatred and parts of our souls resided for hours and hours a day behind these bars, sitting in a harsh sea of cement.

The center strip of the cell was much like the spine. The three-foot wide pathway allowed inmates to walk freely from one end of the cell to the other without encroaching on one another's personal space. My mom's and my personal space consisted of a whopping

187

six-foot square area. You didn't dare enter into anyone else's sphere without permission.

My demeanor started shifting after our bail was denied a second time. I got a bit more territorial and short with certain prisoners.

Mr. Chatterjee visited sometimes to bring us information and occasionally a few goodies like bottled water. One time he brought us some apples and raisins. We were always so thankful for his graciousness, but over time we noticed resentment coming from some of the other inmates.

Often after our meetings with Mr. Chatterjee in the prison office, my mom and I walked back to the cell ashamed to be holding a new plastic bag filled with some eatables. The first thing I'd do when we got back was unwrap crackers or lay some pieces of the fruit out on our metal plates and walk around offering the women something.

At one particular meeting, Mr. Chatterjee tried as politely as possible to explain that Sean seemed a bit out of control and was getting aggressive with some of the employees at the embassy. This was not what we wanted to hear.

We knew my dad and Sean were beside themselves and doing the best they could in the situation. The embassy also had no good news for us, which made for some terrible, long hours of contemplation during lockdown.

The cell lacked the distractions that the yard offered. Instead it offered a whole lot of time to observe and reflect.

One evening I was an emotional wreck. Our bail had been denied for the second time. However we received an emailed letter from my dad that the embassy delivered to us. Sadly it seemed to have a reverse effect on me. Initially it made me happy but with so much anger swirling inside me I couldn't even finish reading it.

I was angry at this situation, I was angry my mom wasn't with my dad, I was angry with my aching body and I was resentful towards the man that I felt was responsible for stripping me of both my fire and racing careers.

I was in a deep, dark place and looking to blame someone. I had such rage in me that night. I wanted to see the night sky. I wanted to see the moon and the stars. I wrestled with deep emotions that consumed my soul. I stood at our barred window with tears flowing down my cheeks. My hands held the bars, and I smashed my head into the metal. I just wanted a glimpse of a star. It was futile, but I continued to push and push. The physical pain didn't affect me. I was crushed and broken.

My mom has always been my rock. She's been there with me through every step of my life, and I know she was concerned for me. She also knows that when I go silent there's some major stuff going on and it's best just to leave me to process. That night, when I turned back from the window, she caught my eye. No words were spoken as I sat beside her, feeling miserable.

My mind scrolled back to a time prior to the fateful day of my accident.

Every morning I felt sick to my stomach as I drove to my station. This should've been my indicator my life wasn't on its true course. Something was deeply lacking inside me. I had no passion left for my fire career. There seemed to be a lack of connection and commitment from me towards this department and this department towards me.

My soul was not being fed. Sure, I had those momentary rushes of adrenalin as I donned my fire gear to rush into burning buildings, but those rushes gave way to the sadness and pain I felt as I would assess a body on a scene and possibly pronounce the person dead, sometimes as their families looked on. I couldn't imagine spending the next

15 years unfulfilled. It started feeling much more like a prison sentence rather than a purpose driven career.

Through the years I've reflected on this period in my life. I see how powerful our words are. Day after day I spoke to God and the universe, like a mantra I repeated these words. " I know this is not my true calling. I don't know what is, please help guide me." Little did I know at the time the universe was aligning a masterful solution.

How could he? How in the hell could someone do this to another person? I was a good firefighter. In my present predicament, I let self-pity lead me back in time.

It was a triple digit temperature day in July. My fire station and other stations were having a big company drill in the San Fernando Valley in Los Angeles.

That type of drill is very physically demanding, made more so by temperatures in the 100-degree range. Various tasks are required, such as throwing ladders, chain sawing, and that day I dismantled a vehicle with the Jaws of Life.

The drill lasted for the better part of the day, and I was drained when we were done.

We had a late dinner at the station that night, and it felt great to sit down. After I washed the dishes, I went into my office, which was the women's bathroom. I was the only female at the station, so I used the bathroom as my study and my place of refuge.

To my shock, at 8 p.m. my task force commander called out over the loudspeaker, "We're going out!" My heart dropped in disbelief, which turned into anger. This could only mean one thing: he was taking me out for another drill.

"You've got to be fricken kidding me." I said out loud to no one.

I called Sean immediately and told him. He advised me to say something to my task force commander. Sean knew I had already tweaked my back a bit from being drilled on the ladder over and over. I had written in the station journals at least three times that excessive drilling had left my spine in pain.

But instead of saying anything, I sucked it up. I kept quiet and played the game.

Before I got hired with L.A City Fire Department I was told it was an old boys network and a lot of them didn't want women in the department. I was naive in thinking it wouldn't apply to me.

Before the city department, I worked a number of years on an engine and a Hot Shot crew with the Forest Service. Plus I had raced on Navy Seal and Marine Corps teams, and I'd never experienced any sexism before. I thought of myself as the mighty Goddess Athena; the Goddess of war and wisdom. Naïve indeed.

It was still partially light out as my entire task force approached the drill area. I was tired from the long day and full from dinner. My commander called out to me, "There's a fire on the south side of the building. Fully gear up, breather and all, and grab the 35."

Holy shit. You've got to be joking. What the F was he trying to do to me? There was no reason on God's green earth for him to be drilling me again after a six-hour day of drilling.

The 35-foot ladder is a monster. It weighs around 200 pounds and is made of solid wood. Old school. I could throw it, but I didn't like it. This ladder had ended careers.

My job was to run toward the building holding the top end of the ladder, while another firefighter held the bottom. When we arrived at the building, my partner would plant the feet of the ladder on the ground and I would clean and jerk the ladder while doing a side break-over head (lift the top over my head), and move my hands rung by rung down its length until it stood against the wall. No small feat.

I donned all my gear, which weighs an additional 70 pounds, and I grabbed that son of a bitch off the engine. As I ran with the ladder in my hands I hit my mark and took a big deep breath to prepare myself to thrust and press this monster above my head. I hurled it into the air and nearly had it upright when I felt the strangest sensation shoot through my spine.

Within a blink of an eye the ladder crashed on top of my head, snapping my neck and pinning it to my shoulder.

I never fell to the ground, but I struggled and struggled to get the ladder off me. It wasn't until I let out a screech, that two fellow firefighters rushed over to remove the ladder from my head.

I bent over knowing something severe had happened and rage filled me. I had worked my ass off to earn this position. I spent years in school getting degrees and certifications.

I had been allowing the commander to slowly tear me down and now he had broken me. A final surge of adrenaline shot through me. I grabbed the rungs of the ladder being held above me. Like someone who finds superhuman strength in a crisis, I drove this ladder to the building. I stepped back, bowed my head in defeat and fell to a knee, never to wear my badge again.

My body shivered and I found myself back in the cell, where I couldn't even see the stars in the sky. I was locked up like a caged animal. What was I supposed to be learning? Was this some cruel joke that God was playing on me? Over and over thoughts spun in my head that night. I silently cried myself to sleep.

There were nights in the cell that weren't all bad. Some nights little Roksona was given permission to come spend time on our blanket. These times were usually fun.

As a young girl my mom had been taught to play a vicious game of poker by her dad. She enjoyed teaching little Roksona how to play many different types of card games.

Roksona was clever. One night I was silently observing the two of them as they played a particular card game. I stared at little Roksona's dirty face, her short chopped hair, and grungy little clothes. I remember drifting off to one of my most powerful and profound moments of myself at her age.

"I am mighty Isis." I called out to God and the universe. "I am mighty Isis, feel my power." I belted this out with the ferocity of a mighty warrior, the body of a nine-year old girl and the openness to allow myself to speak my truth.

There I stood on the rooftop of my childhood home with my beautiful green pendant adorning and draping from my crown to my forehead. "I am mighty Isis." My arms thrusting towards the heavens, my eyes closed, I took a big deep breath into my belly and then with all my knowing I hurled myself off the roof and landed powerfully on the ground below. It was pure satisfaction.

I couldn't help but ache in my heart wondering what would become of this beautiful little soul.

After my mom and Roksona finished their game she headed back over to her own blanket. My mom said with admiration, "She's good. She beat me fair and square on a few of those games." This gave my mom satisfaction. We spent many a night with this special girl playing tons of tic-tac-toe, and drawing lots of very special pictures that I'll cherish forever.

Eating in prison was a very primal experience. I never really got used to it. Every night around nine a deafening silence fell over the cell. The women would turn to face the wall and start eating their dinners. Soon the clanging of the metal bowls hitting the cement floor would start echoing throughout the cell.

Some of the women crushed peppers or lemons on the floor with rocks. There was no cutlery. They reminded us of cavewomen. With one hand they'd grab the rice and shovel it into their mouths. Then the smacking of their chewing would start. It was maddening. Clicking, smacking and slurping of rice, dhal and water. It was fast and intense, and when it was all over the floor of the cell would be covered in copious amounts of food.

Variety didn't exist in prison food. Occasionally, the guards did bring in leftover looking squash. It was soft and mushy. I guess we just assumed it was in the squash family. It most definitely held no nutritional value. My mom and I were really starting to lose weight, and we couldn't afford to lose any. We both noticed that our spines were starting to protrude.

After days and days of the rice I told my mom that I needed to stop eating it because it was hurting my stomach and had led to multiple days of constipation. That's when my mom showed me a horrible rash she was getting on her shoulder, arm and back. We decided not to take any rice that day.

One o'clock in the afternoon rolled around, and the vats of rice and dhal were brought into the courtyard as usual. The chaos of positioning ensued. My mom and I hung out in the back, not looking too concerned, with only one metal bowl between us.

When it was our turn to be served rice, I blocked the bowl so they couldn't give us any. It sent a shock through the crowd. The women gestured for us to take the rice, but I said sternly, "No, thank you."

They looked at us in disbelief and a bit of irritation. Madam Monkey leaned into us and fired off some words in Hindi. She was adamant about us taking some. I pointed to the dhal and said, "Yes, please." Eyes can speak volumes and ours said clearly, "No rice, thank you."

You would think this would've been a short conversation. Instead it turned into a drama. There was no way to communicate what was going on with us, nor did we want to have a conversation about constipation and rashes.

Madam Monkey was beside herself. She strutted around the cell during lockdown like an investigator trying to solve the crime. A few of the inmates came into our space and even picked up our empty metal plate and shrugged their shoulders at us. It got back to the guards and when they tried to ask us about this in Hindi, we simply put our hands in the air.

The rice debacle set us up for a whole new experience.

On the second day of our rice fast, Matajee, the guard, approached us in the corridor and slyly handed us a small plastic bag that contained a hard object. She gestured to her mouth and scooted us back into the cell.

My mom and I were very curious, so we scampered to our space and sat with our backs facing some of the inmates that weren't out in the yard. My mom pulled out a little metal container and opened it. Inside was some glorious looking home-cooked food. It actually had vibrant colors to it. We didn't know how to go about eating it without anyone noticing.

We were hungry. My mom grabbed her pair of pants and rolled the container up inside. We walked out of the cell and looked for a place to hide, but we saw nothing. We paced back and forth down the corridor. My mouth was salivating. We noticed that underneath the stairwell to the second floor cellblock there was a small crawl space. We quickly slid into it.

We popped the metal top off, stuck our grungy hands into the bowl and shoved the food into our mouths. It was absolute heaven. It did happen to be a rice dish, but there was spice and flavor and definitely a different quality of rice.

The space we were sitting under was so shallow that we were leaning sideways to fit. We had to be as quiet as possible. We started getting nervous that someone would notice us missing. I whispered to my mom, "It will be good later. Let's save it." She nodded back at me. My mom grabbed the extra pair of pants off the floor, but before she could roll the container back inside, a pair of feet stopped right in front of us.

I felt like a little kid hiding from a teacher at school. We tried to be as quiet as possible. My mom and I look at each other and held our breath. The person started to push one of the flat woven baskets used for the rice underneath the staircase, but the basket wouldn't fit. The person tried a few times but each time it stopped when it hit our bodies.

As her body bent forward to find the obstacle, my mom quickly tucked the food container between us. Just as we hid it we made eye contact with Bimala.

Her face wrinkled and winced as she stared at us. My mom pressed her finger against her lips, and Bimala looked kindly at us.

She extended her hand to touch my face gently and then walked away.

My mom and I strolled back to the cell and hid the container with the remaining food. Shortly after we went into afternoon lockdown. While my mom was laying down resting, Sophia walked over to our space. She knelt down beside my mom and started rubbing her forehead and hair over and over. As she rubbed she said, "No tension, no tension."

For a fleeting moment she comforted my mom, though we didn't know why. Later that afternoon Sister Elisha came for her usual visit to the ward. She approached my mom and me and asked us if we were feeling okay.

Bimala, she said, was concerned about us after finding us under the staircase. She thought we were hiding and crying because we were so sad and homesick. She wanted to make sure that we were doing okay.

We let Sister Elisha know all was well and told her about the food. The three of us got quite a chuckle as we painted the picture of us crammed under the stairwell stuffing the food in our mouths like animals.

Just as we were grateful to Mr. Chatterjee for bringing us goodies, we were grateful Matajee thought kindly enough of us to bring samples of her home cooked food.

Unfortunately this kind gesture also started causing resentment towards us from the other women. Matajee continued to bring us samples every now and then, but there weren't many places in the compound that we could pass off a container of food without catching the attention of others.

One evening Madam Monkey came over to our space with a grin on her face. She leaned down, grabbed my hand and pulled me up. She walked me down to the opposite end of the cell where I could see Matajee standing in the corridor on the other side of the bars.

As I glanced around the cell, I noticed many eyes on me. Matajee handed Madam Monkey a brown bag. As she turned to me and handed me the bag, her voice took on a funny tone, almost like she had a frog in her throat. She blurted out just one word: "Tasty."

Matajee generally alerted us to her edible gifts while we were in lockdown. Down the corridor she'd walk. Her stick would hit every bar clang, clang, until it caught our attention. She would then make eye contact with either my mom or me. This became uncomfortable for both of us. This caught everyone's attention. The other inmates were not pleased.

It was dog-eat-dog in prison. You never knew what would set off certain inmates, so we tried our hardest to stay clear of those particular women.

One day a new inmate walked in with a bit of swank. Madam Monkey met with her right away and had a civil sounding conversation. I noticed that the new prisoner was pointing to her ruffled and dirty sari.

Madam scanned the woman from head to toe and turned to her stack of saris. She pulled one out and handed it to the new inmate. The new woman nodded her head in thanks and later emerged wearing it. I found out she was a wife of a policeman, which explained Madam Monkey's extra nice treatment.

That evening Madam briskly strutted to the new woman's space and started spewing what seemed to be Hindi vulgarity. She was relentless. Her jaw flapped and flapped as she hacked up mucus from her lungs. The woman backed down to a submissive posture. This must have pleased Madam who turned and waddled back to her own space.

Chapter 8 - Sixteen Hours Of Cement

No more than thirty minutes later, the new woman loudly called out to Madam. Their spaces were on opposite sides of the cell. Of course this caught everyone's attention.

Madam cocked her head in a strange and creepy way and turned towards the woman. As soon as they made eye contact, the new woman held up a lemon. Her eyes widened like she was holding gold. She glanced at the lemon and then at Madam. With the inmate's eyes intently watching, she leaned forward and rolled the lemon across the cement floor towards Madam.

The scene was like a power play in a game of chess and seemed to play out in slow motion as the lemon rolled right into the arch of Madam's foot. Without hesitating, Madam flicked her ankle and rolled the fruit back to the woman. The woman looked at Madam and bowed her head in shame.

The days and weeks passed. Daily life seemed to be a mixture of struggle, sadness, heartache and comedic craziness. Yes, there were those moments of entertainment and connection, but we also saw signs of physical decay in ourselves. More immediately, we had a new and far bigger issue to contend with.

We never found out her name, nor did we care to know it, but we came to call her Cadaver Woman.

I remember the day she entered into our cell. She was escorted in during afternoon lock down. She was a mess. She had cuts all over her face and most of her knuckles were scraped off. She still had dried blood on her skin and cloths. She was mean and surly looking.

Her physical appearance was unfortunate and it's how her nickname was conceived. Her cheekbones protruded and her teeth and gums resembled that of a human cadaver. Bloodshot eyes peered out from sunken eye sockets. Even her toes were mangled. Bloody looking pus oozed from around the nail beds.

She had beaten her daughter-in-law to death. She was put on our "do not associate with" list. We made no eye contact with the women on that list; we just pretended they weren't there. Unfortunately this woman was quick to establish a disturbing issue with my mom. Not only did it shift the dynamic in our cellblock, it also shifted my demeanor.

My nights became more restless. I tossed and turned and felt more on guard then ever. In the mornings I'd wake up tired from lack of sleep. I didn't know what I'd do if something happened to my mom.

During the day in the yard she would watch my mom. When the food was brought in cadaver woman would punk my mom by cutting her off and pushing into her. The first time I saw her do this, I puffed up as large as I could and blocked her back. I certainly didn't want to go this route, but there was no alternative.

Her behavior became more aggressive towards us. She started talking to a few of the other surly women. I could tell she was having conversations about us and could feel the glares from across the yard or cell.

Cadaver Woman got more volatile as the days went by, to the point that I finally had to request a conversation with the warden. Unbeknown to us, the consulate general was coming from Kolkata to visit us at the prison. We were anxious when we heard the news.

The warden and consulate general were discussing our case when we arrived in the warden's office that day. Unfortunately there was no good news for us, except that there would be another bail hearing in the coming days.

I didn't know how much time my mom and I had before either Cadaver Woman snapped or I did. I needed to be able to talk freely to the consulate general without the warden being there. I tried to convey this to him with my facial expressions. I rolled my eyes over and over until he caught on and said, "Under the Geneva Convention I have the right to speak to these woman in private." I thought to myself, how cool is that, just like in a movie.

The warden obliged and stepped out of the room. Once he was out of the room my mom and I started to tell the consulate general about the situation with Cadaver Woman and how it had grown more intense daily. We told him what crime she committed and that her sanity seemed questionable.

We laid all of our concerns out on the table. He answered the few questions he could and then asked the warden to come back into the office. Once the warden sat back down the consulate general asked the guard to take us outside.

My mom and I sat outside the office wondering what was being spoken. After a short time, they ushered us back in. The warden began by acknowledging the situation with Cadaver Woman. He then asked us if we'd rather be held in solitary confinement.

Solitary confinement didn't seem any more appealing than going back into the general prison population. All I could visualize was a tiny dark, smelly cell like the one we'd been held in before entering the prison, and that wouldn't be doable. We didn't know how many more days or weeks we'd be in the facility, so we opted to face the uncertainty of the mad woman.

That evening tensions in the cellblock were the highest we'd ever felt. It had been an exceptionally hot, humid and sticky day and the heat lingered into the night. Sweat kept pouring from our bodies. Around 9:30 that night, shortly after the women had finished their meals, the mosquito nets started to get strung up.

I was writing an entry in my journal when a loud ruckus at the other end of the cell exploded into a heated battle. It was the start of the longest, loudest battle we'd seen.

Of course Madam was in the thick of it. She was screeching at the top of her lungs and poking at Lela's face. Bimala walked over to defend and protect Lela, the sweet mentally challenged gal. Madam pulled what looked like a mosquito net out of Lela's hand, and Bimala started yelling and chastising Madam. That didn't go over well with Madam, so Sopia came over to defend Bimala.

Madam and Sopia started pushing each other. Little Roksona was scared for her mom, so she tucked her head under a blanket. Madam walked over to Sopia's space and ripped the mosquito net strings out of the walls. Bobbi then tried to cool Madam down, but it didn't work. All the mosquito nets were getting yanked down, and total chaos claimed the cell.

The guards showed up, but their attempt to diffuse the situation was futile. I fought the urge to go down and give my two cents, because it wouldn't have helped.

We sat there watching as it turned into a riot. After a solid 30 minutes of inmates yelling at one another, ripping items out of each other's hand and pushing, things started to calm down. Then Madam walked over to our space and put a mosquito net over us. We sat up and told her to stop. In her deep, creepy voice, she said, "No, S.I."

At first we couldn't figure out what she meant, but she aggressively repeated, "No! S.I." Then we realized that she called the Warden S.I. and perhaps if my mom and I didn't have a mosquito net she'd get in trouble. I looked at her squarely in the eyes and said, "If no one else gets a net we don't want one."

She stood above us for quite some time before finally backing down and walking away. You couldn't rationalize what was going on with the other inmates.

Life in prison could take hold of your mind and make you question your own sanity.

Chapter 8 - Sixteen Hours Of Cement

Morning came quickly after the mayhem of the night. The energy of the other inmates was low. No one spoke to anyone else. The women moved methodically as they went about their chores. There was stillness in the air. I wasn't sure if this was a good thing or a bad thing. Perhaps it was neither. It's just what was.

It was the day of our 3rd bail hearing. This time, we were to remain in the prison instead of going to court as we had before. That hadn't sounded reassuring to me when the consulate general had told us, but something felt different when I woke up that morning. Perhaps this would be the day that we finally made bail and got to go home.

At 1:40 p.m., my mom, Roksona and I were out in the yard when the bell at the gate rang. Little Roksona, curious by nature, ran over to investigate. Within a few minutes she ran back yelling, "America, America, America", while holding her little thumb into the air. It was the sign for an inmate leaving. Most of the prisoners were illiterate so they used their fingerprints as their signature.

Sure enough Matajee and another guard walked through the yard with paperwork in hand. I was in disbelief. I wouldn't believe it until I saw it in writing. They set the paperwork down on the cement. At first we only saw my mom's name and my throat choked up. I thought, Oh my gosh, they're not releasing me, only mom. Matajee turned the page and there was my name. My mom pressed her thumbprint to the paper first. I followed.

We were escorted to the office where Mr. Chatterjee, the consulate general and another embassy rep awaited us with smiles. My mom and I were in shock and didn't even know how to respond, so we hugged each one of them.

They informed us that a judge granted our bail and when the paperwork went through that evening or the next morning we'd leave. We later found out that our dear angel Mr. Chatterjee had posted the bail money.

Athena Rising, a Memoir – Heather Bond

Many thoughts swirled in and out of my head as the guards escorted us back to the cell. When we got there several of the women surrounded us and grabbed at our hands so they could see the ink on our thumbs.

My mom and I started to sift through all the belongings that we had acquired over our time in prison. We debated what we'd bring and what we should leave behind. We knew that when we left, it would be a chaotic free-for-all with the women going through our stuff.

That evening, we got the word that it was time to go. The moment we had been waiting, wishing and praying for had finally arrived. The prison had been our home for longer than we'd hoped. We gathered our belongings from the cement floor and looked around to find the cell empty. As we walked out to the courtyard, we discovered all the women lined up to bid us farewell.

We set down our stuff and started hugging the ladies we'd become close to. It was sad. I had visualized myself walking out of the place for so long, but I'd never considered that I would have mixed feelings.

Bimala, Sopia, Bobbi and Hridicka were all tearing up. We hugged many times. I nodded my head and shook Madam's hand. She and I had developed a twisted understanding of each other. I felt like I was a lion and she was a hyena.

Then it came time to say goodbye to our dear, sweet, little Roksona. She brought us a sense of normalcy in this place. I hugged her and kissed her cheeks many times. I didn't want to leave her. What would become of her? She was beautiful, smart and deserved a good life. Just like each and every one of us.

We walked to the first gate and waited for it to open. Tears flowed down my cheeks. After my mom and I stepped through, I looked back and scanned the women one last time, my eyes stopping at little Roksona.

Her dirty little cheeks muddied the tears as they flowed from her eyes. I put my hand on my heart and whispered, "I love you." She turned and ran away. I would never see her again. The gates closed.

Chapter 9
False Freedom

Excerpts from the Times of India and the Statesman
newspaper: Fleeing tourists targeted...Bandh enforcers
target holiday-makers, chaos descends on Dooars &
Siliguri.

Twenty-seven injured in Siliguri violence including
policemen. Former Gorkha soldiers and media persons
were injured today when violence erupted during a rally.

Where does the line in a relationship get drawn? At some point isn't enough, enough? We're free! We've been released on bail. We get to sleep on a bed, eat something different, shower and sleep in, or whatever. I couldn't wait to call Sean that evening. I couldn't wait to hear his voice and let him know I was okay. We were okay. I wanted to know how he was.

As long as I live I'll never forget that feeling of absolute let down. After living in a prison climate fueled by anger, hostility and aggression, I desperately needed some love and compassion. I was looking forward to receiving this from the man I was to marry. Giddy and excited, I stood outside the lobby where we'd be staying for the next few days. I was relieved when Sean answered the phone.

The first words out of my mouth were, "Oh my gosh, I love you my F&L." That stood for friend and love. Our initial pleasantries ended quickly as Sean's focus shifted.

He started rambling about how if I'd listened to him we'd be home by now, how he'd jumped through hoops to find us a lawyer and that my mom and I hadn't listened and insisted on being counseled by Mr. Chatterjee.

Tears welled up in my eyes and flowed down my cheeks. "Stop, stop," I said. I couldn't understand. I felt crushed. He didn't. It became an endless barrage of all he had done for us and why I hadn't done this-that-or the other? My heart felt shattered. All I wanted to do was get off the phone with him.

Two hours prior to this phone call I'd felt pain and sadness in my heart when I looked into the eyes of our fellow inmates for the last time. It was a very different type of pain and sadness. It didn't pierce my heart like what I felt with Sean.

When my mom and I had been escorted out of the women's ward, we were in shock.

We'd been given back our jewelry, camera, wallets and phone. We weren't able to pick up our big backpacks out of the courthouse storage, and we also weren't given our passports. This concerned us. Mr. Chatterjee escorted us out of the prison. Once we got outside, the reporters and photographers were waiting for us. I secretly had my video rolling to capture our release. We were dirty, smelly and skinny. We looked forward to going home soon.

The wind on my face felt wonderful through the open window of the vehicle. Driving to a hotel was surreal. Mr. Chatterjee informed us we'd be going to court the following day about some paperwork. His words were like the ones on the old Peanuts and Charlie Brown shows when the parents spoke and all you heard was, "Wa, wa, wa wa." I was focused on having a shower, a pillow and something other than rice.

Since all we had was a few plastic bags full of belongings from the prison, we quickly settled into the tiny, no frills room. We weren't about to complain. The room had two twin beds with a nightstand separating them and just enough room to walk around them. I remember thinking, we wouldn't even know where to put our luggage if we had it.

After I got off the phone that evening with Sean I had a hard time stopping the flow of tears. I walked very slowly to the room. I didn't want to let my mom know what he'd just said. I pretended I was crying because I missed Sean. I wanted to tell her the truth, but what would she think about Sean talking to me like this? I was going to suck it up and lie, a lie not only for my mom but also myself. Why was I allowing this behavior from him and why would I lie for him?

My mom never suspected a thing that night. We did have a bit of a shock when we received a phone call from the lobby asking us to come down to register with our passports. We tried to explain that we didn't have them, and we were told that we probably wouldn't be able to stay without them. I asked if in the morning we could call Mr. Chatterjee and have him explain the matter. Thank goodness they obliged.

The morning came quickly. We did, however, get to sleep in and wake up in a bed.

We were excited about the day. The judge was scheduled to sign our papers, and our belongings and passports would be returned to us. Since we planned to venture out into unfamiliar streets and walk to the court on our own, we decided to leave quite a bit earlier in case we ran into delays. The directions to the court would have been relatively straightforward in the U.S., but not in India.

Thirty minutes into our walk we started heading under and over train tracks, which led us into an area that seemed less safe. I started questioning our location. Thankfully on the other side of the tracks, we noticed Sister Elisha riding in the back of a rickshaw.

She asked us what we were doing way down there. We told her, and she giggled. She said we were really far off and redirected us. After an hour of walking in a massive circle, we arrived at our destination.

Mr. Chatterjee was waiting, and with no time to spare he guided us into an office and had us take a seat. We sat there for over an hour before he came back in. As we sat in the room, my mom and I heard a lot of noise in the front of the court. We poked our heads out the door and noticed police riots starting to happen. More police showed up as people started shouting louder.

Mr. Chatterjee looked slightly concerned when he came back. He had us follow him to another room to sign out and retrieve our belongings. We were instructed to come back to court at 1:30 p.m.

With our large packs in our possession, Mr. Chatterjee signaled to a bicycle rickshaw to take us to the hotel room, a ride that took four or five minutes. We really had gone way out of our way getting there.

We dropped off our packs at the room and grabbed a quick bite of food before heading back to court. This time we had the correct directions.

As we walked down the main street in town, I noticed the red flag with the hammer and sickle flying. For some reason this made me feel more vulnerable.

Shortly into our walk, we saw a marching demonstration in the streets. My mom and I linked arms and walked briskly towards the court. More and more people and police were gathering on the same road we needed to take to get to court. I questioned whether we should continue, but we agreed that it wouldn't look too good if we failed to appear for our hearing.

The demonstrating was getting bad and looked serious. When we got to the court, we shoved our way through the ocean of rioters, doing our best to remain invisible. Thankfully Mr. Chatterjee spotted us and came quickly. He grabbed my arm and said in his thick Indian accent, "You must get back to the room fast. We skip court because of tension."

My mom and I looked at each other. I thought, Holy crud, this is gnarly. What the heck is happening? Now we've got to fight our way back through this madness?

"Go, go." Mr. Chatterjee insisted.

I grabbed my mom's hand and started to push through the mayhem. My adrenaline pumped as angry demonstrators knocked into us. We pushed and pulled our way through the mobs, never making eye contact with anyone. We didn't stop until we were safely in our room.

Chapter 10
Civil Unrest

Letter that was never sent:

Wow, Sean, I can't imagine or fathom what my dad could have possibly said or not said or done or not done to ever hear you tell me you don't care what happens to him.

I realize that we are all doing the best we can in this situation we're in. We aren't always going to agree but I don't understand how it got so out of control between the two of you. I could never, ever imagine saying that about your mom or dad to you no matter what. When you said that my heart dropped. What on earth does that mean?

Where does that leave us? This set out to be a journey for my mom and me. One that has been in her heart for so long, and I prompted it to happen, and instead of a wonderful experience it's the worst possible scenario. The man that I thought I loved so much and my father, who I deeply love and cherish, have developed such turmoil between the two of them over a situation that was out of our control.

213

I want to make this work between us. You seem to hold so much anger and resentment towards me for not always listening to you and I'm sorry. By no means is it intentional or out of malice, but just the same your frustration towards me is apparent and makes me feel unsafe.

It seems to be the same old song and that's not what any of us need. What's going to happen? What do you want to happen? I want everything to heal on all ends. We have all been affected by this situation, and I am sorry. If I could turn back time so as to not uproot so many people's lives I would. I feel we all feel helpless and uncertain about what's happened and what to do.

I know my mom and I sat in the prison absolutely helpless and concerned more for you and my father. We couldn't do anything except try to relay to the embassy that we send our love and that we're okay. Not having a clue that you and my father were turning into time bombs but both wanting the same thing, and that was to get us home.

All I wanted to do was share and witness my mom in a place that she had dreamed about for so much time. My love has always been true to you. I can only be the person I know how to be and that's me, Heather Bond-the good and the bad.

Written May 25, 2008

From bribe-seeking cops and accusations of terrorism to civil unrest and riots, this was nothing short of an emotional wild ride. This wasn't in our itinerary. But, as I reflect on this now, I can say the crazy part is, it was meant to be.

We hadn't deliberately put ourselves in any illegal or outright stupid situations. But our spoken words are powerful and can manifest. God and the universe don't discriminate between positive or negative words; it's the level of feeling and energy that goes along with the thoughts and words.

So when I visualize the scenarios my mom and I considered while hiking along our mountain roads back home before our trip, our light-hearted role playing, I wonder how much energy we put out to the universe when we said, "Two American women arrested in a foreign country for... Oh my, gosh, could you imagine...? Heck no ..."

Since our trip, I have pondered this deeply. I have sat silently, separate from the outside world and people for ten days at a time in formal meditation, contemplating, processing and trying to heal emotional wounds.

In the days after our release from prison, without the distractions of our fellow inmates and our daily chores, I spent hour upon hour dwelling on the areas in my life that were suffering. It was a form of self-torture really.

We weren't getting answers on our legal situation from the courts, and just outside this small room we occupied, people were being bloodied and beaten in the streets. Many times we were afraid to go out, especially if we needed to get to court. On some days, the entire town was on strike and nothing was available.

With all the turmoil around us, it was hard to believe that my mom and I still faced charges under the Indian Arms Act. It seemed absolutely idiotic to us that the police who charged us with this crime could actually think we were engaged in some form of terrorist act. We were two women from California, my mom with reddish hair and me blonde. Along our journey, we encountered three gals who made us think more deeply on this subject.

Athena Rising, a Memoir – Heather Bond

When my mom and I had first been charged with the crime and held in the tiny, nasty holding cell at the court, we had our first encounter with a few young women. My mom and I had been staring at the walls pondering our dilemma when we started hearing the screaming and crying of female voices coming in our direction.

The guard opened the cell door and tossed in three hysterical young girls in their late teens or early 20s. They created quite a disturbance as they fell directly onto the cement floor.

Hyperventilating and completely distraught, the oldest looking one was in the worst condition. She had snot dripping out of her nose, and many times she'd blow the snot into her hands and fling it onto the floor. She continually slapped her hands on the cement as she wailed out various words in Hindi. My mom tried to comfort them at one point. They weren't in the cell long before being hauled away.

A week later we crossed paths again with the cement-slapping gal. This time she was being escorted into the prison. Her name was Krishna. She was 19-years-old and dressed in modern clothes. She had very light-colored skin and a shorter hairstyle. She spoke very little English, but enough to converse with us.

She was in with us for a few days before she was taken somewhere else. Learning what landed her in the prison helped us to understand our own situation better.

She had been accused of being part of a bombing that killed three people. We never found out specific details due to language barrier, but this young gal that I wouldn't look twice at walking down the streets of my hometown was in prison on terrorist charges.

How could my mom and I think that in the eyes of the local authorities and in this political climate and region we would be immune to such allegations?

There were many layers to the civil unrest affecting us.

I found out from Sean that back home there was major tension unfolding between him and my dad. I did my best to cover this up from my mom to keep her from worrying, but my own tension with Sean was taking root. My emotions continued to affect my physical wellbeing. I was getting weaker and sick feeling.

I started losing chunks of my long hair. My mom, too, was beginning to lose her hair. I had extreme headaches and intestinal issues. As the days slipped away, I felt as though I was spiraling into a deep dark hole.

The outside strife seemed to fuel my internal struggle with how I got injured. I was constantly trying to rationalize why it happened to me. I couldn't shake the thought, if I ever were to get out of India what was I going to do with my life, my career?

My ego felt like I was deliberately robbed of my fire and racing careers, but I also had a deep inner part of me that felt otherwise. This was my battle. As I would sit in the hotel room on the bed, for hours I would reflect on how for months before my injury I talked daily with God and the universe about my fire career not being my souls' purpose.

Unbeknownst to me, these conversations would become the start of a 10-year journey through the deepest depths of my being. Emotionally and spiritually I was going to need to die and be reborn.

When my accident with the Fire Department took place, my soul was crying out for guidance. I guess God had sent me signals but I was either too stubborn to listen or never sat still long enough

217

to hear him speak. He had to send a more abrupt message by way of a 200-pound ladder falling on my head. I had no choice but to sit still after that. Then it was up to me to listen. But as I was held captive in a foreign country with riots and bloodshed around me, I struggled with the question, Why me?

The brief moment of splendor we'd felt walking out of the formal prison had evaporated. My mom and I started feeling like we had hopped out of the frying pan and into the fire. Perhaps we weren't heading home as quickly as we thought.

Chapter 11
Second Cell Living

Letter that never got delivered: Happy 70th Birthday Pa

Happy birthday to my dearest father! I am sad to say that court wasn't in the stars for us today.

Today was a very low day for me. I had a huge breakdown, my heart's been hurting too. My head has been pounding. It doesn't stop, and my stomach is so sick feeling. I actually have a bit of diarrhea.

I just feel so helpless at times and there's so much stress. I look at mom and want more than anything to transport her back to you pa...

Written May 27, 2008

My mom and I had to become familiar with a whole new region, political climate and the ins and outs of daily life. We occupied a small room in a modern hotel. The hotel was located in a town called Siliguri in West Bengal. It was an outpost town without many tourists, just a trickle of the visitors coming to visit the hill villages like Darjeeling.

219

Athena Rising, a Memoir – Heather Bond

It wasn't colorful nor did it have an appealing landscape. It was dry, dusty and lackluster. The wires that strung from one building to the next created a tangled web that bundled together all of the electrical, telephone and who knows what else. Multiple daily power outages occurred. They were more common than not, so if a full day came and went without an outage, you noticed. Those were the small victories.

The main street was lined with shops and pushcarts. The back alleys held the bazaars and tiny stalls. One day we strolled through an area called the Hong Kong market. Unlike the bazaars with different fruit and vegetable stands, the Hong Kong market had cages filled with chickens and other animals that would be slaughtered right there.

I couldn't hang out very long around there because the smell of blood and intestines triggered my gag reflexes. Thanks to the scraps of entrails, the dogs that claimed this territory looked a lot healthier than the poor malnourished dogs a couple blocks away.

My mom and I felt much like tiny fish in an aquarium. We were able to move around the area freely if riots didn't stop us. But even though we could see through the glass to the outside world, we couldn't swim beyond the boundary of the tank, which happened to be a restaurant called the Conclave. It was on the outskirts of the town at the opposite end from the court. We managed to navigate this a few times. It took courage and smarts to dodge all the sharks along the way.

However, the sharks I speak of came in the form of crazy drivers on rickshaws, tuk-tuk's, beggars, children wanting your watch or sweets, men fighting to get you as a customer when you're not even looking to buy, and thousands of people crossing a bridge with about a two-foot walkway.

My mom and I would always stop halfway and look down into the river, which seemed to be a lifeline to the local people. On the edge of the river was a shanty village that was teeming. The river embankment was muddy. This seemed to make a very good place for the village pigs to dwell. Children would be crouched down along side the water bathing and women would be washing clothes. Everywhere you looked along the river it was occupied with a person doing something.

Along our venturesome travels, which encompassed encounters with various forms of vehicles, my poor mom had the misfortune of having her foot rolled over and her body run into by rickshaws a couple of times. One time the hit resulted in blood loss but no apology from the driver.

The walk to the restaurant took us about an hour each way. Once we got inside we'd deliberately take a few deep breaths, since the restaurant had a calming atmosphere that we enjoyed and it put us at ease. It was the only place we found that was void of loud noises we didn't have the luxury of a noise-free zone in our room so we always took our time eating before tackling the gauntlet back.

As time passed, the boredom of everyday life became daunting to us. We started looking for small pleasures in every possible thing. That's certainly not a bad thing, but when most of the hours in your day are confined within a 10- by 10-foot room there's not too much to draw from; but we did find an entertaining daily ritual.

Since our room didn't have a refrigerator, we had to get our meals outside. The hotel had a very small menu for room service. A few of the breakfast choices were beans, toast with butter, corn flakes and tea.

Every morning like clockwork I called the front desk and placed the usual order, "Good morning, I'd like to put a breakfast order in." I'd say this very clearly and slowly so they'd understand.

"Yes, yes. What can I get you madam?" The person on the other end always had a thick accent but I could understand.

Then I would try to put our order in; it never changed between three items. Somehow they never seemed to understand. As the days went by, my mom and I developed a system. If I looked at her a certain way while placing the order, she'd know they didn't understand. She'd put on her flip-flops and head down to the front desk with the menu and point to the items.

A knock on the door would follow shortly. Depending on the day, we would get one of three workers. Each one of them had their own personal way of presenting the tray of food. We had a favorite who put on quite a show. Setting down the tray and walking away would have been too simple. The more food on the tray, the bigger the production would be.

If he brought us tea, toast with butter and corn flakes, the performance would look much like this: He'd place the tray at the end of one of the twin beds because there was no table. He'd scan the tray to see its contents. First the saucers that were stacked on the tray would need to be put in place. The first two for the tea would be set on the bed. The remaining saucers would be put to the side for a moment. The two teacups would then be placed in the saucers and twisted to adjust the direction of the handle for no apparent reason.

The sugar was next. It also got a saucer. He'd look for a spoon on the tray and place it next to the sugar. The milk was in a tin, but it too was worthy of a saucer. By then, a couple of minutes had passed.

The toast plate would come off the tray and it would need to be accompanied by two more saucers. The last saucer would be strategically placed to hold the bowl for the corn flakes.

After the tray had been stripped and everything placed on the bed, he would stand back and scan his placement.

He was never quite pleased with his first placement, so he'd follow up with a few minor tweaks. Some twists and turns of the cups or moving of the spoons would finish the performance. When he was satisfied, he'd look at us proudly with a big smile on his face, tilt his head towards his shoulder and say, "Yes?" We would smile back in grateful approval and give him a tip for all his hard work. Meal after meal, day after day, they never slacked in their performance.

How do you salvage your sanity when everything around you is falling apart? Just as we'd established an exercise program in the prison, once we were out, my mom and I started going to the gym. This gym, however, was located within the walls of our 10-foot-square room. Again, it was nothing fancy, but it was ours.

This is how the routine went: "Hey mom I'm going to go to the gym. Do you want to come?" I'd stand up off my bed two feet away from my mom pretending like I was holding a gym card you had to slide through a machine.

Some days she'd join me. When she did, she'd stand up from her bed and I'd say, "You've got your gym card, don't you?" My mom would usually laugh, and we'd walk to the end of the bed. We'd flick our wrists through the air as if swiping our gym cards. Then we'd either lie back on our beds like they were a gym mat or we'd do some exercises off the ends of our beds. On the days that one of us went to the gym alone, we'd say to the other, "Okay, bye, see you in a while."

Such is life; in every moment of every day we can experience a multitude of emotions in very short periods of time. We all have magnificent days and moments, and then we all face moments that really challenge us. How are you going to choose to react?

One morning as I sat quietly on my bed, we got a call from my older brother in the U.S. Having lived out of state for over a decade, he'd moved back home to Santa Barbara to be with my dad during this trying time. He became a buffer between Sean and my dad.

I answered the phone and my brother mumbled something about my dad being in the hospital. My senses heightened into alert mode. I couldn't understand what he was saying, he was slurring his words; he'd been drinking.

This really pissed me off. My posture changed and my jaw tightened. I have an absolute zero tolerance rule when it comes to people wasting their lives away by drinking; sadly I've lost friends from alcoholism.

I asked Ian to repeat himself so I could understand him. Then two key words popped out of his mouth, heart and hospital.

The thought of my dad's heart giving way under so much stress and tension had me beside myself. It wasn't just the fact that his wife and daughter were in a troubled situation, it was the turmoil between him and Sean hitting an all time high.

I love my brother, but in that moment I wanted to reach through the phone and smack him hard. I wanted to shake him and say, "This is our dad you're talking about help me understand, put me at ease!" I kept asking him questions, and he'd repeat himself over and over without giving me specific answers. Perhaps he didn't know the answers.

Meanwhile, my mom was on the edge of her seat waiting to hear what was happening. She could only hear what I was saying, which wasn't very encouraging. Rage coursed through my body as I hung up the phone. I remember thinking if anything happens to my dad someone is going to pay for this.

Chapter 11 - Second Cell Living

I didn't want to tell my mom that Ian was drunk sounding but I told her what I knew and said to her, "We need to call the embassy now." It broke my heart to see the pain and concern in her eyes.

Chapter 12
The Communist Party and Hare Krishna

There is sacredness in tears. They are not the mark of weakness, but of power. They speak more eloquently than ten thousand tongues. They are the messengers of overwhelming grief, of deep contrition, and of unspeakable love. –

Washington Irving

A week or so prior to getting the phone call from my brother about my dad, my mom and I started hearing both the embassy and Mr. Chatterjee start to speak about a particular man. We were desperately looking to get answers about our case and wanting to know when we'd get our passports and go home. No one seemed to know.

I found it interesting the way everyone spoke of this man; it sounded mysterious. It also sounded like he was a powerful person, although we didn't like the sound of what we were hearing. Who was this man they spoke about? Could he be the one to answer our questions?

We'll call him Mr. S. That definitely keeps it mysterious. My mom and I found out his full name and that he was one of the leaders in the Communist Party. It appeared to my mom and me that somehow he was controlling our situation, but what did he have to do with our case?

At the time there was both internal civil unrest happening in the region of India where we were being held, and there was also political and economic unrest between the United States and Indian governments. My mom and I started feeling like pawns trapped in the middle of this game.

My mom and I made great efforts to call as many U.S. government officials as we possibly could. Most of the time it seemed futile. Even with the internal turmoil back home, we knew that everyone there was doing the best they could for us.

At one point my father reached out to my former boyfriend, who was a high ranking officer in the United States Marine Corps, to see if he could get any answers. I had a few phone conversations with him as well, but everyone seemed to be hitting dead ends.

One afternoon I was on a phone call with an U.S. Embassy official, when they informed me that they believed the phones were being tapped and we'd need to cut our conversations short.

My first thought was, they didn't just say that, did they? You've got to be kidding me. Now the phones may be tapped?

I told the official that I needed to find out about my dad. I couldn't reach him or my brother. I had no idea what had happened with my dad. The last thing I'd heard was my brother saying the words "heart" and "hospital."

After the abrupt end to the embassy phone conversation, I called Mr. Chatterjee. I told him my mom and I wanted to set up a meeting with Mr. S. and I wasn't going to take no for an answer.

Chapter 12 - The Communist Party and Hare Krishna

Mr. Chatterjee diplomatically told me that Mr. S. was a very busy man and it wasn't easy, nor was it protocol, to meet with him.

I dug in my heels and told him I didn't care. I insisted that it needed to happen. I didn't know who he was, and I didn't care who he was. I just knew I wanted to look him in the eyes. Mr. Chatterjee told me he'd try to arrange a meeting.

After my mom and I had been released from the prison into our second cell living situation we were introduced to a man whom we were told we would need to report to. This may sound vague but, like many things, we weren't exactly sure what was going on. I certainly wasn't in a place to be Ms. Smiley and pretend that everything was hunky-dory. I wasn't rude to him, but I was carrying so much heavy, negative energy. We'll call him Inspector D.

We learned that Inspector D was the head inspector of the intelligence department and we were in his jurisdiction.

When he walked into a room he was confident. He was a charming and pleasant-looking fellow and definitely not afraid to use his power and authority He was an intelligent man. My mom later said that he felt he wasn't living his full potential.

One morning the front desk called us and told us that a policeman had dropped off something for us to come down and pick up. My mom and I thought this to be a bit strange, but perhaps it was paperwork that needed to be signed.

My mom said she'd go down and pick it up. I was shocked when she came waltzing in the door with a mini blue cooler in her hand. She set it down on the end of the bed and opened it. Boy were we surprised when we saw a couple bottles of what appeared to be fresh-squeezed juice.

My mom was excited. I was very leery. I thought, Perhaps it's poisoned? Who would send this to us? Why would they send it to us?

"Mom, we can't drink this. We have no idea of where it came from." To me it felt like a bribe of some sort. I remember feeling irritated by this. My mom hesitantly agreed with me that we didn't know where it came from and that perhaps we should hold off drinking it.

We put in a call to Mr. Chatterjee to see if by chance he'd had a policeman drop the juice off for him. I didn't really believe that was the case, but he was the only kind person we knew there.

Later that afternoon we received a phone call. It was Inspector D. asking us if we'd received the fresh juice. We informed him that we had and that we appreciated the gesture. He also gave instructions to take the cooler and bottles back to the front desk when we'd finished.

I still didn't want to drink it. It looked tasty, but I insisted that no one was going to bribe or buy me. My mom, however, indulged in the fresh watermelon juice.

This continued on a regular basis. The cooler started appearing in the hallway right outside our door. They cut out the middleman- the front desk clerk. In retrospect, I believe it was an act of kindness, but in those moments it sadly got under my skin. There were other goodies that appeared in the cooler as well. Everything that came in that cooler bothered me.

One morning I woke up, and my jaw was in a lot of pain. My mom told me that we'd better monitor it and if it continued we'd have to figure something out. The pain worsened in the next few days, and my jaw became noticeably swollen. The pain shot into my ear and sent excruciating pains throughout my entire face. As if things weren't bad enough with my hair falling out and persistent headaches. I had no idea what was wrong with me. Never in my life had I been under so much emotional stress. It was horrible. I wasn't sure what to do.

The evening of the day we noticed the swelling I started thinking back to one of my adventure races in 1995. I was on a Marine Recon team, "Team Semper-Fi" for the first X-Games ever held. We were one of the top twelve teams racing against each other on a 350-mile course.

First three days we never slept. We hiked, climbed, kayaked, white water rafted, mountain biked and canoed. My feet where constantly wet. Unfortunately we made a navigational error that got us lost deep within the bogs and marshes of northern Maine.

My team and I all sported the traditional military camo-pants and our race jerseys. Both my dad and brother are Army vets and my brother spent months in Desert Storm. I felt like I was a soldier in Vietnam the way we were slogging in circles in these dense bogs, water to our knees. We could rarely see the sky.

It was coming up on day four or five and I remember thinking, gosh, one of these guys reeks and I didn't mean like body odor, I meant like rotting death.

Subsequently my left foot had been in tremendous amounts of pain for a couple of days and I was stupidly sucking it up and not saying a word. I finally mentioned this to one of my teammates who was a Navy Seal corpsman who wanted to take a look.

Taking my shoe off was torturous. With each lace that had to be loosened because of swelling the odor I was previously smelling got closer and closer until it revealed its ugly head. I peeled my sticky deathly smelling sock off my foot and there we saw the flesh on my three small toes being eaten away; just like so many soldiers, I too had gotten trench foot.

It's fascinating how much physical pain a person can endure. Unfortunately my shoe never fit the same again. For 16 hours we spent lost down in the bogs I had to call upon some higher powers to get me through the miles and I believe the painkillers helped the situation.

We finally heard helicopters and knew we had to be getting close to the next checkpoint. However, I still had to finish this leg of the race and had one more ahead of me, the kayak portion.

Race officials were now aware of my condition and with my mentality of never throwing in the towel, I continued racing under the careful watch of my team corpsman. Each team had a private plane fly them to Martha's Vineyard for the final leg of the race, an 80-mile open ocean kayak leg to Newport, Rhode Island.

I felt confident because I'd just be paddling and could manage the pain to the finish line.

We launched our kayaks into the mighty Atlantic Ocean from the small island of Martha's Vineyard, off the east coast, at 2:30 in the morning.

The following evening my team along with other teams got caught in rough seas and fog so dense I couldn't see my teammates. It was an uncomfortable and scary situation.

We knew we were getting close to our next checkpoint and from there it was only another six miles to the finish line.

"Hey, can anyone hear us?" my captain blurted out into the darkness of the night. "Hey, we need help, is anyone there?" the voice of concern toning out from his lungs. Our five-man team was huddled in three kayaks trying to hang on to one another.

Chapter 12 - The Communist Party and Hare Krishna

We thought we saw a dim light in the distance. We had had a few times of major hallucinations throughout this race already so we were trying to figure out if this was real.

We all started yelling. We heard a voice respond, "This is the check-point. Paddle towards the light." A sense of relief flooded over us as we quickly paddled towards the light on the sandbar. We were met by race officials and were shown where we could set our sleeping bags to rest until it was safe to continue.

I kept my wetsuit on as I lay down to keep the pain in my foot to a tolerable level. I knew that a race medic would be coming to check on me. I didn't want him to find me. I knew he was the only person that had authority to pull me out of the race. I hid under my tarp in my sleeping bag.

I heard a voice say to another, "She's under there." I thought you idiot why would you tell him that? I got a knock on my tarp and a voice sounded out, "It's the medic, I need to check out how you're doing."

I wanted to stay hidden but I popped my head out from under the tarp into the darkness of the night sky with the medic's headlamp shining on me. "You're going to have to take your wet suit off so I can check out your foot." He said this in a rather serious tone.

After my wet suit came off the medic and I went back and forth in a debate on why I should or should not continue this race. My side was simple. I only had six miles left and I had already come 350 miles and the rest I'd be sitting in a kayak.

The medic's side was a bit more direct, "Are you willing to lose these toes for this race?" He showed me how bad the infection had become. It had shot up as far as the middle of my shinbone and the pain was something fierce. I responded to him with a simple yet stupid response,

"Yes I am willing to lose these toes." He smiled at me and said, "I can't let that happen. You're out of the race and off to the ER."

Once I was loaded into the ambulance everything went fuzzy as if my body started to shut down. I vaguely remember reporters waiting at the hospital to get a chance of an interview with me. I remember waking up the next morning with tubes in my arms, a cross above my hospital bed and wondering where the heck I was. I still had all five toes on that foot, I just ended up losing all the toenails until they and my skin, thankfully, grew back.

Now I lay there on my bed In India with this jaw pain saying to my mom, "I'll never forget when I called you from the hospital that time and you asked me where I was. I had no idea. I remember you telling me to look around the room to see if I could find something with the name of the hospital on it, but all I could tell you at that moment was there was a cross hanging over me."

On day three of this pain we received an invitation to accompany Inspector D to some sort of gathering. This, of course, didn't sit well with me. I believe the pain amplified the irritation. I told my mom that I wasn't going to go. I really didn't want her to go either, but she was a big girl and could make her own decisions. I understood that we were going stir crazy in this room, but if she went I felt I wouldn't be able to protect her if something were to happen.

That evening my mom was picked up by a red police van and escorted by two policeman and Inspector D. to the gathering. I used my jaw pain as an excuse not to go. Upon reflection had I not been in pain I probably would've forced myself to go so that I could have been there for my mom.

Chapter 12 - The Communist Party and Hare Krishna

For the couple of hours my mom was gone that night I felt like a worried mother. I couldn't imagine all the nights my mom sat up worried sick about where I was in my teenage years. This was payback.

Once she returned, I felt much more at ease. She proceeded to tell me about the evening. She said that over all it had been nice. It turned out to be a birthday party for a family member, but whose family we have no idea. My mom really came alive when she told me of a situation that happened along the way to the party.

Her eyes lit up while giving me a look like, hold on to your seat. " You're not going to believe this. On the drive over, Inspector D was talking about the musical 'Gone with the Wind' and then, all of a sudden, the police van that we're driving in comes to a halt as it collides with a motorcyclist.

The driver of our van leans out the window and starts beating on the motorcyclist. Then Inspector D says something in Hindi, and the passenger of the police van jumps out of the vehicle and runs around to the poor fellow on the motorcycle and starts beating him up more!

After a while Inspector D yells, 'That's enough', and his man stopped and hopped back into the car. Inspector D turns to me and says, "Don't worry, this is India, just like Rodney King in America."

My mom had a perplexed look on her face, and she said, "What could I say?" Then she proceeded to tell me that the food was tasty and she learned a lot more about the Inspector. After hearing the story, I was just grateful my mom was back in our little room safe and sound.

My jaw situation wasn't subsiding. We thought it would be a good idea to call Sister Elisha and ask if she could recommend a good dentist. The last thing I wanted to do was to go to a dentist in a foreign country, but what choice did I have? Sister Elisha was kind enough to walk us to what I believe was her own dentist's office. They allowed me to do a drop-in check-up to see what was going on.

The room was very primitive looking, and the tools looked like they were from a different era. I have to say I don't care for the dentist to begin with, and this place had me feeling a bit more vulnerable than usual. The dentist informed me that I needed a root canal.

I remember thinking, Oh hell no! I am not having a root canal done here. I didn't want to appear rude, so I let them know that I'd be going back to the states soon and wondered if they could recommend anything to manage the pain. They suggested clove oil.

Of course I had no idea when I'd be getting back to the states, so I really hoped that the clove oil would help. I thanked them and paid for the diagnosis. Sister Elisha kindly gave us instructions of where we could find clove oil in the marketplace, and we went our separate ways.

The clove oil turned out to be a great solution for the pain. However, the poor tooth no longer resides in my mouth. It didn't need a root canal. From being under constant states of stress, I had clenched down through my jaw region so hard for such long periods of time that I'd split the tooth right down the center into the root.

Six days after we got that phone call from my brother about my dad we were given a green light for a meeting in the chamber of Mr. S.

I remember feeling anxious. I had butterflies in my stomach and used the toilet multiple times before we left to meet him. I wondered what he'd look like? I had created a vision in my head of a very gruff and hard man. I was concerned about how he'd react to us when he saw us in person.

We left early so we'd have plenty of time to get there. We definitely didn't want to be late to this meeting.

Once we arrived, we were asked to sit and wait in a room, and after 30 minutes we were called back. The waiting had intensified my anger and frustration. My palms were sweating and my heart rate was high when his secretary walked us back to his chambers.

I felt like leaders of opposing armies were meeting before the battle commenced. I could hear the beat of my heart like a drum inside my head.

There he sat in his chair. Stone-faced and emotionless, he gestured for us to sit in the two chairs provided. There were no pleasantries, just straight to the facts. The energy that he exuded was negative and dark. His eyes were very piercing and intense. He exuded a sense of superiority with the first few words from his mouth.

He started off the meeting on the wrong foot by saying in his deep voice, "You technically should be in the prison still. You are looking at a sentence of three to seven years and definitely a minimum of a year."

All that came out of his mouth for the first few minutes was, jail this, prison that, six months, seven years, over and over without stopping. It was as if he was trying to frighten and intimidate us. It was crushing me.

I felt all the rage that was built up inside of me intensifying until finally I couldn't take it any more and I abruptly pushed my chair back from his desk. Tears started flowing uncontrollably down my cheeks and my eyes swelled in pain. I said with both my jaw and fists clenched, "My biggest priority is to get home to my dad!" My heart and head were ready to explode. I remember looking at the man's neck and wanting to crush his esophagus with my bare hands.

I'd hit my threshold. I couldn't stop my crying. He was absolutely the wrong person to sit across from you when you feel like you're having a nervous breakdown. He was abrasive and didn't seem to have a compassionate bone in his body.

Out of nowhere he threw an entirely new twist on this whole case by saying, "Your best option is to put an application in to withdraw the prosecution!"

My mom and I were dumbfounded by all this legal-turned-political mumbo-jumbo. I saw my mom's jaw clench and the little blue vein on her temple darken as she said, "What does this mean to us?" At this point my mom was holding my hand as it rested on top of my thigh.

He proceeded to tell us that this would mean skipping the judicial system entirely and going between the American and the Indian governments. He might as well have been speaking Hindi to me. I couldn't comprehend anything he was saying. I still didn't know who this man was. He certainly didn't seem to be on our side, and I don't even know if he was.

My mom asked questions, but unfortunately it was too much for us to grasp in the meeting. Nonetheless, he wanted an answer. We felt pressured. We couldn't imagine how much slower things could possibly move, so, just like a game of Russian roulette, we made our choice and agreed. My mind flashed to a childhood memory I experienced more than once with my dad.

"May-day, may-day, this is whiskey- zulu- victor... The boat engine has seized and we're going to need immediate assistance from the Coast Guard, these are our coordinates. I have two small children on board the fishing vessel and the seas are rough." My dad's ice blue eyes and English accent showed a commanding presence as he spoke into the CB radio of his fishing vessel, The Fagin.

At that moment, sitting in front of this man's desk, I felt my mom and I needed to send out another may-day, but to whom? We walked out of the meeting that night not knowing what we just agreed upon.

From fresh-squeezed juices to invitations from inspectors to gatherings, mysterious pastries at our doorstep, phones being tapped and high-powered Communist Party leaders, it seemed as though things couldn't get any stranger.

It reminded me of times when things aren't going well and you look to the heavens and say, "Is that all you got for me?" Of course God and the universe always seem to respond with, "No! I've got a whole lot more." No matter how bizarre things were, the bar always seemed to get raised on us.

One early afternoon, as my mom and I were coming back from picking up some supplies, the man at the front desk of our hotel informed us we had a message. The written note requested our presence to accompany Inspector D to a Hare Krishna temple that evening.

In that moment I thought, what does that mean to accompany him to a Hare Krishna temple? Is he a Hare Krishna? I have to say I was both intrigued and puzzled at the same time.

I was a bit curious as to what the Hare Krishna people and temple would be like. Thankfully the clove oil I purchased in the marketplace had really helped reduce my jaw pain so I couldn't use that as an excuse. I was at the stage where I was thinking, If I can't beat them, I'll join them.

That evening we got a knock on the door. It was our police escort coming to fetch us. I have to say most of the time I wasn't sure how I should feel with all this. I mean why were we getting all these various treats and attention? It just didn't sit well with me.

Inspector D wore a dress uniform, and my mom and I wore the finest Indian shirts we had. On the drive over, Inspector D told us that we'd be having a private audience in the chamber of a world renowned Swami guru of the Hare Krishna religion. My eyes widened and I'm sure my jaw dropped as he said this.

I immediately started thinking about proper etiquette and protocol. Do we bow? Do we kneel? Do we shake his hand or is that taboo? Was the swami going to try to convert us into the Hare Krishna religion? Was this a cult? Did he think we were heathens because we were in prison? I wanted to know why were we getting this special meeting?

Talk about VIP treatment. When we pulled up to the temple, the driver of the police vehicle pulled so close it appeared to me that we were on one of the lawns right at the base of a long staircase to the Iskcon temple.

The sun was setting as we arrived. The hues of oranges and reds from the sun washed on the side of the massive white and light peach accented temple.

There was a familiar feel in the air. It was quiet and still. I felt at ease. The temple was three levels high and had a massive dome on the top that was shaped like a pineapple with miniature domes around the base of it. On the first two levels there were around a dozen arched doors running the length of the building. The grounds were immaculate. In between the main temple and a pagoda-looking building, a beautiful green lawn and a pretty good-sized pond spread out across the grounds.

We entered the main temple where a ceremony was being held. The sound of the music was rhythmic, and the devotees seemed to be moving methodically in a trance like motion. The room was hot and humid. People were sweating. It seemed as if this ceremony wouldn't end anytime soon. We participated for a couple of rounds as we twisted and turned to the rhythm.

After our initiation in this rhythmical ceremony we were escorted to the private chamber of the head swami. Inspector D seemed proud to introduce us to him. He was nothing like I had envisioned. My vision was a lean, fit wise-looking Indian man. To both my mom's and my surprise he was a heavier set white guy.

He was very relaxed in his posture and wore a beautiful garland of flowers around his neck. He made us feel comfortable. He anointed us with holy oil. We swapped stories and found out he was originally from Wisconsin and had moved to San Francisco in the 1960s, came to India in the 1970s and had never left.

We enjoyed hearing how he came to India and the Hare Krishna religion. As I reflect now, I realize that this was a great privilege to have been invited to a private audience with this man. But with the impending legal issues that confronted us it was hard to embrace what should have been a beautiful experience.

Chapter 13
Secret Documents

I have survivor skills. Some of that is superficial- what I present to people outwardly- but what makes people resilient is the ability to find humor and irony in situations that would otherwise overpower you.

Amy Tan

The brief moment of distraction and what little pleasure we got from the private audience with the swami of the Hare Krishna temple was soon another blur in the chaos happening around us and back home.

Everything was unraveling. The days of our lives were just withering away. We had missed out on celebrations back home. We had missed Sean's birthday, Mother's Day, my father's birthday, Father's Day and it looked as though we would miss my parents' anniversary as well.

Division was happening all around me. The embassy had given orders to the U.S State Department to have Sean removed from any further control or contact regarding our case. He was not only

243

a wildcard, but he was volatile. It wasn't helping our situation. I know he was doing the best he could with his tools. Unfortunately he was pissed off at everyone and acting out in very inappropriate ways. My contact with him became less as time went by. It was an unfair and cruel burden for me to have him use me as a verbal punching bag.

During one phone call I had with Sean in our room my mom couldn't take hearing me defending myself anymore. She turned to me and said, "That's enough. Hang up the phone!"

I felt trapped between my parents and Sean. I didn't want to choose. I don't think I had ever cried so much in my life. The most heart-wrenching part was that it divided my mom and me.

For the first time in my adult life I was angry with her. I wasn't angry at any one thing because she hadn't done anything. But she was pissed off at Sean, with good reason, for what he was unnecessarily putting me and my dad through. I know she had to be absolutely shocked when she heard the way he spoke to me. She had never heard this before.

Sadly it was my dirty little secret, and now my mom was calling me out on it. She was standing in the truth. She was standing in her rightful ground as a caring, loving, supportive mother. And as a strong woman, she was letting her daughter know that the behavior was not okay. I've reflected on all the verbal abuse I endured it makes me shudder.

I was overwhelmed by the lack of integrity I had been experiencing the last couple of years in my life. First there had been the Fire Department, then Sean, then this whole legal nightmare; I felt there was no justice.

While my body was physically broken from my injury, I'd had to fight to defend myself against the legal system within the Fire Department. Being denied what I was entitled, I saw no justice.

244

Chapter 13 - Secret Documents

I had been fighting a battle of a shattered heart with the man I thought I loved even though I knew the relationship wasn't for my highest good. I was pleading to be released and sent home from a nightmare that never seemed to end. I wanted so desperately to stand in my truth and power, but I felt weak and broken.

After the chamber meeting with Mr. S, my mom and I started hearing our case spoken about differently. There was a special application that was going to get submitted to the proper authorities and this supposedly would withdraw us or have us bypass the judicial system with the courts and judges.

Our case would then move to a higher level with the governments of the two nations. The Home Secretary, State Department, Governors and District Magistrates would all be playing a part in it somehow. Mr. Chatterjee informed us that Mr. S. was heading back to Kolkata to show this new application to the U.S. Embassy.

Another week had gone by before we heard the news that Mr. S had arrived back from showing the application to the Consulate General in Kolkata.

While he was away, the civil unrest in our area heated up again. It had escalated to such a level that my mom and I received news that Mr. S. was being requested to travel to another region. At first we didn't realize how this was going to affect us, but we soon found out that these mysterious case-sensitive new documents needed to be delivered back to the proper authorities in Kolkata and with Mr. S. leaving there was no one to take them. This was a devastating blow to my mom and me.

My mom and I were getting desperate to get out of India. I'll never forget one afternoon while the whole region was on shut down my mom said to me in a very serious tone, "Heather, maybe we can flee and escape." I tried not to laugh. But she wasn't smiling. She was serious. She hadn't been feeling or sleeping well for some time. Our situation was taking a toll.

I looked at her and smiled and said, "Mom there is no way this would ever work. First of all we are surrounded by the Himalayas, Pakistan and the Bay of Bengal, and secondly we have no identification. I don't see any of these as good options."

She stared at me as if in a trance, then did a quick little headshake and said, "No, I guess none of those would work." She finally made eye contact with me and a partial smile broke over her face. This broke the ice enough for me to start laughing. However, she was quite serious about the entire conversation.

Chapter 14
Frantically Fleeing

In all chaos there is a cosmos, in all disorder a secret order.

Carl Jung

Desperate times call for desperate measures, and this was one of those times. My mom clearly knew that making any attempt of an escape would be insane. It took awhile, however, for my mom to come to this conclusion.

Even after I gave her the geographic visuals of our options, she still had a conversation with my dad and he even discussed this with my former military boyfriend. The consensus confirmed to my mom that this was not a good idea at all. However, we came up with the ludicrous idea that since there was no one to make the long journey to Kolkata to deliver the secret documents, it was up to us to get them there.

After my mom and I came up with this crazy idea, we thought the notion of us even asking the embassy officials would probably seem insane to them. I remember role- playing the conversation

247

with my mom. We did have a few good laughs at what we were about to ask, but we were quite serious and desperate. I remember playing the role of the authorities and saying to my mom, "Sure no problem. That would actually be very helpful. We realize you're political prisoners and have no identification, but this could work."

We laughed at the insanity of it. We weren't willing to let any more time slip by if we could help it. We called Mr. Chatterjee and ran the idea by him. It didn't sit well. I believe he was afraid for us. However it wasn't his decision and we insisted he go through the proper channels to find the answer for us.

One thing we were learning is that we'd most certainly never get a quick answer on anything, and our patience muscle was fatigued. While we waited to hear if this crazy idea would manifest I did as much writing as I could to keep my brain occupied. I needed all the distraction so that the battles I was fighting in my head didn't consume my thoughts.

One day I wrote a letter to Oprah Winfrey. I felt very strongly that she would find our whole story very fascinating. I remember thinking to myself, she'll probably never even see this letter but then again crazier things have happened. I thought, gosh, maybe Oprah could help get us home.

Then, (The gods must be crazy because) my mom and I got a green light on transporting the documents. We would travel with no identification, and we'd be taking a 10-hour train ride into an entirely unknown region. I was both excited and nervous at the same time. However we didn't get an official green light until a few days after the initial approval.

The embassy was aware of what we were attempting to do and no one was comfortable with this scenario. We'd been watching the local news the last few days, and unfortunately for us, the riots were at an all time high in our area. Thousands of tourists and others were fleeing. Tourists were being stoned and beaten in violent rioting. My mom and I second-guessed what we were attempting to do, but in our desperation, we felt it was our only option.

It was now at the height of monsoon season and when it rained it flooded. Mr. Chatterjee gave us directions to the train station where we could purchase our tickets for the following day's departure. The rain was not only torrential, it was relentless. We waited as long as we could to see if it would let up before tackling the walk to the station a couple of miles away. As hard as the rain was falling, we thought surely we wouldn't run into any of the rioters. Were we wrong!

With our infamous umbrella in hand we trudged through the ankle-deep water. The rain hit us from the side, which made the umbrella useless. We were soaked to the bone.

With the constant poll positioning through the hoards of people, it took us almost an hour. My mom and I were shocked when we saw three lines of men forming outside the station doors. It wasn't long before frustration kicked in.

As we stood there waiting, we watched over and over again as various men walked up to the line and went in front of us as if we weren't even there. I mumbled something to one of the men that cut in front of us, but all it got us was a dirty look.

Men were shouting in Hindi, gesturing with their hands and waving them in the air. It was chaotic. I started to question if we were in the right line or place. I felt we were at a horse race with bets going on around us. We looked high and low to see if we could spot a sign that indicated train tickets or something.

Yes, we were indeed in the correct place. However we found out that with all the thousands of people trying to escape, there simply were not enough trains to evacuate the numbers, and local hustlers were taking advantage by purchasing multiple tickets to earn a profit.

I started feeling our glimmer of hope slip away. We weren't feeling comfortable with all that was going on around us. We'd been standing for over an hour in the pouring rain and had only moved a foot.

I finally turned to my mom, and with a semi-defeated tone, said, "Mom, there's no way we're getting out of here by train." I remember thinking, f#@k! Now what? My mom and I had a long stare into each other's eyes.

"This is just all wrong," my mom said with an overwhelmed look on her face. Then a thought crossed my mind, "Mom what if we took a plane?" She looked at me like I was insane. She was correct; I felt I was a bit bonkers. The question now was would we be able to fly without any identification? I had great doubt that we'd get there, but what other options did we have?

Weeks prior to this we'd found a back alley place that had computers and access to the Internet. I thought perhaps we could purchase airline tickets to Kolkata online. We left the madness of the train station and headed back an hour through the pouring rain only to find out the shop was shut because of the riots. Everything was closed down.

We called both the Embassy and Mr. Chatterjee and let them know that it wasn't going to be possible to get out by train and that perhaps we could fly. There was always uncertainty with everything that had to do with our case. But nonetheless we were willing to take all the risks we could to assure the safe delivery of the documents that could lead to our freedom.

Once my mom and I were given the okay for us to try to fly, we packed our few belongings. We were concerned that we wouldn't even find anyone to take us to the airport given all the chaos of the riots. We did however find one brave soul willing to attempt this mad run to the airport with us on his tuk-tuk. We agreed on a much higher price than we'd ever paid, which was just fine given the situation.

With our packs clutched in our hands and resting on our laps, we watched our driver negotiate his way through the madness of thousands of people rioting and vehicles burning on the sides of the roads.

My mom and I had no way of knowing if this was all for naught. We didn't have any idea if we could even purchase airline tickets let alone be allowed to fly without passports or any other identification.

As we drove through the madness, I couldn't help but think of how lucky we have it back home in our beautiful small town of Santa Barbara. We had never experienced turmoil in our backyard like this!

It was the longest white-knuckled, 45-minute drive I had ever experienced. As we rounded the corner and saw the airport come into view, my breathing started to feel labored. I was nervous and had a feeling of guilt come over me. It didn't look like the same airport my mom and I unknowingly strolled into with gun ammunition in my pack on that fateful day a couple of months back. Today this place was mobbed with staggering numbers of people trying to flee and escape. I felt like a lamb walking into a lion's den.

Chapter 15
Tourists or Terrorists

In the midst of movement and chaos, keep stillness inside of you.

Deepak Chopra

As I watched our driver disappear back into the sea of madness I couldn't help but wonder what lay ahead for us. My mom and I hurled our packs onto our backs, I took a big deep breath and we started to maneuver through the hoards of people.

My body felt like it was walking awkwardly. I felt tight and tense. I felt that people were looking at us suspiciously, like they knew our situation. Then the thought crossed my mind perhaps they recognize us from all the pictures of us in newspapers and media. I had a hard time shaking my feeling of guilt. I usually look everyone in the eyes, but for some reason I wasn't making eye contact.

The airport was loud and teeming with panic. I stood in the line rehearsing how I was going to ask the clerk to purchase airline tickets to Kolkata. I didn't know what I would say if they asked for

253

our passports. My mom and I weren't having any conversations at this point. I think we were holding our breath and hoping for the best.

We got waved to the window. The worker asked us how they could help us, and as confidently as I could I squeaked out, "We'd like to buy two tickets to Kolkata, please."

The clerk looked me in the eyes as his head started to tilt towards his shoulder and go into the famous Indian nod. The question in my mind always was, Will that head nod that usually mean no in the states become a yes or a no?

"Yes, yes, ma'am."

I waited for him to ask for our ID next, but he didn't. I nudged my mom's leg under the counter. While he was looking on his computer screen, I pulled out my debit card.

"Yes ma'am, we have two seats available for Rs 7,787." Since we had been here for such a lengthy period we had references to the exchange rates and did a quick calculation. My mom and I had agreed ahead of time that we'd put this on my debit card.

"Okay, thank you I'll use my debit Master Card, please." I thought that at any minute he'd ask us for our identification.

"So sorry, ma'am, we don't take credit cards." My mom and I turned towards each other with lost looks in our eyes.

"Good fricken grief, Mom, what is God asking of us?"

I love my mom for so many reasons, and in this moment she was as cool as a cucumber. She immediately pulled her little worn wallet out and started scrounging through her cash. She calmly said to me, "Heather, how much cash do you have?"

Once again, the gods were on our side. What are the odds that between the two of us we would manage to have just enough for the tickets? It did, however, wipe us out.

We felt a small victory as we walked away from the counter. Not only did we manage to pull off the money situation, we also never got asked for our IDs.

The lobby of the airport was almost out of the league of even being a standing room only. It was very difficult for us to find a place to stand especially with our packs. It was so hot in there I actually had sweat dripping down my back under my shirt. The flight time came and went. All we could do was wait and hope that we'd actually get on a plane.

We not only managed to make the last flight, but we even got to Kolkata with a bit of daylight left. We felt reassured that the embassy had at least given us the name and address to a hotel they recommended.

After a 45-minute taxi ride, we were relieved when the driver pulled in front of the hotel. We were hungry and exhausted. We'd been looking forward to grabbing a bite to eat and collapsing on our bed.

Unfortunately my relief gave way to annoyance. We were absolutely shocked when the desk clerk told us the cheapest room they had would cost 150 American dollars.

We had just emptied our wallets of all our cash, and I knew that my funds on my debit card were in a critical state. It was now dark and here we were in the heart of Kolkata. We had no reference to where we were or what better options we had.

By the time morning came around, we were another 200 dollars poorer. However, as always, we tried to find the bright side of the situation. It this case we looked at our complimentary breakfast as being a win. Unfortunately the breakfast wasn't as pleasant as it could have been. Not because of food choice; that was lovely.

It was a nice buffet-style breakfast with was a variety of egg dishes, French toast and other goodies. When we walked in the nice dining area there were only two of the tables filled with people. We set our travel satchels on the table and went to get our plates.

I was looking forward to this yummy looking food. It had been a long time since we'd laid our eyes on such great looking breakfast options. As we turned to head back to feast, I was absolutely floored to notice that four people had sat in our seats. It was very awkward. I thought, surely they saw our stuff sitting smack dab on top of the table.

We walked up to the table and I said, "Excuse me, this is our stuff on the table and we're sitting here." They looked like a well-to-do Indian family. The older woman whom I assumed was the mother looked at me briefly with a demeaning look. She then gestured to our stuff as if to say, "Take it and leave."

There stood my mom and me at the edge of our table holding our food plates and this family wasn't budging. We were dumbfounded. One part of me wanted to make a stink, but my higher self kicked in and I thought, Thank goodness we are not like them. I said, "Excuse me," as I reached across the length of the table and picked up our items. I turned, and we walked away and sat at another table.

My mom and I had two primary missions our first full day in Kolkata. The first one had just been added to our itinerary and that was to find us an affordable room to stay in. The second mission was actually our only true mission: to deliver the secret documents to the American Embassy.

Chapter 15 - Tourists or Terrorists

All we knew was that the embassy was located on Ho Chi Mihn Road.

After our unpleasant breakfast experience, we grabbed our packs and checked out of our room. We set out onto the streets of Kolkata with a small map and our belongings.

I saw a street sign across the road that read Sudder Street. By the looks of our map, it appeared we were in somewhat of a central location. We felt we'd have a good chance of finding a room in the area. There was a mixture of nice and not-so-nice all mingled up together.

As we walked along the bustling road, a particular building caught our eye. It had the same aesthetically pleasing look to it as the prison with its persimmon colored paint and banyan trees. We were in luck. It happened to be a hotel called the Astoria. From the outside it appeared suitable to us and would save around $130 a night compared to the place we had just stayed. I am certainly not a math wizard but $20 a night sure beat $150.

We unloaded our packs inside our new room at the Astoria. Mission one had been completed. Before we could tackle our main mission we looked at our map and found the location of the United States Embassy. As soon as I felt confident with my bearings and the direction we needed to go to get us there we called and informed them they could expect our arrival in an hour and a half. We also let them know that we'd be traveling by foot.

As we walked along the streets, I couldn't help but feel like I was a tourist in this distant land. But fleeting thoughts of our journey and being associated with terrorism kept popping into my head as we walked through both the slums and the roads that looked like Park Avenue.

I started having scenes flash like a film projector running inside my head. I felt as though I was having an out-of-body experience watching all we'd been through up to this point. Tears flowed down my cheeks as one scene faded into the next. I saw my mom and me months earlier so excited to be embarking on this mother and daughter journey.

As that vision faded, another one popped into my head. This time it was my mom and I being thrown into that dirty, smelly holding cell, and as fast as that came into focus it faded into to us being escorted through the night into the prison.

My dad's eyes pierced my thoughts and the words I'd spoken to him haunted me. "Don't worry, Dad, I'll bring Mom back safe and sound." But here we were emotionally and physically beaten walking through the streets of Kolkata.   I thought, Dear God, please let us go home.

The landscape of the buildings shifted with every block we walked. A little over an hour had gone by before we turned onto Ho Chi Mihn Road. The road had English architecture and was lined with trees.

After walking a few blocks down this road we noticed what appeared to be a roadblock in the distance. Soon public driving access came to an end and the road became lined with staggered cement barricades. We started noticing many security cameras and a few watchtowers on the sides of the road.

When we got to our first security check and were asked for passports, I thought, oh shit, here we go. We spent the next handful of minutes trying to explain ourselves without getting any understanding from the guard, so he made a call. The next person to arrive better understood our explanation about our passports, and he too made a phone call. The third person to arrive understood the procedure and the person we needed to see next.

Chapter 15 - Tourists or Terrorists

After we passed all the security checks and formalities, we met up one by one with the embassy officials. I thought it was interesting that we met them in the order of their rank.

I remember the largest office of the Consulate General was quite nice, but only the American seal on the wall stood out to me. Once we got in front of the Consulate General it was time to hand over the thick large envelope, the secret documents. We didn't know exactly what the contents included but we did know it contained the possibility of sending us home.

My mom and I had traveled far and had made some major decisions to deliver these documents. It was no easy undertaking dodging our way through the mayhem and riots of the civil unrest. Our mission was complete, but what did that mean?

The embassy gave us little bits of information, but it wasn't as if they themselves had a clear understanding of where the case was going from here. We sat for a bit of time with all of the officials going over certain actions that had already been taken and ones that needed to get done.

We heard talk of the paperwork needing to get in front of the Chief Minister as well as a few others. So, again, it was as clear as mud. It's times such as this when you just need to surrender.

As the meeting came to an end, we all stood up and shook hands. Just before we were escorted out, the Consulate General informed us that we'd need to stay in Kolkata for an unknown time period. This comment did not sit well with me, but, like I said earlier, you just need to surrender.

My mom and I left the embassy in a bit of a fog. Once we got out of the confines of the Embassy, my mom turned to me with a questioning look and said, "Okay, well now what?" She cracked a smile and laughed.

Athena Rising, a Memoir – Heather Bond

I quickly came to the realization that we could actually be tourists and explore Kolkata, so I said, "Let's find a bookstore." My mom looked a bit surprised by my response "The travel section. What better place to find information we need to explore?" We both concurred this would be a good place to start.

As we wound our way back through the neighborhoods, we noticed a very modern looking shop-lined road. We felt this would be a great place to start searching. We noticed a gentleman that looked as though he could direct us to the proper location. Sure enough he told us that in another block or so we'd see a bookstore.

Once inside the shop, I felt as though we hopped into a bookstore back in the states. People were relaxed. Some were wandering and others were lounging. My mom and I found a few good books that gave us some great visuals and ideas. We wrote them down in my trusty little pocket notebook. Once we were finished researching we thought we'd head back to have a little rest at the Astoria.

We had a funny experience along the way. Through our time in India I had become quite used to my mom and I not being able to walk side by side. Due to the sheer numbers of people, she'd usually be off to either my right or left.

We'd become accustomed to keeping a conversation going even when we couldn't see one another. This time we'd been walking down what appeared to be the quietest street in India and having a conversation for quite some time. Then I noticed my mom wasn't making any of her usual small comments.

When I turned to look at her, she wasn't there. Instead a pretty healthy looking dog stood in her place. It caught me by surprise. Then I looked farther back and saw my mom. I was relieved. I couldn't understand where she had gone.

Chapter 15 - Tourists or Terrorists

As crazy as it may sound, I thought for a second she'd turned into a dog. When my mom walked up to me she told me something had caught her eye, so she stopped to take a look. I gestured to the dog and told her I thought she'd turned into this dog. We laughed so hard. The whole scenario was curious and it actually opened up a deep conversation, all the while the dog sitting, waiting patiently right between my mom and me.

He'd been looking at us as if he'd understood the whole conversation. The three of us continued down the road. Our new friend followed at our side like a loving pet and then, poof, he was gone.

With it being the height of monsoon season, we took heed of what one of the American Embassy officials had told us. He was a local from Kolkata. He let us know that as funny as it may sound we really needed to be careful not to fall into any open man-holes in the streets. He told us a few stories where people got seriously hurt. This was definitely not a scenario we ever needed to think about back home. We appreciated the heads up.

We soon realized that the height of monsoon season definitely wasn't the height of tourist season for a very good reason. It was difficult to get around in the torrential rain. Even with an umbrella, you'd be soaked to the bone within five minutes.

My mom and I made a command decision that we wouldn't let this rain keep us trapped inside. I remember us laughing in our room as sheets of rain kept coming and not letting up. In my best English accent I said, "Damn it, this rain shall not defeat us!"

We laughed and laughed. I don't think it was so much what or how I said it, it was the fact that there we were again. A different location, different time and God and the universe were still saying,

261

"Okay, now what ladies? How are you going to react to these cards we're dealing you?"

We all have different ways to make ourselves feel a bit better. Sometimes just a long hot wonderful bath infused with essential oils does the trick for me. Unfortunately I didn't see that happening anytime soon. I don't recall any hot water up to that point in the entire journey.

However, what popped into my mind was a hair cut. It had been close to a year since I'd had it trimmed. I had many split ends, and it just felt horrible from losing chunks of my hair due to all the stress. Thank goodness I had a lot of it to begin with. The idea of a haircut popped into my head when I saw a fancy looking salon.

With umbrella in hand, we set out to get a price check and to see if I needed an appointment for a trim. Just for reference, I'm not a gal who fusses with any type of product or styling, but I really was hoping that the feeling of healthier hair would perk me up.

I was in luck. They had a stylist available for a walk in, and the price was affordable. When the gal came out to get me, I felt like a giddy little girl going into a fancy-looking place to get my hair done for the first time. I looked back at my mom as I followed the gal to the back. My mom smiled and gave me the good luck gesture with her thumbs up.

With the language barrier I tried my best to explain to the stylist that I wanted her to trim off the dead ends.

"Little, just a little", I told her while my thumb and index finger displayed about an inch apart for measuring purposes. "I have very curly and frizzy hair." She did a few of those uncertain looking Indian head nods. I really was hoping that hers meant Yes, I understand.

She took the first cut, and I felt a weight difference. I thought, Holy moly, this sure felt like a big chunk. I gazed down at the floor and saw a rather long chunk of my hair.

The stylist saw my look and said, "Much more healthy now." She'd cut about five to six inches in length. My heart skipped a beat. Then a voice inside my head said, what do you expect? She must have thought you needed it.

She continued to cut. I didn't look into the mirror until she was done blow-drying it.

Holy shit, you've got to be fricken kidding me! I looked like Krusty the Clown. I turned quickly away from the mirror. It was so frizzy and short. When I came into the salon my hair was halfway down my back, and now it was shoulder length and sticking out wider than my shoulders.

After I thanked her, she walked me to the front. When I came into view of my mom, her jaw dropped. Her eyes widened and she knew not to laugh, at least not anytime soon.

When the cashier saw me I got a similar reaction, only she said to me, "Are you liking?" Of course I don't like this. Who in their right mind would like this? I look like a demented clown. But what I really said was, "Yes, it's fine, thank you."

I walked out of the hair salon feeling disheartened. It wasn't even the fact that my hair looked crazy. It was all the other uncertainty that I'd allowed to consume my life.

Of course the whole situation we were living out here in India seemed like a strange time-warp experience to me. I wasn't upset with my hair or the gal; I was upset at myself.

I knew my hair looked horrible and with the look on both the cashier's and my mom's faces, I knew they thought the same. Yet I chose not to say anything. This was another example of me trying not to make waves with others, but always at my expense. It was just like with my relationship and the Fire Department.

I had wished I said something to the salon about not being pleased, because that was the truth. Instead I smiled and laughed, "Oh, yeah, no, it's fine. I, I like it."

"Heather are you sure you don't want them to fix it?" My mom said with a perplexed look on her face. I knew I was heading straight back to our room to wash my hair out and responded to my mom by saying, "No, let's just go."

The rains had been relentless while we were in the salon. The knee-deep water in the streets was rising. Thoughts of uncovered manholes filled our heads.

As we waded through the streets, my mom sent out an alarm, "Oh, shoot. My flip-flop just broke." I turned to see her reaching into the water. She was elbow deep and fishing for her shoe. I looked at her with so much love and admiration. She's so emotionally balanced.

Then a smile broke over her face. "Aha!" she said as she pulled her hand out of the dark water with her flip-flop in a tight grasp. She quickly removed her other sandal and proceeded barefoot through the unsanitary-looking water.

The rains never seemed to let up. It made me wonder about all the thousands of people living in the poorest slums. Some of them had nothing more than a cardboard box shelter covered in plastic. Witnessing this as we walked the streets really struck my heart hard. I had a very hard time seeing the massive number of people that live this way. Yet I was intrigued as I watched them go about their daily lives.

Chapter 15 - Tourists or Terrorists

One of the primary places my mom and I wanted to experience while we were stuck in Kolkata was the famous Howrah train station. It's the largest train station in the world, and up to 3 million people per day go through it.

We had watched a great video about it on our National Geographic Great Railways of India video. Before we could start out on our adventure, we needed to find my mom a pair of flip-flops. We found it quite humorous to watch the beggars look and gesture at my mom walking barefoot through the streets. They must have thought she was a crazy red-haired woman with no shoes.

We walked along little stalls until we came upon one that sold shoes. I think in the Indian culture they have smaller feet because it took quite some time before we found one that was close enough to fit my mom.

As we set off towards the train station, my mom and I discussed our most recent conversation with the embassy.

We had been informed that we'd done all we possibly could, and now it was up to the powers that be. We also found out we were not able to leave the following day as planned due to the 1,000 extra paramilitary troops that were brought into Siliguri. All services would be cut off for at least 48 hours.

It had become quite an adventurous journey to get to the train station. We passed through what looked to be fields of shantytowns. The trash piled around us was insane. We passed by a giant wall with a beautiful old gate, and just near the entrance a placard read The Mother Theresa Foundation. We would have loved to have a peek inside, but we continued on.

In order for us to get to the train station, we had to cross over the Howrah Bridge. It was absolutely mind-boggling. It's a steel suspension bridge that spans 2,313 feet over the Hooghly River. It is said that 100,000 vehicles and 150,000 pedestrians cross the bridge on a given day. It teemed with life. It was quite an experience in itself to walk over.

Just as we neared the opposite side of the river, the most amazing sea of orange caught our attention. My mom and I headed to the side of the bridge to get an aerial view. It was a feast for our eyes. It was the most brilliant flower and vegetable market we'd ever seen. I had never witnessed so many orange marigolds in one location in my life. It was mesmerizing.

People were busily working and purchasing fresh goods. There was something captivating to us in this scene. It made us want to be down among the colors and the crowds. It was a photographer's dream, and I captured some amazing and beautiful aerial view pictures.

After quite some time had passed we left the enchanting view and continued our journey towards the station.

When we got to the end of the bridge, we turned around to grasp the magnitude of its size. Boy, what an engineering feat! As we gawked over the bridge, I noticed a sign that said, "No photography allowed on the bridge." I looked at my mom and said, " Oops. Oh well. Not much we can do about that now." We both thought it was very odd that photography wasn't allowed, and we never did find out why.

Just in the distance stood the train station. It was most impressive. I thought it looked more like a massive fort or castle. It was a bright mango-looking color and built in 1854. It felt like a small town when we got inside. As we wandered, I got very sad and lonely.. I was watching thousands and thousands of people coming and going.

Some of the people were moving with intention and purpose and others just drifting. Drifting with no purpose. I felt like I was drifting myself. I was just going through the motions of the day with no direction, intention or purpose, and it felt so wasteful. We had watched days turn into weeks, and weeks turn into months, and still here we were standing on a train platform staring at a woman sitting in a train car with the words Women Only written on the side.

Eight hours later my mom and I dragged ourselves through the door of our room at the Astoria. We were soaked to the bone, hungry and ready for a hot shower. We knew we wouldn't be getting a hot shower, but at least we could get our wet clothes off.

We were again getting low on our cell phone minutes, but we agreed we'd each make a phone call that evening. I was glad when my mom was able to talk to my dad on the phone. We were happy when we heard he only had to stay in the hospital for a few days while they monitored his heart issue. That was a huge relief for both of us.

As my mom spoke to my dad that evening, she suddenly started laughing and said, "Oh my gosh, these flip-flops are two different sizes." We both continued to laugh as she said, "One is a size eight and the other is an eleven." The belly laughing continued and tears flowed down our cheeks. Neither of these sizes was correct, she needed a nine. She finished up the conversation with my dad and handed the phone to me so I could call Sean.

Our conversation started off with any news we needed to report. I also wanted to share what my mom and I had done that day. As I told him about the amazing bridge experience, I mentioned the sign I saw later at the end of the bridge. Our conversation got ugly very quickly.

He started chiming in. "What the f#@k are you doing? Can't you listen? Can't you read what the sign says? If you could, maybe you should do what it says! Maybe if you could, you and your mom wouldn't be stuck over there in the first place!"

He went on and on. I hunched over in the chair. I felt pain in my heart. The pain was actually physically manifesting in the organ of my heart. This told me something. I couldn't even get two words in edgewise. What was there to even say? I had given this man my heart, but the words I love you didn't seem to mean anything anymore.

That's not love. I didn't feel safe with him. He was heavy, and there was darkness. I knew I couldn't live my life like this. I hung up the phone not wanting to make eye contact with my mom. My head was totally confused and my heart physically sick.

Chapter 16
The Godfather And The Terminator

If you want to awaken all of humanity then awaken yourself; if you want to eliminate the suffering in the world then eliminate all that is dark and negative in yourself.

Truly the greatest gift you have to give is that of your own self-transformation

Lao Tzu

Another week of our lives had gone by before we finally got the green light we needed to fly back to Siliguri.

We understood once we got back we'd be waiting on a court date. We weren't even sure what exactly the court hearing would be about. We just wanted to go home. The way I saw the whole court situation was this: I'd believe it when it happened. We were glad to at least be getting back to see Mr. Chatterjee. We had corresponded with him the whole time we were in Kolkata.

269

When my mom and I arrived back to our room in Siliguri, all the workers were happy and surprised to see us.

That night we placed our usual room service order and happened to get our favorite guy. As usual he didn't disappoint us with his poetically wonderful presentation of the food.

The phone rang shortly after dinner and it was Mr. Chatterjee. He sounded very excited. He told us he'd be stopping by for a quick chat. Curious as to his excitement, we sat on pins and needles until he arrived.

It wasn't until around 9:30 that night that he rang us. He came to our room for the meeting. The anticipation was killing me, and then he said, "We have court date in the morning."

We all looked at each other. Then my mom hesitantly said, "Will this decide if we get to go home?" He looked at both of us and drew himself up a bit. "Yes, yes this could mean that the papers were approved."

I heard a keyword in that sentence that made me a bit leery. "What do you mean, could?" I didn't like the sound. We'd had our hopes up so many times I wasn't about to be let down again.

Mr. Chatterjee side nodded a couple of times and said, "There could be some conditions, but I don't know." Oh boy, I thought to myself and said, "What kind of conditions do you think there could be?" Both my mom and I took a deep breath. He continued to explain that our case was so far out of his hands at that point that he didn't know.

The morning came quickly. We left extra early for our walk down to the courts. We had walked this route so many times that it felt comfortable to us. We had become regulars on these streets, and we waved to various familiar faces. We arrived with plenty of time to spare.

270

Chapter 16 - The Godfather And The Terminator

There was no sign of Mr. Chatterjee for some time. It made us a bit nervous so we put a call in to him. No answer. Just as I hung up the phone, he came driving up on his scooter. He was dressed really sharp. He was very focused and I think a bit nervous. I know I was incredibly nervous.

Mr. Chatterjee had both of us sign a document, and then he disappeared into one of the rooms. My mom and I waited outside. A short while later, he emerged from the room and had us each sign two more papers. Again he turned and walked into a different room.

It was nearing 11 in the morning when he popped back out. This time he said with a very serious tone, "Mr. S. will be here in the upper court room at 12:30." It was interesting the energy that was held in that comment. Mr. Chatterjee informed us he'd be back to get us at that time. So, as always, my mom and I sat and waited.

I wasn't sure if Mr. S. would already be in the upper room waiting. We had never been in that area before. My heart rate sped up as we got close to the doors. My last encounter with this man left me wanting to choke him. My mom and I linked arms as Mr. Chatterjee opened the door.

I did a quick scan of the people in the room but didn't see Mr. S. This room was very different than the ones downstairs. This was bigger, cleaner and had more of an official presence to it. There were cases already in session and being heard. We found seats and sat down.

The double doors swung open. A man in a nice suit walked into the room while being escorted by two guards. The entire courtroom stopped. A silence came over the room. I could hear the tapping of the men's feet as they walked by us. Every person in that courtroom stood up except for the judge. The guards stopped.

The man approached the judge, who sat higher up on a raised platform.

The man handed the judge a piece of paper then turned to the audience and looked out towards us. It was Mr.S. like the Godfather himself.

Mr. Chatterjee handed us a duplicate of what the Godfather delivered to the judge. The judge looked in awe at the paper. My mom and I glanced down at our copy. We noticed, it had been signed by The Terminator, the then governor of California, Arnold Schwarzenegger.

It was time. The conditions were read. "Yes, your honor, we understand."

Yet I didn't understand what he was reading. I heard that we would be getting our passports back and would be cleared to leave the country. The conditions were spoken.

Mr. S approached us outside the courtroom. Stern, direct and impersonal, he said, "You understand that you are being given three months return to the U.S. on a humanitarian leave to take care of personal affairs. You will return in September and relinquish your passports back to the authorities and stand trial for your crime. Remember this is a charge with a sentence of three to seven years."

My heart dropped and tears flowed down my face. I didn't remember hearing the judge say all that. I looked this cold-hearted man in the eye and said, "Yes, I agree to that."

Three days later and passports in hand, we were told the conditions again. This time they were delivered by one of the kindest souls I had met, Mr. Chatterjee. Without the presence of this man, our time in India would have been far more challenging than it was.

Chapter 16 - The Godfather And The Terminator

From the beginning he made himself open and available to us. He was always professional yet his heart was warm and caring. There was something special about this person. He was able to open his heart to two unknown women and support them on their difficult journey. We honored him for being real and authentic.

When it was time for him to deliver our legal conditions in his own words, it was challenging for me. He had driven his scooter over to see us off to the airport. It was awkward I'm sure, for all of us. I had absolutely no intention of coming back to stand trial. I knew I'd cross that bridge when the time came. Yet I didn't want to look my friend in the eyes and lie to him. So I created an energetic message.

I wanted him to know my intentions without saying the words. I forged the clarity and energy strong from within me. He surely was going to feel the message. He looked at us with a look of kindness and friendship. The look that said, "Wow, what a journey this has been. I will never forget you" But what he really said was, "So, we'll see you in three months time?"

I sent him my energetic message as powerfully as I could with as much love and appreciation and said, "Yes."

I felt he got my message. I then redirected the conversation by talking about me writing this book. We thanked him for everything he'd done for us. He had probably done more than we'll ever know. We both gave him a huge hug, and he drove away.

I sat silently staring out the window of the plane as we headed home, back to the states. I felt empty and sad inside. There was a heavy, unspoken division between my mom and me. It was heart wrenching. I was so confused about my relationship with Sean. I was confused about everything we'd all just gone through, and I wasn't sure how to deal with it.

One part of me was saying that the relationship between Sean and me was over. Then, this weak, broken voice in my head that had arrived alongside my injury would try to justify and make excuses for him. I cried and cried.

We were supposed to have a massive, joyful welcome home party, like the one we planned months ago in prison. We had visualized everyone being so happy with all kinds of our favorite foods and us hugging everyone over and over. But that was not to be.

I know now that the higher powers within me and around me had only begun the journey.

Epilogue

Tears of complexity flow down my cheeks as I sit here in one of my favorite little coffee houses in my beautiful hometown of Santa Barbara.

It's been almost 10 years to the day since my mom and I boarded a plane that sent us halfway around the world.

For me it was a spiritual quest, and for my mom and me it became a mother and daughter's odyssey that would change our lives forever. I cry for our journey and I cry for the process of my internal struggle that took me into my darkest depths, places so ugly that I never could have imagined them. I was stripped down until there was nothing left but my magnificent soul.

I was forcing myself to put on a happy face. I was anxious and my heart was pounding. I had a little sense of relief to know we were back on American soil and that my mom would be home safely with my dad. But I was devastated by the feeling and visual that pierced through me when my mom and I walked out from behind the doors at the airport.

I saw my dad, my brother and Sean all spread out and standing alone in different areas. I scanned back and forth looking at each one of them. My dad had tears flowing down his cheeks and a warm, wonderful, welcoming smile.

My brother stood happy and neutral in the situation.

Sean had that all-too-familiar strained look on his face that didn't feel welcoming. In his own way and mind he may have been really happy to see me, but so much had happened.

My mom and I walked to my dad first, and we all hugged and cried. Then I felt almost obligation rather than wanting to go to Sean and hug him. All I can say now is I felt awkward, empty and extremely confused. I walked towards him. I wanted so much to feel happy. I wanted everything to be great. I wanted to be happy and joyful, but I wasn't. But like I had been doing since my injury, I pretended I was. I put on my "fake happy."

The reality of the division hit really hard when my mom walked over to me and said, "We're leaving now. We'll talk later." We held each other. She turned, and I watched my brother, my father and my best friend, my mother, walk away and leave me standing there to face my demons.

I wanted so badly to be walking away with them in a safe, loving environment. But the universe works in mysterious ways. It listens to our deepest desires. It has the ability to answer those desires although it may not be the way we envisioned it.

Sean's and my conversation on the way home was strained. I didn't have much to say. I'd like to have thought it was the shock of being back on American soil that had me tongue-tied, but it was deeper than that. We were about 30 minutes from being home and we were driving along a beautiful ocean stretch of the freeway when I noticed Sean get a bit fidgety. He put on his blinker to exit the freeway.

My heart started to speed up and not in a positive way. I felt that he was going to pull off the road and want to have sex. I say "sex" because there was no love or passion.

Shoot, I no longer felt safe with him. Then that internal overriding voice interrupted my gut feelings and said, "Just do it and get it over with. It's been months."

I had absolutely no desire to have sex with him. I wanted to make love to a man who made me feel safe and loved me for all that I am. But at that time in my life I didn't even know who I was myself.

Then I knew. I knew in that very moment that Sean had impregnated me. But there was a negative charge connected. It made me cringe. Even knowing what I know now, the thought still makes me shudder. I felt like he had the energy of revenge on his mind. Not love. I believe I felt the energy waves he sent out to the universe with his energetic scream. It said, " F@#k you, Larry, I'll always be a part of Heather's life." (Larry is my dad.)

I tried to push the whole experience aside. I wanted to focus on finding a sense of normalcy. There was no warm, welcome home party or yummy food and balloons. I continued to struggle to find my place among all this destruction.

I listened to Sean demean my parents while I defended them. Then my dad would barrage me with all the crazy things Sean had said and done. I found myself defending him too. I felt trapped in the middle of a tangled web.

One day shortly after my mom and I had gotten back, Sean asked if we were still planning on having a wedding. I let him know that with all that was going on it wasn't going to happen without my parents. He told me, if we're not getting married now, with or without them, we're not going to get married at all.

I wasn't one of those little girls that dreamed of having a big wedding but I did know this: if and when I was to get married, my parents would be there.

Again I dismissed that conversation and brought in excuses for his behavior. Maybe it's me, and I'm overreacting. Maybe I am being sensitive and making it into something it's not. Perhaps this sounds familiar and some may relate. Maybe if I just talk a bit softer or dumb down my vocabulary he'll love me more. Yet all this was doing was having me shrink and give my power away to someone else. Piece by piece my heart continued to shatter.

Why does one stay? I couldn't answer that question then, but I can now. We've all got our stuff and our stories. Hopefully you're strong enough to get through the tunnel to the light. There are certain people in life that are like vampires. They're those individuals who seem to thrive and prey on people when they are weak. They will keep kicking you when you're down and make you believe it's you with the issues.

Within a week or so of getting back home, Sean had done a great job of making me feel so uncomfortable about my relationship with my parents that I walked down the road in search of consolation from my lifelong friend Blue.

He happened to be my first love. He and I dated from age 15 to 26 and I had known him since I was 11 years old.

I remember telling Blue and his then girlfriend that what was happening at home with Sean was so ugly I'd rather be back in the prison.

They were a bit shocked by that statement, but it was the truth. I appreciated them listening to me vent. After I got home from their place, Sean questioned where I had been. I told him. He then accused me of going down there to sleep with Blue. I was in complete shock. Where does that mentality come from? I thought, you've got to be fricken kidding me. But, with my weak state of mind, I quickly thought, what more can I do to make him know that I love him. Or loved him.

In our tumultuous relationship, the one place that we could find a sense of peace and common ground was on our adventures. At least while the endorphins were in full swing. So we decided to pack up his truck and try to make things better by taking off on a 10-day, adrenaline-packed adventure. But though there were moments of fun there was an ever-present fissure between us.

Like many parents with their kids grown up and pushing into their late 30s, my parents had been waiting years for me to have a child. If they had had it their way, it would have happened years prior when Blue and I were together.

When I got the official confirmation that I was pregnant, in some deep emotional way I felt like I had betrayed my parents' love. In the past I had visions of me running to my parents, excited, happy and full of joy. But again that wasn't to be. Instead I contemplated how I was going to break this news to them. I couldn't get myself to tell them.

The vision etched in my mind of the night of conception haunted me. Then I remembered my sacred ceremony I performed high in the mountains in Darjeeling. I prayed to have a child. I remembered I had made an agreement with God and the universe that if I was to be blessed with that great gift, I would love that child with every ounce of my being, with or without a man by my side.

So, on a warm, bright, sunny morning in October of 2008, right around my mom's birthday, I finally got the courage to tell her

I was already over three months pregnant, and that she and my dad were going to be grandparents. I wasn't attached to a certain reaction. I knew that she would be happy for me. She was happy that her daughter would get to become a mother and experience its joys. But she was heartbroken for the situation that existed around such a sacred gift.

There was never a word spoken between my parents and Sean throughout my entire pregnancy. Many times I questioned myself as to what I was doing staying in this divided relationship with Sean. I deliberately spent hours alone in nature. I hiked and explored while humming. I wanted to give this magnificent little creature growing inside me the tranquil beauty and peace that is found in the rhythms of nature.

Keely Shay was born at 11:05 p.m. on April 25, 2009, ten months almost to the minute of her conception. She came into this world loved by all. She had 10 family members waiting to see her in the waiting room. She had both sets of her grandparents, her uncles, auntie and two cousins. I will never forget that moment when the doctor set her on me. Her plump, fresh, collagen-filled cheek rested on my lips, I inhaled her smell, and I whispered the words, "You are a silent warrior, and I love you with all my potential."

When my dad first held Keely, he called her the peacemaker. Ironically on the day she was born there was a picture of his Holiness the Dalai Lama on the front of our local newspaper. When my dad said these words, my gut reacted. I thought to myself, No, she's not the peacemaker. We all need to find the peace within ourselves.

The road to peace and forgiveness is a process. It can be a long, lonely and painful journey. I was desperately searching to find this within myself. I was embracing being a new mom with an open heart. Unfortunately my heart had been shattered. I was not able to give myself to her fully because I wasn't whole. Sean's and my relationship continued to decline.

I constantly searched for ways to make our relationship work. I knew I needed help. I befriended a beautiful woman I had met through a networking event and she became one of my spiritual mentors.

She suggested when the time was right I should look into participating in a 10-day silent Vipassana meditation retreat. It's a very challenging undertaking for most. The retreats are held throughout the world, and there happened to be a center deep within the mountains, about a five hour drive from home.

The many retreat participants take a vow of silence for 10 days and learn the deep process of Vipassana meditation.

Letter to my parents February 7, 2012

Dear Ma & Pa,

It is my sixth day at Vipassana. Today has been a big day for cleansing. It's raining and I started my period two weeks early. I have shed many tears. We meditate approx. eight-ish hours a day. Today we got to go into the new pagoda.

It's a beautiful white temple that has a maze of single cell rooms for isolation. They're not more that three feet wide and not much longer really.

Vipassana is one of India's most ancient meditation techniques. It was rediscovered by Gautama the Buddha more than 2,500 years ago. Vipassana means seeing things as they really are. It's the process of self-purification by self-observation.

One begins by observing the natural breath to concentrate the mind. With a sharpened awareness, one proceeds to observe the changing nature of the body and mind and experiences the universal truths of suffering and egolessness. The truth realization by direct experience is the process of purification.

Today I cried for all of us, mom, dad, Sean and myself, over our reactions to India. I felt the pain, anger, sadness, hurt and helplessness for each of us at the deepest level. As I sat there in a dark cell crying, I visualized us all wanting the same common goal but being four totally different souls we all reacted differently and that's okay.

I'm sure we all felt like a dagger plunged through our hearts and planted a root of pain very deep within our souls. This is a big part of why I'm here. To uproot the guilt, anger and pain of what transpired. I asked today to leave or uproot these feelings and to know that, that's what was, but this is what today is.

I wish to be free of these feelings of the past. As much as I love what was said about Keely being the peacemaker, the real peace must come from within each one of us. That's what I am seeking for myself. I love you both more than words could ever say and I hope that if I've said or have done anything to hurt you I ask for your forgiveness.

Forever & Always
Pauge Wauge xoxoxo

It was a deep and profound experience for me. The surprising thing was when I sat and contemplated on the final day, the message I received from myself was to have a wedding. How crazy that sounds to me now. I wanted for this relationship to work for our daughter's sake. For us to be a loving family unit like the one my brother and I grew up in. But, again, it's a journey.

When I suggested to Sean that we get married, his response was, "Well, I don't want to get legally married." Alarms sounded in my gut.

My nagging voice of justification set in. Well you know there are a lot of people that don't get legally married, even when I couldn't think of anyone. But I shrank. Who was this wedding really for? Now we had our precious little daughter, and a part of me held on to the hope that perhaps this ceremony would fix it all.

I wasn't the only one in my family struggling with demons.

My brother, Ian, had hit rock bottom with his drinking; it affected everyone. Soon after I got back from Vapasana he informed me he was going to turn himself in. My first thought when he said this was, what did you do?

I thought he meant turn himself into the police for a possible crime. It turned out he'd come to a place of realization; if he didn't get help and stop drinking he was going to die sooner rather than later.

I was a bit cynical about his initial announcement. I had watched his torturous attempts of self-detoxification. I had been an enabler to him for many years but after Keely was born and I was sinking in my own turmoil, tough love became the answer. The only positive part I could see at the moment was his admission that he had a problem. Furthermore he needed and wanted help.

As my mom and I drove away from dropping Ian off at a local detoxification center in our hometown, I turned to my mom, shrugged my shoulders, and in a snarky tone said, "Well, we've seen him detox himself many times, we'll see what happens."

My mom's eyes looked sad but hopeful, "Well you just never know. This could be the start of a new beginning for him," she said in an optimistic way. In my heart I agreed. I just knew he would need help after he detoxed.

Humans have an amazing capacity and ability to change our circumstances. We need only to recognize the problem and create a new reality for our life. This is exactly what Ian did. He spent the next year and a half living at the Santa Barbara Rescue Mission where he learned new tools and ways of being a proactive human free of addiction. But could he sustain this? Many don't.

His internal journey when he moved back home continued. While living at the Rescue Mission he had put on a solid 25 pounds of extra weight. He'd always been lean built so this was different. Once he settled into daily life I started nudging him to come train with me.

Our training started off as gentle hikes for the first week or so. Ian's pace started picking up. On the way back from a hike one afternoon he looked at me with a familiar look, and said "I think I need a goal."

I felt he had me in mind to be a part of the plan. "What were you thinking? I said with a bit of excitement in my voice.

"Well, what would you do now race wise?" he said this with concern for my spine injury. At this point I had definitely healed from my fire department injury yet had resigned myself to the fact I'd probably never race again.

However, I got butterflies just thinking about the possibilities. "Well, I'd have to really put my thinking cap on and see what's happening these days on the race circuit," I said with a bit of trepidation.

The next day on our hike we were like two school kids talking about our new bicycles. We both had done tons of research the evening prior. We named a few options of possible smaller adventure races but none seemed to light us up until Ian said, "I was looking at this 7 day stage race through the Sahara Desert called Racing The Planet; The 4Deserts Series."

I could see him watching for my reaction as he continued to say, "It looks pretty cool, it's all running." I couldn't believe what I was hearing "Oh my gosh!" I blurted out. "This has been on my race bucket list". We both lit up; it was a done deal. Now all we had to do was get the race organization to accept our applications and start training hard.

By the time Ian and I stepped foot on a plane to take us to the 4Deserts race we were heading to the Atacama Desert in Chile and not the Sahara in Egypt. Due to the civil unrest that was happening in Egypt in 2014, the race moved to Jordan, and we thought it best to switch race locations given my imprisonment.

Ian and I clocked thousands of miles running, hiking and sometimes crawling by the time we boarded that plane. We raced in a number of ultra marathons along the way. We were prepared and ready. For me the training process with my brother was an amazing and special journey unto itself. We trained like soldiers; focused and deliberate. Though it was grueling at times we always seemed to be laughing and smiling. I watched and witnessed his metamorphosis.

The race was a seven-day, self-supported stage race through the Atacama Desert, the driest desert on the planet.

No small feat, but we were ready. In this race the competitors carry all their own gear, food and water for the duration of the race while running a minimum of a marathon everyday.

The terrain that we'd be running through can only be described as looking like Mars; harsh, barren, desolate land. Actually this is where NASA does their Mars training. Though at first glance it may seem void of life, vegetation, or water, it has hidden wonders.

It is a high altitude desert and the starting line sat just below 12,000 feet. Ian and I had set daily goals. A trick of the trade in racing is to get your pack as light as possible.

We had ripped the labels from most of our gear to shave off ounces of weight. This wasn't camping. We had done a great job of compiling high caloric healthy foods that could sustain us and didn't weigh a ton. Our goal was to start and finish the race together.

The Atacama Desert is extreme in many ways. When it comes to the weather, it's no different. While day temperatures soar into the high nineties plus, the nights dip to freezing levels.

Each racer is assigned a specific tent to sleep in throughout the duration of the race, eight of us per tent. Only a thin layer of canvas separates you and the permafrost ground below which made for an extremely long cold first night. Temperatures rose as we dropped in elevation along the course.

Grateful for morning light, I couldn't shake the pain and cold I felt in two of my toes. Later on I realized they had succumbed to a mild case of frostbite but thankfully I only lost my toenails.

On day one Ian and I surpassed our goal time. We were excited about our position we established and felt strong regardless of the toes.

Day two was a longer day. The first section of this twenty-eight mile leg took us into a magical slot canyon filled with freezing cold temperature water. Quite a shock on the body but Ian and I were in our element. We preferred scrambling on various types of terrain rather than straight running.

I led the way into the canyon that morning; I felt alive. We were doing a good job at passing others and maintaining a nice position through this section. Ahead of me I noticed the competitors getting into a bottleneck at a technical section.

Ian blurted out, "Go to your right." I didn't question his call. Without delay or breaking my stride I shifted my direction back into the river to avoid the bottleneck. As my left foot plunged through the icy water it got wedged between two rocks and with my body's momentum my right foot slipped, forcing my body to snap forward over my trapped leg. I heard a noise and felt pain shoot through my knee as I lay in the water.

I looked at Ian as I pulled my foot free and said, "I think I've done something to my knee."

He quickly started helping me hoist my body from the frigid waters. He knew that I wouldn't have complained unless I felt I had sustained some form of injury.

"I should be okay, maybe we just slow it down for a bit." I said with a slightly agitated tone. He had a concerned look on his face but agreed.

I was wearing a special type of compression legging that not only helps keep the muscles compressed, they also help in cold conditions. However, from being completely soaked to the bone in the water it took me a while to warm up. As my body thawed I felt my knee start to swell and throb.

As I struggled through the miles the pain worsened and I ignored it, pushing the pain aside. I have trained myself to mentally endure tremendous amounts of physical and emotional pain. It can help at times but not when you're inflicting more harm to yourself.

I stared up at a massive razor-like ridgeline that lay ahead of us and told Ian I was going to take off. He looked at me like I was crazy. But as strange as it sounds I needed to go at my own pace to get to the top. I saw a string of competitors slowly death marching this hill and I made it my mission to pass as many as I could. I think it helped keep my mind off the pain.

I pole positioned most every person I saw on that hill that day. But we still had some of the hardest miles to cross over the giant red sand dunes. They were a sight to behold.

Unfortunately it came at a painful cost. My knee had started bruising and I couldn't keep the swelling down. I felt as though I was on a forced march through the hot barren desert. I couldn't wait to get into camp and elevate my knee and have the medic take a look.

After twenty-five miles of misery I saw the white-tented camp in the distance. I know my brother was relieved to finally get there too. He had endured the painful, slow crawl alongside me for the last ten miles when he could have jogged. I felt bad.

I was also hopeful that an evening of rest and some good pain pills would do the trick and have me back on my feet for the morning.

Unfortunately the swelling didn't go down through the night as planned but I got some rest and it was a new day.

Day three had begun and I found myself standing alongside my brother with my pack on, race ready but wounded. The swelling had increased through the night and left my calf, ankle and foot feeling as though they were going to burst. Ian wasn't convinced with my decision to continue but he supported me.

As we took our positions at the start line I asked Ian if we could stand off to the side; I didn't want to be in the thick of the pack. We had been warned about the terrain we were going to encounter for the first ten plus miles.

Racers refer to it as frozen broccoli. They're mounds of permafrost earth that jut from the surface of the ground like a giant head of broccoli; it can be hazardous to uninjured knees and ankles.

As the starting gun fired to get the third leg of the race underway I knew it would be a long day. Within a few hundred yards we hit the hellacious terrain. My already compromised pace shifted into a lower gear. I've raced through many types of terrain but never had I experienced anything like this unpalatable broccoli.

With no trail to lead the way my gait veered in many directions to avoid the bigger chunks of earth mounds. I started feeling as though I was in a nightmarish virtual reality video game as the miles came and went. I watched my brother full of energy and free from injury moving efficiently ahead of me. He'd stop to wait and check on my wobbling failing body. I would tell him, "I've got this. I'll just be slower." With a strained smile he'd take off again.

Ian became a blur in the distance and no one else was around me in this stark landscape. My mind started to get angry and wander. The past two years of training had brought my brother and I closer than ever. I cherished that. However through this time the turmoil from Sean and India still haunted my personal life and took me deeper into a hellish nightmare.

The odds had been stacked against me. It was amazing I had even made it to the race.

Six months prior to our race departure I had finally had enough of Sean's behavior.

Sadly, three-year old Keely had to endure two people that happened to be her mommy and daddy become ugly with one another. Yes, there had been a non-legal wedding ceremony and had two people been madly in love with each other it would have been a magical day.

Sean's accusations of me having multiple affairs had gotten out of hand. Our daughter witnessed me become a punching bag for his verbal abuse. His behavior got so bizarre I questioned my own sanity. I slowly grew numb, and what little light that was left in me went dim.

The stress started physically taking a toll on my heart, not to mention that I was still pushing hard training miles through this time. I was physically weak and severely anemic.

Both my parents and I felt I could have a heart attack. I told myself, "If you don't leave this relationship you're going to die." I sought medical attention.

Back on the frozen broccoli of the Atacama Desert I was in a battle; my heart and my ego where having a show down. My heart was starting to show signs of physical pain as these thoughts swirled. My leg was so painful that I was taking one step forward and literally two steps sideways to counter the pain of hitting that foul broccoli.

I am grateful that Sean and I never legally married. When he moved out we made a handshake agreement on 50/50 custody of our daughter. There was nothing else, and I mean nothing.

Uncontrollable tears flowed down my salty cheeks in that dry wasteland. I started losing my composure. My attention was being pulled to the most heart shattering experience to date. It had happened four months prior to leaving for the race, two months after Sean moved out.

It was June 28, my parent's anniversary; I had just finished a two-day vision-quest. I had numerous messages waiting on my phone. I received a call that rocked me to the core. I was told that my life-long friend, my first love, was found dead.

I cursed to myself and God in the desert that day. I screeched out, "Why?" No one could hear me. At this point Ian looked like a mirage.

I wrestled with thoughts of death and regret. How could my oldest friend on the planet be dead? I'd never see him again. I had just spoken to him. He was a new dad. He just told me what a wonderful father's day he had. I hit absolute rock bottom.

That day in the desert became another layer ripping away from me towards my own transformation.

I struggled back and forth with this pain of loss, separation from Sean, all the time and money that went into this race, and now my leg.

My mind raced. How could I get injured in water in the driest desert on earth? My ego didn't want to surrender. Then this softer more wise side of me, probably my soul, shouted back, "What more do you have to prove?"

It caught me off guard. "Yeah, I'm talking to you, what more do you have to prove." I started to listen.

There was a demon and an angel having this conversation. I became the observer. I cried as I stumbled around. I thought to myself, what do you have to prove?

This has been Ian's journey for his recovery. Growing up I always felt he took a back seat to my competitive exploits. One of the voices chimed in, yeah, this is Ian's journey. He's come so far. You're slowing him down. Let him run this race. My ego was testing me. This isn't about you, Heather. This is about helping someone, your brother, do the impossible. This is his time to shine, let him go.

Calmness came over me with this realization.

As if choreographed Ian began running back towards me. He had no idea of what had been transpiring the last eight miles. As he neared I could see tears rolling down his checks.
"You know Heath you don't have to do this," he said with concern written all over his face. I looked at him with a smile and said, "I know, I'm done."

He looked shocked at my quick response. I told him I'd pull out at the next checkpoint. It was another half mile or so in the distance. He told me how much he loved me and didn't want to see me damage myself anymore.

Since injuring my knee I had pushed thirty-six painful miles. I told Ian to run ahead to the CP and let them know I was dropping out. As he turned to run away he looked back and said, "Do you want me to take your pack for you?"

I looked at him and laughed and said, "Hey, I've still got some ego left."

Sadly I did not finish the race. I did, however, continue to rove with my brother and tent mates. When Ian left me at the checkpoint that day he was in second to last place due to my injury. That afternoon when he finished that leg of the race he had moved up from the back of the pack to 82nd out of a field of approximately 170.

Four days later when Ian crossed the official finish line no words could describe how proud I was of his journey.

Shortly after my return from the Atacama I received the most disturbing text message from Sean accusing me of being an unfit and dirty mother to Keely. It was graphic, and it disgusted me to the core. These accusations continued. I threatened to take legal action, but I wasn't strong enough at the time. So I did nothing.

He still had a hold on me and we didn't even live together. I continued to engage in self-help groups and seminars. I spent thousands of dollars trying to find and own my power.

Some would fire me up for a short period of time. I was trying to understand that I am inherently worthy of a beautiful, joy-filled life, as all of us are. But I continued to flounder with my business and personal life.

I was supporting my daughter and myself, but just barely. I had no clarity of vision. No matter what I tried, I wasn't shifting my life force to where I wanted to take it.

I continued to be concerned for my daughter's mental wellbeing while in the care of her father. This was eating at me. His behavior was so bizarre at times it frightened me.

When outside sources started speaking about his behavior, I knew this was another sign that I needed to step out of my comfort zone and do something about it.

I had always been a strong, independent woman before my injury. People had no idea how weak-minded I had become. I couldn't believe it myself. I felt like I hid it well, always putting on my happy face. But I was struggling to find peace within myself. I certainly had more work to do before I could forgive Sean or myself.

I met someone shortly after Sean moved out who became one of my spiritual guides. Actually he's more like a strong, ass-kicking guide. He's passionate about guiding others to know their inherent worth. He gave me a compass, but not in the physical sense. He didn't physically hand me a compass; he gave me tools and taught me a process to reclaim my power.

It's called the True North Compass. It's a tool that every human being on the planet can utilize so they can live their life in integrity and to their highest potential.

Guess what I learned: I am that gal who wants to live her life to her highest potential. I am that gal who has run into burning buildings while others ran out, who has pronounced other human beings dead on tragic scenes, who has jumped off two-story buildings and landed on a small airbag below. I am that gal who has jumped out of planes, who has rappelled out of helicopters, who has raced thousand of miles through third world countries with Navy Seals and Marine recons. I am that gal who sat in prison with her mother in a foreign country. I am that gal that gave birth to the most magnificent little soul and I refuse to give away my power any longer.

What does a person need to do to emerge back into their light? They need to confront their demons and fears head on. So I looked myself in the eye through a mirror and said, "No more will I give my power away to anyone else. This is where it stops."

I found a wonderful paper given to me, written by a dear friend and it speaks volumes:

Epilogue

Heather's energy is a mysterious force with phenomenal power.

It was last seen in and around a beautiful woman. Her force can be recognized by a flowing grace and elegance that is encased in rainbow like hues and features.

The power created allows her to walk tall and perform almost magical physical feats. You will be able to pick her out of a crowd because she will have a smile and a sense of confidence that exudes from her very being. Her mind will be full of songs and she will be dreaming of a world to be explored.

Unfortunately last reports of Heather's wellbeing are less than encouraging. Her aura was characterized as faded and her eyes lacked the usual luster that normally glistens in the sunlight. Her thoughts have been cloudy and consumed with negativity and self-doubt.

If Heather's energy is found it needs to be reacquainted with her immediately. The universal consciences are greatly affected by her loss. The implications of this drop in the force can have profound consequences. The results of which may manifest themselves in the form as an increase in natural disaster's, governments being over thrown, football seasons being canceled due to lack of interest, or worse!

Heather herself will stop dreaming. If this trend is allowed to continue the forces of evil will be strengthened by this apparent loss of her energy within the cosmos.

A word of warning; Approach her cautiously. She may not recognize that you are there to help. While her life energy is low her power is still great and it may be under the influence of the dark side. The dark side realizes she is vulnerable and is doing everything in its power to take advantage of this disturbance within the galaxy.

So how do we get Heather back before it's too late? The council has determined that there is only one way to break her out of this fog of despair. Take her by hand, carefully, and gingerly guide her to the nearest mirror of truth. The mirror does not judge it does not lie it does not pretend.

The mirror of truth makes you take a long look, not at what you can see at the surface but at what you see when you look beyond the corporal image and begin to see what lies within. Have her focus on not the visible but on the invisible. Have her feel the life force that lies silently waiting to be rediscovered. She will begin to realize that she has lost none of her energy. Her energy is right in front of her it has always been there, she need only peer deep within herself to find what she never lost.

But be prepared for possible resistance from her. She has been consumed with less than positive affirmations for sometime now. Therefore, do not let her wander off do not let her do anything else but stare deep within the mirror of truth until she begins to smile again at who she truly is.

Watch her body language, as it will begin to relax, as if she has found an old friend within herself. Have her notice the colors that surround her begin to brighten, her eyes will begin to reflect the energy within and her thoughts will begin to flow freely toward eternity. Remind her the mirror will always lead her back!

With the full love and moral support of my parents, on July 11, 2017, I had Sean served with official "court ordered" papers. I was filing for full legal and physical custody of our daughter. Along with the papers, I also had them deliver a heartfelt, handwritten letter of my intentions. I wasn't planning on taking Keely's dad out of her life. I wanted him to get professional help. His delusional thinking and volatile anger had hit an alarming level. I needed to protect my daughter and myself at all costs.

When I arrived at this decision to file, it was absolutely the last thing I wanted to do. I had no desire to drag my personal affairs into the convoluted legal system. But I realized on a much deeper level that if I didn't, my life would continue to swirl around the thoughts of good enough is good enough. And it's not.

So I made another agreement with God and the universe. My agreement was this, "I am doing this for the best and highest good of all involved in this no matter what the outcome." I felt the entire universe shift when I declared this. I was in absolute earth energy and with every ounce of my being I declared these words. These words became my mantra morning and night.

The key piece to this agreement was, "No matter what the outcome." I had to release and surrender to all that was.

I couldn't be attached. I became a powerful warrior and mama bear. I held my daughter from seeing her father for 40 days. He claimed I'd kidnapped her. I didn't care. This became the hardest part of this decade-long journey, and it got ugly.

Given my situation at the time, I had to go the route of self-representation in court. Most people said this was a terrible idea. They thought I would be eaten alive by the opposing attorney. I did, however, get legal aid through the family courts.

Sean hired a cutthroat attorney. We'll call her Ms. C. She was tall and slender. I stand five feet seven inches tall and she towered over me in height. She was morally and ethically bankrupt.

I knew from the very first contact with this woman I had a challenge ahead. She seemed just as power hungry and manipulative as Sean, if not more so. She tried to intimidate me and threw around her legal authority from the beginning. She accused me of kidnapping my own daughter. Then she threatened me to drop the case or she'd have charges pressed against me. I looked her square in the eye and let her know that I was fully prepared to face any and all matters regarding this case.

We never know where life is going to lead us. What I do know is that we can't control what life or other people may throw at us, but we can absolutely control how we react and respond. This is our responsibility as individuals. This is where we need to strengthen our emotional muscles. The stronger that muscle becomes, we find that we stop living in the past and replaying our old stories.

We can't change others' perceptions and beliefs, whether morally or ethically. This isn't our job. The greatest gift we can give to others and ourselves is to become and live in the states of peace, joy and happiness.

With the help of my mom and dad, I spent hours compiling mind-boggling, destructive, and compelling evidence to present the court. I was embarrassed to hand over the graphic evidence written by the father of my daughter, someone I used to love. I became totally exposed and vulnerable by sharing how I allowed this person to treat my daughter and me so poorly.

I prepped, prepared and studied as much as I could about the legal aspect for the big court date. On a personal level I spent hours in silence building my strength to withstand whatever came my way. I continued to speak my mantra.

Going through this legal journey brought my mom, dad and me as close together as we'd always been prior to India. My mom and dad never knew what a true nightmare my relationship with Sean had become. The way I explained it to my mom was there was nothing new in this madness because I still was in the darkness. She was just now seeing the full magnitude of his behavior.

I felt badly for my mom through this time. She endured listening to Sean say terrible things to her about her own daughter, foul, insulting names and lies. Things like I am a pathological liar, a cheat, a druggie, even a dirty piece of shit.

He threatened my parents' home and land of almost thirty years by turning them into the county. My mom's health definitely suffered through this time. She allowed him to rant many times until one day she snapped. She stood up and actually called him out for what he was, a bully and a coward. That's the nice version.

When I made the decision to file for full custody, I was under the impression that the legal journey would be a long process and not cut and dry. Sean and I had never stepped foot in front of a judge for any reason. It had been three years since he'd moved out, and it was time for me to face his cutthroat attorney and the judge. I could only pray and assume that the judge had read all the nasty evidence that had been submitted by me.

When I recall that morning of our first court hearing it seems like a blur. Not in the sense that I don't remember what happened but in the sense that what transpired in the courtroom was a fast moving ambush that totally caught me off guard. (No, I will never forget what happened that morning. It's actually hard to even fathom.)

My mom, dad and I walked into the courtroom and sat down together. My heart raced as I visually scanned the courtroom. I was wearing my power slacks and shirt, a nice professional look. I took in some big deep breaths to help ground myself for what lay ahead. I noticed Sean and his parents all sitting separately. Up to this point my family had always gotten along with Sean's family, but this situation created a fissure between us.

I saw Sean's attorney along with the other attorneys checking in with the court clerk nearest the bailiff. I watched the other attorneys return to their seats but noticed that Ms. C. stayed behind. The judge quickly said into her microphone that there'd been a case pushed up the priority list, which is when Ms. C.

walked to the microphone at the podium and launched into our case without either Sean or me being present.

The judge asked if the plaintiff was present. I jumped out of my seat and headed to the low swinging doors as I responded, "Yes, your honor, I am here."

I then rushed to my microphone and adjusted it to my height. Before I had my folder open, Ms. C. started the most hurtful character assassination. I was absolutely dumbfounded. I stood strong. I listened to a woman who had no idea who I was insult me with an awful rant. She spoke so many lies to the court in an effort to convince the judge of what a horrible mother I am to my daughter. She even told the judge that my daughter was so dirty because I had barely enough water at our home to bathe her.

The saddest part was the fact that Sean and his family supported this attack. It made me sick to my stomach. I had a hard time understanding that they actually thought this beautiful, bright-eyed girl fit the picture this woman was painting. Do they actually believe this?

When I look at the legal systems from my mom's and my case in India compared to the custody case here in the states, I can see that they were two totally different experiences.

In India it may have been long and drawn out, but it never got vindictive. We knew we were guilty of possessing the bullets and ammunition and the authorities were going by their judicial system. They weren't contriving anything. It may have been a painful process, but we never felt like we were being lied to.

Yet when I stood in that courtroom in Santa Barbara, Sean's malicious attorney engaged like she had a personal vendetta against me. It seemed to me that all she cared about was winning. I would hardly call such a person an advocate for children.

Approximately eight minutes into her assault, the judge finally stopped her. She cut her off and explained that she'd already come up with a ruling. My jaw dropped to the floor.

The judge continued to say that she saw a lot of "he said, she said." I hadn't even said one word at this point. I was convinced that she hadn't seen the particular file I submitted. I asked if I could speak.

I started off by asking the judge if she'd had a chance to view the particular case-sensitive information. She stated she didn't recall seeing anything in the file regarding this. I was now more convinced than ever that she'd missed the most pertinent information. Surely if she'd seen it we'd be having a totally different conversation.

Sean's attorney continued to tell the judge that I'd somehow fabricated all the texts and email messages and that none of the information should be admissible.

The judge abruptly stopped Ms. C. from speaking. The judge said she'd already come to a decision. I braced myself as the judge ruled. I held my breath as she said, "Continuation of 50/50 custody. One week on, one week off." I thought to myself One week on, one week off? This was an entirely different schedule from what we had before. It would be the longest time period my daughter had ever been away from me.

I felt a pit form in my stomach. I felt like I was going to vomit. I wanted to scream. I wanted to cry. I couldn't understand. I thought, what's wrong with people? This isn't right.

I turned and walked back to my parents. I looked them in the eye and said, " Let's just go; I feel sick." We walked out of the courtroom.

Sean, his parents, and his attorney and her assistant were all smugly standing outside doing their victory dance.

I said nothing as I walked by them. My mom on the other hand felt compelled to speak her mind to Sean in two quick words, and we continued to leave the courthouse.

Before I knew it his attorney approached my mom and, like something out of a movie, she got into my mom's space. My mom put her hand in the air to block the woman from being in her face. What happened next looked so contrived.

Ms. C jumped back away from my mom as she screamed, "Assault! Bailiff, this woman just assaulted me!" I did a double take. Did she just really say that? No sooner had the words come from her mouth, than a bailiff came over and intervened. I stood there shaking my head in disbelief.

Ms. C formally pressed charges against my mom. Of course it ended up being dismissed and a waste of everyone's time. As Ms. C. walked away being escorted by another bailiff, I was compelled to say six words to her in a calm voice. "Thank goodness I am not you." I meant that through and through.

Shortly after shaking off that absurd situation and wanting to vomit, plan B went into effect. There was no way I was going to accept that ruling. I went into full warrior mode. My mom and I were absolutely convinced that given what the judge said about not seeing these particular items in the files we feared somehow the most pertinent evidence was over looked. My mom and I sat in our car and wrote out a list of what we needed to do. We were going to file a Motion For Reconsideration.

I never lost sight of my purpose. I spoke with a number of adults who as children had suffered abusive situations they voiced their encouragement to me because they wished that their parent had had the courage to speak up.

302

I knew I had to follow through no matter what the outcome. However, I didn't feel I was participating on a fair playing field. I needed to make sure that the referee, in which in this case was the judge, hadn't been blindsided by the tactics of my opponent, Ms. C. It's hard to believe that a ruling such as this was made in a 15-minute time span.

We made sure all the t's were crossed and the i's were dotted when we filed and served the Motion For Reconsideration.

Upon delivery to Ms. C's assistant she noticed what the paper work was and refused to accept them from me. In the past this never had been an issue. After I called my mom who was sitting in our car waiting, she walked into the office. I handed the papers to her, and she then turned and handed them to the assistant.

Within a few days I received their response to the motion. Just when you think things can't get any crazier, they usually do. I was in absolute shock as I read over the papers.

In their response, they claimed that my mom assaulted Sean's attorney and also supposedly verbally assaulted Sean. My father supposedly verbally assaulted Sean's father and I, too, verbally assaulted someone. Although I am not sure whom I'd allegedly assaulted, it all seemed like a sick circus show.

The day was October 11, 2017. I didn't know what to expect on that day in court. Perhaps the judge had a chance to read the evidence, and she would change the court ruling as quickly as she made the first. Maybe the judge would decide that this case needed more time given the evidence, and we'd set a trial date.

I knew, however, I was going into this prepared to face Ms. C. head on. I now understood how she played and I wasn't going to let her throw me off course. I was going to start the show this time.

Athena Rising, a Memoir – Heather Bond

I had five items lined up to support my Motion For Reconsideration. I started the show off with confidence.

Ms. C set in on her first ambush tactic. She sure loved to object and use the word hearsay. At one point, after I read the first court hearing's transcripts, I questioned my mom whether she actually thought Ms. C. knew the true meaning of the word hearsay.

I kept with my notes. She kept objecting. It went back and forth many times. I made sure I completed my entire list. It was a battle. My heels were dug into the ground and I wasn't going to let her legal mumbo-jumbo intimidate me. I don't believe I ever looked at Ms. C.

The judge finally stopped us. She looked at me and said she had seen these items originally and had not missed them the first time. Ms. C, in her fashion, had filed a sanction against me for $2,500 for wasting her and the court's time. The judge quickly denied the sanction. There was nothing more I could have said. I had rolled the dice and now it was in God's and the universe's hands.

The judge looked at me in what I thought was sympathy. She gave Sean an opportunity to speak.

After a few negative and insulting comments the judge stopped him. I felt the judge was energetically telling me her hands were tied. She looked down at her screen for a moment. As she looked up, we locked eyes and she said, "Former judgment stands, 50/50 custody. Reconsideration denied."

There was no pitted feeling in my stomach like I wanted to vomit. I didn't feel like screaming or crying. I wanted to be silent. I wanted to go home and be alone. I wanted to be in the elements of nature and sit on one of my meditation rocks to process all that had transpired.

Epilogue

I changed my clothes and walked barefoot out onto my favorite boulder. The ocean appeared calm on the horizon. I sank my hips down upon the powerful rock, inhaled a deep breath and looked to the heavens.

My eyes closed as I called out, "I am doing this for the best and highest good of everyone involved no matter what the outcome." I inhaled. I felt the breath bathe over my body as I repeated the words. My lungs filled with more oxygen than I had felt in years. My stomach softened as my body relaxed.

Tears began to flow down my cheeks. I was beyond emotion. I repeated my mantra one more time, and sat silent, feeling content. No thoughts entered my mind.

A vision appeared. I observed a cork popping from the crown of my head. It was vivid and alive. Over a decade, turmoil had imprisoned my mind. With every swirling arm of sludge that left my energetic body- pain, anger, resentment, destruction and betrayal- a familiar force filtered in. I watched the sludge flow away and disappear into the ether. I felt it dissipate.

Three hours had passed before I reopened my eyes. A surge of energy shot through me and I witnessed my innate life force reawaken. I felt freedom and knowledge that anything I desire is possible, and I was ready.

No, the court ruling didn't go as expected; it was not meant to be. I had no attachment; I couldn't. I had to confront my fears. If I hadn't my life would have stayed in a stagnant state, a life where good enough is good enough. I don't believe it is. We are all inherently worthy.

I started writing this on a bitter-cold cement floor in prison. Nine years I spent writing and re-writing various parts of the manuscript. Frustration always set in; there had been no closure. The lessons of this story couldn't unfold and become clear until I endured this final painstaking leg of forgiving not only those who wounded me but forgiving myself.

Before the betrayals that left my spine and heart shattered I was whole. I felt I'd lost that; Athena had broken. It has taken me over a decade to realize that I am far more magnificent than I could have ever imagined.

While my freedom and worldly possessions had been stripped from me in prison, the stories of my fellow cellmates impacted me deeply and me taught me to have compassion towards myself, and others. My spiritual practice and the art of self-observation expanded as I sat for hours alone in silence.

The individual I felt hurt me the most in my life, (Sean) turned out to be a worthy teacher. When we play the shame and blame game, we give our power away. I had given mine far too long. Even with the best of intentions, we can't change people's perceptions. This isn't our responsibility.

I am proud and honored to be able to demonstrate to my daughter what a compassionate and powerful human being looks like, and I continue to expand daily; she's a light that shines through the darkness.

As for my mom and me going back to stand trial in India, well, that wasn't meant to be. But when my daughter gets a bit older, we will take a mother, daughter, and grandmother journey through India.

Ah, India, it was written.

" FORGIVENESS"

The End

Photos

Shafi Shalla- AKA "AL" "I give you my best driver." Look him up at Email Shafishalla786@gmail.com or +91 9810144598 for a grand adventure.

Picture of my mom with Kahn "The Best Driver" He took care of us like we were family. Made us feel safe and kept our journey fun.

Mr. Abhoy Pada Chatterjee- A wise and kind man who selflessly and generously gave himself to supporting and representing my mom and me through this time dark time.

The paddy wagon that transported my mom, myself and other prisoners between court and prison.

My mom and I on our overnight camel safari in the great Thar Desert.

Me and my mom in holding cell before being sent to prison and having all our possessions taken.

My favorite picture of my mom in India in our favorite place in Jodupur AKA – the Blue City.

Me rappelling and training for a race.

About the Author

Heather Bond is the creator and owner of *Bond Fitness and Adventures* and the lead adventure and body guide. *Athena Rising Journeys* was birthed from years of guiding and training others in a wide variety of life experiences and adventures. In September of 2019 she was one of six people selected to be on an international logistics team for *The Toughest Race, the Eco-Challenge*, which was held in Fiji. It is set to air as a ten part documentary series on Amazon Prime in 2020.

Heather's service work and introduction to non-profit organizations started at 13 when she was issued a special work permit to start training as a C.I.T, (counselor in training) at the Goleta Girls Club in Santa Barbara, California. She was later hired by Girls Inc. of Greater Santa Barbara as assistant gymnastic coach. In recent years Heather has been a mentor for the "Take Your Daughter's to Work Day program". Her passion for serving others runs deep.

She earned a coveted position as a fire fighter with the Los Angeles City Fire Department, one of the highest trained departments in the world. Prior to LAFD she was a type 1 Hot Shot with the United States Forest Service, and when not fighting fires I was helping operate the Smokey Bear program for the inner city youth.

In the early 2000's Heather launched *Adventure Odyssey Quest*. These 2-3 day journeys were designed for women only. The adventures included, hiking, rappelling and other fun outdoor activities. Glamping at it's best.

For over two decades Heather has been a multi certified fitness trainer and nutrition coach, not only for private clients, but also volunteered at the local Santa Barbara high schools as a pre-season strength and conditioning coach for young athletes. She developed the 5Elements Academy for elementary schools which encompassed both physical strength, coordination and emotional intelligence training.

Heather is the author of the inspirational memoir, Athena Rising, and co-hosting on the Santa Barbara Teen Sports radio show.

Heather's passion for guiding women to live a life of purpose without fear has only grown stronger, but also to inspire individuals to reconnect with their full potential and with nature. There is much joy to be found.

About the Author

Athena Rising, a Memoir – Heather Bond

Made in the USA
San Bernardino, CA
09 July 2020

75173874R00182